Understanding Digital Culture

Understanding Digital Culture

Vincent Miller

Los Angeles | London | New Delhi
Singapore | Washington DC

SAGE Publications Ltd
1 Oliver's Yard
55 City Road
London EC1Y 1SP

SAGE Publications Inc.
2455 Teller Road
Thousand Oaks, California 91320

SAGE Publications India Pvt Ltd
B 1/I 1 Mohan Cooperative Industrial Area
Mathura Road
New Delhi 110 044

SAGE Publications Asia-Pacific Pte Ltd
33 Pekin Street #02-01
Far East Square
Singapore 048763

Library of Congress Control Number: 2010932501

British Library Cataloguing in Publication data

A catalogue record for this book is available from the British Library

ISBN 978-1-84787-496-2
ISBN 978-1-84787-497-9 (pbk)

Typeset by C&M Digitals (P) Ltd, Chennai, India
Printed by the MPG Books Group, Bodmin and King's Lynn
Printed on paper from sustainable resources

MIX
Paper from
responsible sources
FSC® C018575

Contents

Acknowledgements

Top of the list, I have to dedicate this to Kate. Thanks for putting up with this.

I also dedicate this to my mother.

In addition, I would like to thank people who have commented on previous drafts of this book, or in general just been helpful colleagues. So I would like to thank Ryan Conlan, Majid Yar, Monika Krause, Adam Burgess, W. Shatnah, Chris Shilling, Rohit Sharma, Phil Carney, Keith Hayward, Johnny Ilan, and Mila Steele.

INTRODUCTION

We live in a world where the internet and the world wide web have, in the matter of only two decades, shifted from being at the forefront of a new frontier of communication technology, to being for most people an incredibly unremarkable part of our culture and daily life. Many once held an optimism that the internet would, for example, revolutionise work and office life, and create active, engaged citizens instead of the passive subjects of the broadcast media age (Poster, 1995), or lead to the creation of alternative communities, worlds and even identities free from the prejudices of offline society (Rheingold, 1993).

However, as the internet has become something used by the majority of the population in advanced economies, that population has brought with it all of the habits, inclinations and prejudices which are endemic to society as a whole. As a result, much of this early optimism that the internet would radically change our culture in some sort of knowledge revolution has begun to fade in light of the realisation that our culture has perhaps transformed the internet more than vice versa.

The internet has now become a major part of work, leisure, social and political life, for most people in advanced economic nations. It is no longer its novelty, uniqueness, or potential to transform life, but its mundane nature and pervasiveness that now gives the internet its significance. Not in the sense that it has profoundly 'changed' the world, but in the sense that it has become enmeshed within the enduring structures of our society. As such, the online sphere is no longer a realm separate from the offline 'real world', but fully integrated into offline life.

This integration has only been enhanced by the massive popularity of mobile technologies, particularly mobile phones, the latest generation of which allow almost perpetual contact to the world wide web, as well as to our friends, relatives, bosses and significant others. As a result, digital culture now involves more than merely sitting at a computer terminal, and studies of the information age are moving on from the preoccupation with 'internet studies' to consider the pervasive use of mobile phones and other wireless Information Communication Technologies (ICTs). What this means practically is that this is not simply a book about 'internet studies', but a book that considers many wider forms of digital culture, including mobile communications technologies, gaming and technological bodies (to name a few) within and beyond the internet, to demonstrate how digital technology in a broad sense is used within the wider contexts of everyday life.

REVOLUTIONARY TECHNOLOGIES?

In 1975, roughly two decades after the rise of television as a mass medium in Britain was ushered in by the coronation of Queen Elizabeth II in 1953 (the same time as 'the golden age' of television in the United States), acclaimed cultural theorist Raymond Williams wrote *Television: Technology and Cultural Form*, an investigation into the cultural influence of television as a form and practice in British and American cultural life. He begins by introducing a set of statements that were representative of how television was seen as 'changing' the world:

i   Television was invented as the result of scientific and technical research. Its power as a medium of news and entertainment was then so great that it altered all preceding media of news and entertainment.

ii Television was invented as the result of scientific and technical research. Its power as a medium of social communication was then so great that it altered many of our institutions and forms of social relationships.

iii Television was invented as the result of scientific and technical research. Its inherent properties as an electronic medium altered our basic perceptions of reality, and thence our relations with each other and with the world.

iv Television was invented as the result of scientific and technical research. As a powerful medium of communication and entertainment it took its place with other factors – such as greatly increased physical mobility, itself the result of other newly invented technologies – in altering the scale and form of our societies.

v   Television was invented as the result of scientific and technical research, and developed as a medium of entertainment and news. It then had unforeseen consequences, not only on other entertainment and news media, which reduced in viability and importance, but on some of the central processes of family, cultural and social life.

vi Television, discovered as a possibility by scientific and technical research, was selected for investment and development to meet the needs of a new kind of society, especially in the provision of centralised entertainment and in the centralised formation of opinions and styles of behaviour.

vii Television, discovered as a possibility by scientific and technical research, was selected for investment and promotion as a new and profitable phase of a domestic consumer economy; it is then one of the characteristic 'machines for the home'.

viii Television became available as a result of scientific and technical research, and in its character and uses exploited and emphasised elements of a passivity, a cultural and psychological inadequacy, which had always been latent in people, but which television now organised and came to present.

ix   Television became available as a result of scientific and technical research, and
     in its character and uses both served and exploited the needs of a new kind of
     large-scale and complex but atomised society. (Williams, 1990 [1975]: 11–12)

The reason I have quoted this passage at length is because I find it fairly striking how
all of the characterisations of the effects of television on society Williams lists (apart
from perhaps point viii) are today levelled at the internet, two decades after it was popularised through the invention of the world wide web (WWW) in 1991. In fact, many
of these statements speak directly to the content of some chapters within this book.
This highlights the point that perhaps we have been here before, many times. New
technologies always breed anxiety about their consequences, and certainly the internet
and mobile phones have bred both anxiety and optimism in their potential to shape the
future. However, like television (but perhaps more so) it is important to realise that the
internet, the web, and mobile digital technologies are more than just 'technologies',
they are a set of social relations which incorporate the use of technologies with various
results.

Determinisms

It is almost inevitable that any significant new technology will be predicted to transform
society, or at least to embody the potential to transform society, for better or worse. It
is often said, especially in the initial stages of the adoption of a particular technology,
that the technology will generate social change based upon the implicit values, virtues,
or vices possessed by that technology. This line of thinking is often referred to as _tech-_
nological determinism and, in this respect, the development of networked ICTs is no
exception.

Raymond Williams (1990 [1975]) defined technological determinism as suggesting
that new technologies set the conditions for social change and progress. In such a view,
technology is seen as a law unto itself, in the sense that technological innovations are
seen as drivers in the 'progress' (or sometimes 'decline') of society and culture. When
Time magazine produces a headline such as 'How Twitter will change the way we live'
(Johnson, 2009), they are engaging in a form of technological determinism which suggests that, in the relationship between technology and culture, culture is the passive
agent and technology the active one: culture and society 'react' to technological developments in a cause-and-effect manner.

Implicit in this view is the vision of technology as something separate and independent of society. Inventions can merely 'happen', and then society has to deal with the consequences of that happening and the new ways of life that follow. Or, one can see science
and technology as following some sort of inevitable path or autonomous logic (what
Bimber (1990) refers to as a 'logical sequence') in which new technologies are part of a
process that not only directly effects change on society, but also sets in motion the direc-
tion for future technological changes, as well as the necessary altering social forms and
organisation. So the invention of the incandescent electric light bulb by Thomas Edison

in 1879 can be seen as the inevitable next stage in development from the gas lamp, and both inventions created fundamentally new ways of being to which people, businesses, and governments had to organise themselves around.

On the surface, technological determinism seems to make sense, and indeed as Mackenzie and Wajcman (1999) (from whom I borrow the light bulb analogy) suggest, it contains a partial truth. No one would argue that the invention of the light bulb was not a significant event in terms of the following consequences: extending our days, influencing the design and structure of buildings, revolutionising transportation, shaping the development of entire cities to sizes never thought possible, changing our work patterns and leading on to further innovations in lighting and electricity more generally.

Within the context of digital culture, technological determinism has been rife, especially in the early days of internet studies (Bingham, 1996). Many authors that are seen as central in this book, including Karl Marx, Marshall McLuhan, Manuel Castells and Mark Poster have been accused, rightly or wrongly, as following this logic. For example, in Chapter 1, Poster is quoted:

> Electronic culture promotes the individual as an unstable identity in a continuous process of multiple identity formation. (Poster, 1995: 59)

Poster here is promoting an anti-essentialist view of identity, but in doing so, could also be accused of technological determinism, by insinuating that identity formations are directly linked to technological developments in 'electronic culture' and encourage the formation of multiple identities, or a certain *kind of person*. It is important for the reader to be critically aware of such logic when it is at work.

The social determination of technology

Putting Edison's invention of the light bulb into a social context reveals another view of the relationship between technology, society and culture which might be called *social* or *economic determinism*. Extreme ends of this view would characterise technology as the passive partner in the culture–technology relationship, and is referred to as 'symptomatic technology' by Williams (1990 [1975]). This refers to a form of determinism whereby social conditions create environments in which technologies are seen as either necessary by-products of social processes or, as early sociologist of technology William Ogburn argued, were *inevitable,* given the correct set of social conditions (Mackenzie and Wajcman, 1999: 8). From this perspective, new technologies *become necessary* at certain points of cultural development. So in the case of the light bulb, its invention becomes a symptom of wider social changes. Given what was going on in society at a particular time and the general march of 'progress', the light bulb *had* to happen.

This view is not particularly prevalent in contemporary popular or academic writing, but it arguably does make an appearance on some of the arguments of extropian posthumanism (see Chapter 9). Futurists such as Ray Kurzweil often make evolutionary-style predictions about the advancement of society more generally. In *The Singularity is Near* (2005), he suggests that an evolutionary jump in human society, the singularity, is an inevitable future occurrence: this is a point in the evolution of humanity in which technological advancements occur so rapidly, that humans themselves will not be able to keep pace and will be out-evolved by machines that are more intelligent than humans. Ultimately, in the 2040s, the singularity will spell the end of 'human' history (as humans will no longer exist outside machine-human hybrids), and the eventual transformation of the universe into a giant computational body. While in one sense this smacks of technological determinism, these transformations are seen by Kurzweil as *inevitable* epochal stages in human history.

Such evolutionary discussions are problematic. If inventions are basically inevitable, this gives very little agency to the inventions or the inventors themselves, and also little agency towards society itself or the people that make up society. Both are passive in the face of some sort of predetermined narrative of 'progress' or 'decline'. In Kurzweil's view of the future, it doesn't really matter what inventors of new technologies or businesses, governments and individuals *want* to see happen, what will happen is going to happen.

Technological enablement

In Williams' (1990 [1975]) view, both technological determinism and symptomatic technology approaches are as bad as each other, in that they depend on the isolation of technology from society either by viewing technology *creating* new ways of life on its own, or as simply providing materials for new ways of life already in formation. When considering the light bulb example above (or even 'the singularity'), one major piece of the puzzle missing is the notion of *intention*. As Williams suggests, new technologies are *looked for* and developed with purposes and practices in mind. These purposes are intended to change things and influence society: that is their point. In general, one can suggest new technologies are developed to:

- Fulfil a need or solve a problem.
- Bring about a certain condition in the future.
- Create a profit or some sort of personal gain.

All of these are interrelated and are motivating factors that have their basis in social circumstances and the desire to change those circumstances. Edison was trying to solve a problem (safe lighting), but his motivations, and the resources he was able to muster, were the results of a particular social context (capitalism), which values profit and makes profit possible. He also undoubtedly had a vision of how his invention could shape the future, but likely had no idea what myriad of uses eventually would develop out of his creation. Thus, technologies can be seen to set up a system of enablements with two potential outcomes: 'preferred', conventional or intended uses, as well as unexpected applications and novel cultural forms (Hayward, 1990).

The Edison example speaks specifically to the role of economic contexts within the technology–culture relationship, which naturally leads on to a discussion of Karl Marx. There is considerable debate as to whether Marx was a technological determinist or the opposite (see Resnik and Wolff (1982) and Shaw, (1979)) for good examples of either side). Bimber (1990) provides a thorough commentary which suggests that Marx viewed technology as an *enabling* factor within economic structures. While technological application is dependent on the material conditions of production (economic systems and labour relations), the presence of science and technology helps to enable these particular systems and relations, through first, the accumulation of capital by the bourgeoisie, and second, through the creation or alteration of labour markets. This is well illustrated by Marx's phrase:

> When capital enlists science into her service, the refractory hand of labour will always be taught docility. (Marx, 1990 [1867]: 564)

Within the contexts of capitalism, new technology is most often created with the implicit (and sometimes explicit) intention of creating wealth, or adapted for such ambitions. Thomas Edison did not just happen to invent the electric light – he planned to invent it. He wanted to find a way to sell electricity and provide light to people in order to make money for himself (Mackenzie and Wajcman, 1999). His research was funded by businesses who also intended to profit from his innovations. Edison was an entrepreneur, and was operating within the social environment of capitalism. This environment provided him with the means to develop a technology, and the motivation for him to sell that technology in a competitive market which already included gas lights, oil lanterns and candles. The market helped to determine the nature of his invention (it had to be cheaper and safer than gas), and helped to steer the course of its eventual use in society. Far from a separate world of science and technology, Edison's invention emerged and was constituted by a set of social and economic arrangements.

This enabling view within many Marxist approaches becomes clearly evident with regard to information technologies in Chapter 2, where the influential work of two Marxists, Manuel Castells and David Harvey, are discussed in relation to the economic foundations of the information age. Harvey (1989) proposed that capitalist enterprises continually look to increase profit through the opening up of new markets of (cheaper) raw materials, (cheaper) labour, or new consumers. For Harvey, these are inherently spatial concerns as such operations involve the increasing of spatial scales of practice, and this is seen in contemporary times in the process of globalisation.

The problem of increasing spatial scales is distance, and the time it takes to travel long distances (the friction of distance). Increasing this time cuts into profit by increasing 'turnover time' (the time it takes to turn raw materials into sellable commodities and ultimately receive the profits from these goods sold to consumers). Thus, capitalist enterprises are always looking for ways to reduce the friction of distance: to metaphorically pull the locations of raw materials, labour markets and consumer markets closer together in time, while being able to increase their distance apart in space. New communications technologies allow this to happen by speeding up communications and transfers of money, as well as providing global access to certain types of labour and new consumers through *time–space compression* (Harvey, 1989). Castells (1996/2000) refers to this overcoming of distance and the resultant ability to communicate in real time on a global scale as *the space of flows* (see Chapter 2).

Base, superstructure, infrastructure

What can be gained from the discussion of time–space compression and the space of flows is the further consideration that digital communication technologies have importance as a system of *infrastructure* that enables certain practices and social relations. Infrastructure refers to the underlying framework or basic foundation of an organisation or system. Infrastructures are the basic facilities that enable something to function.

Marxists would suggest that, in the context of capitalism, the functions that are enabled are primarily intended for the practice of economic enterprise. Infrastructure can be seen as contributing to the economic *base* of society (the relations of production) upon which the *superstructure* of society (culture) is built, thus enabling both economic relations and ways of life. Marx himself illustrates this in his popular writing, in 'The future results of British rule in India' published in *The New York Daily Tribune* in 1853. He proposed that the British exploitation of India as an economic enterprise will revolve around the creation of a 'modern' infrastructure of railways and communications:

> The millocracy have discovered that the transformation of India into a reproductive country has become of vital importance to them, and, to that end, it is necessary above all to gift her with the means of irrigation and internal communication. They intend now drawing a net of railroads over India. And they will do it. The results must be inappreciable. (Marx, 1977 [1853]: 333)

Once the infrastructural base was laid, Marx predicted that the introduction of new infrastructures would enable new forms of work and labour markets:

> The railway system will therefore become, in India, truly the forerunner of modern industry. This is the more certain as the Hindus are allowed by British authorities themselves to possess particular aptitude for accommodating themselves to entirely new labour, and acquiring the requisite knowledge of machinery. (Marx, 1977 [1853]: 335)

In a more contemporary context, Graham and Marvin (1996, 2001) have recently re-inserted infrastructure back into the consideration of social scientists by brilliantly examining the changing form and constitution of cities within the wake of economic globalisation and the new configuration of telecommunications infrastructure which enables that process.

As discussed in Chapter 2, the infrastructures of digital communications were not only developed to enable a particular set of economic initiatives (the need to globalise in search of profit), but also encouraged those initiatives at the same time. In turn, this infrastructural base provides a framework under which new forms of organisation, relationship and experience (culture, including virtual cultures) can emerge. In Chapter 4, the significance of infrastructure is perhaps most apparent in the discussion of digital divides and the role that mobile phone infrastructures are playing in the African context.

The creation of mobile communications technologies and infrastructures that support mobility has become a significant and increasing factor of contemporary life (Urry, 2000). Indeed, demands for mobility in many respects have been put forward as a primary impetus in the development of ITCs and their subsequent adoption and use. This is the case both in terms of production, with a demand for a more flexible, efficient and productive labour force (see Chapter 2), and in consumption, with increasing access to consumers and ease with which consumers can purchase and use (especially media) goods (see Chapter 3).

We all experience the increasing mobility of information technology in our use of an array of digital devices: mobile phones; PDAs; WiFi-enabled laptops and notebook computers; iPod's and many others. The most popular of these devices, mobile phones, have evolved through a series of generations, which have seen them move from instruments of purely voice communication, to ones that include SMS text, as well as image production and consumption, to their current state (typified by the iPhone) of embodying a full set of multimedia technologies, and full-blown access to the web.

These mobile technologies help to support certain ways of living that were intended by their inventors. However, this relationship is far from straightforward. No-one would have intended, nor expected, that the telecommunication structure of global capitalism would be used to buy and sell virtual clothing and sexual aids for avatars in the virtual world of *Second Life* (Meadows, 2008), and no-one would have expected the mobile phone infrastructure of the Philippines to be used as a way to send text messaged to God (Roman, 2009). Still, the notion of ICTs as an enabling (and now, thanks to mobile technologies, ubiquitous for many) infrastructure is something that readers should consider throughout this book. In some ways, it's difficult to imagine how digital culture can become much more 'mobile'. But it can.

In another example, recent innovations in computing infrastructure in the form of *cloud computing* have the potential to greatly increase mobility by unburdening computational devices from the need to maintain their own locally-installed software and storage capabilities. Cloud computing is a fundamental shift in how networked computers operate. At the moment, most networked computing uses an extremely decentralised infrastructural model. People are in the possession of powerful devices (such as PCs), which have their own individual sets of software installed on them, and have large amounts of storage capability to be able to run software as well as store data for the individual. In the cloud computing model, data storage, software provision, server provision and the maintenance of all these is centralised to a provider whose business is the maintenance and provision of these infrastructures. The provider then allows individual customers to use them, much in the same way as an electric utility company allows individuals access to a centralised power supply (Carr, 2008).

What this means *practically* is that individuals and organisations are freed from the costs and responsibility of buying software that may or may not be used very much, and the maintenance and security of that software, as well as the need to replace computers and devices which go out of date two years after their purchase. Organisations are also potentially freed from the burden of having to buy and maintain server systems. What this means *conceptually* is that individual devices have the freedom to be less powerful, because there are fewer demands on storage and computing power. Devices instead become more reliant on strong network connections to be able to use and access centralised software and data. These devices have the potential to be smaller, cheaper, easier to use and, perhaps most importantly, more compact and mobile. Cloud computing may have the potential to enable new ways of living but how, when, and in what matter this is realised is a matter for 'culture' to decide.

THE STRUCTURE OF THE BOOK

In order to fully understand the digital culture, it is important to examine not only the economic and social impacts of an 'information society', but to examine these alongside the shifting and emerging cultural forms that are already playing an increasing part in mainstream consumer and media cultures. Thus, this text strives to integrate and make explicit the link between the more economically-based 'information society' literature and literature emerging from cultural studies that focuses on the production, use and consumption of digital media and multimedia. The aims of this book are to:

- Provide a balanced, yet critical account of the economic, social and cultural dimensions of the information society.

- Situate these developments within wider sociological debates around globalisation, individualisation, and consumerism.

- Emphasise and contextualise the increasing importance of mobile, wireless and converged media technologies and forms in everyday life activities.

- Examine the ways in which the rise of the information society has posed new challenges and transformations of older socio-cultural topics such as inequality, power, identity, community and belonging.

- Map the transformations of cultural forms associated with the rise of new media and its consumption.

- Illustrate the above through a series of contemporary case studies of digital culture.

This book can be informally divided into three sections. The first section (the first three chapters) articulates the base–superstructure–infrastructure argument by examining the technological and economic contexts from which the innovative elements of digital culture emerge. The second section (Chapters 4 to 6) then goes on to examine the sociological questions of inequality, politics, privacy and how these are problematised in the information age. The third section (Chapters 7 to 11) will focus on 'culture' in the information society and will examine identity, community, and the body in the information. Interspersed among several chapters are four contemporary case studies of digital culture, illustrating how the issues raised in the previous sections manifest themselves within everyday, 'digital culture' life contexts. More specifically:

Chapter 1, in many respects, is the foundation for the book and sets the ambitious task of reviewing the key elements of digital media. Through discussion of such authors as Lev Manovich, Roland Barthes, Gilles Deleuze and Jean Baudrillard, this chapter lays out an understanding of digital media based on three themes that, in combination, present digital media as innovative as compared to media of the past: technical processes, cultural form and immersive experience. It then examines the case of video games as cultural products that are uniquely created through contemporary digital media technologies and thus defy traditional cultural categorisation.

Chapter 2 discusses the economic foundations of the information age. It reviews the concepts of post-industrialism, the information society, post-Fordism, globalisation, and the network society as economic conceptions, through discussion of the work of Kondratieff, Schumpeter, Bell, Castells and others. This leads onto a discussion of 'weightless economies', intellectual property and a consideration of the consequences of weightless economies.

Chapter 3 examines the issue of media convergence by looking at the changing structure of the media industry (media industry convergence) in the face of technological innovation (technological convergence) and neo-liberal globalisation (regulatory convergence). It will then discuss converged media experience by focussing on Henry Jenkins' notion of 'convergence culture' and participatory media practices, as well as Axel Bruns' concept of 'produsage'. It ends with a close look at the music industry under the auspices of convergence culture.

Chapter 4 looks at the more sociological question of inequality through the concepts of domestic and digital divides. It will make the point that inequality is not merely a question of economic and infrastructural access, but also a socio-cultural question of use, and will finish with a discussion about the potential of mobile phones to help overcome economic and infrastructural barriers in the developing world.

Chapter 5 looks at the concept of privacy and how contemporary technology is challenging modern Western conceptions of privacy and the right to a private life. In keeping with the theme of the first half of the book, its focus is largely on how commercial imperatives, particularly practices of personal data collection for use in marketing, are driving changes in contemporary notions of privacy.

Chapter 6 provides a general discussion of how protest, politics and warfare are conducted in a networked digital age. First, a general discussion of identity politics and new social movements will preface the topic of 'cyber politics and protest' where the tactics, ideology and organisation of ICT-based social protests will be examined. The emphasis will be on the concept of networked decentralisation. This concept will then provide the backdrop for the additional discussions of Cyber warfare.

Chapter 7 considers the theme of 'identity' as it has been presented in discussions of digital media thus far. It presents a narrative of how identity has been discussed as it related to cyberculture since Sherry Turkel's early work on Multi-User Domains (MUDs), through to personal web pages, blogging, social networking and, finally, to avatar use in online worlds and Massively Multiplayer Online Role Playing Games (MMORPGs). It then considers the phenomenon of 'cybersex' as a case of contemporary identity processes at work in digital contexts.

Chapter 8 looks at the concept of community in the digital age. It approaches this subject within a wider discussion of the role of 'space' in the formation of relationships and social organisation, and how such relationships can be transformed when space becomes less of a determining factor through the use of communication technologies. The notion of 'community' is discussed alongside considerations of 'mobility' and 'individualism' and ultimately contrasted with 'network'. The conclusion being that it is perhaps best to view both online and offline forms of contemporary belonging in terms of increasingly a-spatial 'networks', rather than 'communities'. This chapter ends with a case study discussion on the value of social networking and microblogging in establishing and maintaining 'presence' in a network society.

Chapter 9 considers the relationship between technology and the body, and how technology is helping to reshape conceptions about what it is to be 'human'. More specifically, it investigates several varieties of posthumanism that can be considered within the context of digital culture: cyborg relationships, extropianism and disembodiment and technological embodiment. The last two in particular critically examine the idea that humanness (as a 'mind', or as a 'body') is reducible to information that can be manipulated and altered. The chapter then looks at technological embodiment, as an approach which suggests that the use of technology is a part of humanness itself and, using the examples of mobile phones and 'ambient intelligence', demonstrates how the use of new technologies allow us to alter our embodied relationship to the world around.

While broad-ranging in scope, the subject matter dealt with in this book is not exhaustive. Since more focussed treatment is given to 'culture', this book will focus less on topics such as 'legislation', 'crime', 'distance education' and 'e-commerce' than books with a similar subject matter, although all of these topics do make cameo appearances at various points. Hopefully, it will provide a useful and considered account of not only digital culture as a description of contemporary society, but also the economic and social processes that have got us to where we are now.

1

KEY ELEMENTS OF DIGITAL MEDIA

This new revolution is arguably more profound than the previous ones, and we are just beginning to register its initial effects. Indeed the introduction of the printing press affected only one stage of cultural communication – the distribution of media. The photograph affected only one type of cultural communication – still images. In contrast, the digital media revolution affects all stages of communication (acquisition, storage, manipulation, distribution) and it effects all types of media – texts, still images, moving images, sound, and spatial constructions. (Manovich, 2001: 19)

Mark Poster (1995) was one of the first theorists to provide an insightful discussion about what was, at the time, the emerging communications revolution of 'new media'. He argued that the main difference between old broadcast media and new media was that new media was 'active', whereas old media was 'passive'.

Poster associated broadcast media with modernism, in the sense that it was part of the development of modern industrial capitalism and the nation-state. In that respect, the structure of broadcast media reflected its role in the modern nation state: a small elite group of producers, because of their wealth and privilege, had the access and ability to shape the public sphere of broadcasting, and thereby sent one-way communication to the much larger mass of receivers (see Figure 1.1a). The model of communications here is a hierarchical one, with those in power, or at least representing the interests of those in power, creating hegemony through the ownership and distribution of a popular culture that encouraged audience outlooks that were favourable to the status quo. This sort of critique of modern media and popular culture is epitomised by the Frankfurt School, and particularly by Adorno and Horkheimer (1991), in that this type of broadcast model is said to promote a passive audience, vulnerable to the herd mentalities which make nationalism, and even fascism, thrive.[1]

By contrast, Poster argued that the new 'internet model' of media promoted a more active and critical subject. Interactive, two-way communications such as those implicit in internet architecture suggest a collapse of the distinction between consumers and producers, and a more decentralised model of media production, less hierarchical and more akin to a network (Figure 1.1b). This structure therefore allows the audience the

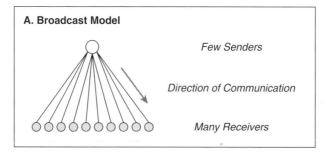

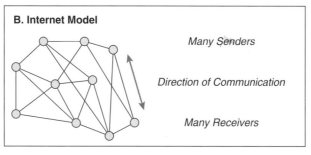

Figure 1.1   'Broadcast' versus 'internet' conceptual models

affordances of increased choice, and the ability to 'answer back' or produce their own media: 'The shift to decentralised networks of communications makes the producers consumers, senders receivers, upsetting the logic of the first media age' (Poster 1995: 33).

Poster associates his decentralisation and two-way communication with a more active, engaged and aware audience or subject, one that has to make choices, make decisions and formulate opinions from the wide variety of information sources at his/her disposal. Media in the digital age becomes a 'lean forward' instead of a 'lean back' medium, and Poster associated this more critical thinking, actively engaged subject with the contexts of multiple and diffuse identity formation associated with postmodernism: 'Electronic culture promotes the individual as an unstable identity in a continuous process of multiple identity formation' (Poster, 1995: 59).

Whether or not these somewhat optimistic predictions have panned out quite the way Poster first envisioned is the story for other chapters (Chapters 6 and 7), but his thoughtful analysis of the differences in, and the effects of, new digital networked forms of media set the basic groundwork for many later discussions of the characteristics of digital media. This chapter will examine the changes in media, and the experience of media that has been occurring for two decades now and are still taking place.

Since Poster's early work, the 'differences' between old and new media is a topic that has been discussed by many authors and on many media industry web pages. As a result, many definitive lists have been offered. For example, Lister et al. (2009) follow a more mainstream or conventional approach to describing these differences, suggesting that new media is digital, interactive, hypertextual, dispersed, and virtual, whereas

Manovich (2001) takes a more novel approach. Echoing Marxist base/superstructure theory, he builds from the technical elements of digital media production and turns them into cultural categories, arguing that new media is numerical, modular, automated, variable and transcoded.

I plan to take a route between these two approaches, considering the groundbreaking work of Manovich (2001) in detail, but stopping short of the technological fetishism that is sometimes present in his work.[2] In the rest of this chapter, I will attempt to summarise the essential features of digital media within three major themes where, in combination, digital media can be seen as innovative in comparison to the media of the past: technical processes, cultural form and immersive experience. Technical processes refer to the technological building blocks of digital media, cultural forms refer to the ways in which digital media objects are created, encountered and used, and immersive experience refers to the environments that digital media can create. The last substantive section will examine the case of video games as contemporary media products, created from contemporary technologies, which defy traditional cultural categorisation.

It would be a mistake to suggest that these are all fundamentally unique to digital media, in the sense that, as Bolter and Grusin (2000) suggest, setting up a false binary between digital or 'new' media and 'old' media is unhelpful, as new media is made up of a recombining or 'remediation' of content and other aspects of old media. At the same time, it is necessary to point out how significant the switch to digital culture potentially is. Manovich (2001) recognises this when he suggests that the computer screen (whether on a desktop or laptop monitor, mobile phone, PDA interface, or television games console) has become the primary way in which mediated culture is experienced in technologically advanced countries. In that sense, the computer has moved from being merely a tool, such as a calculator or processor, to being a filter for all culture and has started to replace the cinema screen, the television, the gallery wall and the book as our primary interface with mediated culture, with the internet itself becoming a repository for all culture and cultural forms.

TECHNICAL PROCESSES

The first set of ways that digital media is in many respects novel as compared to previous media paradigms, such as broadcast or print media, come under what I am referring to as technical processes. By this I mean the technological aspects of production, distribution and consumption which contribute to the shape, character and potential of digital media.

Digital

The first of these, digitality, will be discussed comprehensively in Chapter 3 on convergence, and so will only be mentioned briefly here. Suffice to say that digital media is by nature a numerical representation (Manovich, 2001) in that all information is represented in 0–1 digital code. Manovich suggests that numerical representation makes digital information programmable, alterable, and subject to algorithmic manipulation. Thus, digital media can be 'tinkered with' in a way that is extremely difficult with traditional analogue media (as any user of Photoshop is aware) and is alterable in several ways. It can be *compressed* and *decompressed* using *algorithms*, allowing for large amounts of data to be stored and distributed in an efficient manner. It can be easily manipulated or copied, and is transferable between different sources, objects and means of technological delivery.

Networked

Digital media tends to be *networked* (produced, distributed and consumed through two-way networked infrastructures) in a variety of ways such as the internet, mobile phone, or WiFi networks, whereas broadcast media tends to be consumed on one-way analogue infrastructures. Conceptually, much digital media is more akin to the telephone than television broadcasting or cinema screening. In that sense, digital media, as Poster (1995) suggests, tends to follow a more decentralised network architecture with many producers and consumers in a constant dialogue with each other, as opposed to a more pyramidal model of broadcast media in which an elite of producers sends out one-way communications to many receivers.

This decentralisation of media production means that, with many more producers and sources of information, there is a greatly enlarged element of choice when consuming digital media as compared to the broadcast media of the past. Whether it be the multitude of web pages, blogs, forums and the like on the internet, or the hundreds of channels available on digital television, digital media expands choice immensely compared to the previous broadcast era where choice available for sources of information was severely limited to, for example, five terrestrial television broadcasts on the analogue spectrum.

This diversity of choice then becomes a fundamental characteristic of new media that follows on from networking, convergence and the blurring of producers and consumers. The audience is given immense choice and, because of digitisation and convergence, the user has the capacity to choose from all available forms of media and content which are deliverable over any device or channel.

Interactive

Manovich (2001) proposes that 'interactivity' is a meaningless term, since the ability to manipulate and customise information is the most basic fact about computers. He further argues that almost all previous forms of media could be considered 'interactive' in the sense that they have called upon the audience to do some sort of 'work' in the consuming experience.

However, despite these caveats, interactivity is still an important part of digital media to acknowledge even if, to a certain extent, the term is somewhat watered down. 'Interactivity' can be defined in a number of ways, most generally as 'responsiveness'; as in the responsiveness of a media object or piece of information to the preferences, needs or activities of the user.

Interactivity has been a notoriously difficult term to pin down more specifically, especially its use within the context of digital media. Kiousis (2002) and Downes and McMillan (2000) both provide comprehensive discussions which attempt to establish a coherent definition. Kiousis (2002) argues that interactivity has been spoken about in three thematic ways. First, interactivity can be seen as implicit in the technological structures of computer mediated communications. This is reminiscent of Manovich's point above in that 'interactivity' is seen as something embedded in the structure of the media or in computer technology. Thus, it is the deterministic structure of the technology which creates the affordance of 'interactivity' and interactive media, in a sense that there is a technological potential for a user to modify their mediated environment, as they use it.

The second theme is more sociologically oriented and relates to the context in which communication of any sort occurs, and the results of that communication. Here one pays attention to the *context* in which messages are exchanged. Some communication settings, such as a telephone call, tend to promote two-way communication or interactivity more than others, such as a speech involving a large crowd. It can be seen as the way people adapt their actions to a particular social situation (Jensen, 1998).

The third theme is more of a psycho-socially oriented aspect of interactivity relating to the perception of the user or the 'state of mind' of the audience in terms of taking a 'passive' or 'active' role in relation to the media, or the extent to which they feel invited to participate in an interactive experience. This approach tends to be used when evaluating web site design, where some sites are better than others at establishing an active role for the user of the site, creating a more interactive experience.

Overall, perhaps the simplest but most useful definition of interactivity in the context of digital media is provided by Jensen (1998): 'A measure of media's potential ability to let the user exert an influence on the context and/or form of the mediated communication' (Jensen, 1998: 461, cited in Kiousis, 2002: 368).

What this demonstrates is the socio-technical relationship between the user of media and the media itself. The user has the potential – and can be invited – to have some sort of influence on the presentation of the media, or feedback upon it. In this respect, interactivity is seen to be one of the more 'value added' characteristics of digital media (Lister et al., 2009) in that business and industry find it useful for marketing purposes to know as much as possible about how their products are perceived and can be improved. Interactivity provides business with the means to tailor their products more effectively around the 'needs' of the user, making them more desirable. Thus, 'interactivity' was a much-hyped phenomenon in business and marketing throughout the early development of the web, and helped drive the development of the internet as a business-led phenomenon.

Hypertextual/Hypermediated

At the close of World War Two, Vannevar Bush, military science advisor for US presidents Roosevelt and Truman, published an article in *The Atlantic Monthly* which suggested that with the war over, America should turn its efforts towards organising the substantial amounts of scientific advancements taking place in such a way as to make the increasingly vast panoply of human knowledge accessible to all. He argued that science was advancing at such a rate that it had already outstripped the ability of scientists themselves to keep up with the advances taking place.

Bush's proposed solution was what he called the 'memex'. This was to be an inter-linked archive of human knowledge which would work by association in a manner simi-lar to the understandings, at that time, of how the human mind operated. This memex would thus consist of a 'web of trails', which could theoretically link any one document to any other, based on some set of relevant criteria at any given time.

> Thereafter, at any time, when one of these items is in view, the other can be instantly recalled merely by tapping a button below the corresponding code space. Moreover, when numer-ous items have been thus joined together to form a trail, they can be reviewed in turn, rapidly or slowly, by deflecting a lever like that used for turning the pages of a book. It is exactly as though the physical items had been gathered together from widely separated sources and bound together to form a new book. It is more than this, for any item can be joined into numerous trails.
>
> … Wholly new forms of encyclopedias will appear, ready made with a mesh of associative trails running through them, ready to be dropped into the memex and there amplified. The lawyer has at his touch the associated opinions and decisions of his whole experience, and of the experience of friends and authori-ties. The patent attorney has on call the millions of issued patents, with familiar trails to every point of his client's interest. (Bush, 1945: 7–8)

Bush's prophetic ideas were later influential on Ted Nelson, the info-tech pioneer who coined the term 'hypertext' in the mid-1960s (Landow, 2006). What Bush actually did was lay the conceptual foundations for 'hypertext' as we know and use it today: the sys-tem of links and databases that allow us to navigate from one bit of content or web page to another on the World Wide Web.

Hypertext is a form of text that is composed of *nodes* or *blocks* of text (or media, in the case of hypermedia) which form the content, the *links* between these blocks of content, and the *buttons* or *tags* that enact the link from one node to another (such as the links or tags embedded in web documents). As one follows the different links, paths are created within the *network of nodes*. The fact that the choice of paths is normally up to the reader means that hypertext by nature is a *non-linear* form of text, and it begins to blur the distinction between 'writer' and 'reader'. Thus, hypertext combines traditional text with interactive branching to create a non-linear text which is difficult to conceive of within the notion of a 'traditional' printed page (Conklin, 1987: 1).[3]

Landow (1994, 2006) was one of the first, and still is one of the most comprehensive works to examine digital media from a literary theory perspective. He, and many since, have pointed out how hypertext is very similar to Barthes' notion of *writerly text*. The writerly text for Barthes is an ideological tool that he promotes in contrast to the *readerly text*, which he associates with most forms of classic literature and the notion of 'the book'.

In brief, Barthes suggests that classic literature has two elements which inform an ideological position:

- *Authorship*   In that the production of meaning resides within the author and the reader is obliged to follow under convention.

- *Linearity*   In that the sequence of events is set up and determined by the author and presented as a material whole which itself constitutes a beginning and an end.

These elements suggest 'possessiveness' on the part of the author and, ideologically, an attempt at enclosure of meaning by allowing the author the power to present an authoritative, definitive, linear voice of 'reality'. In contrast, Barthes champions the writerly text, which attempts to erase the authority of the author as some sort of definitive voice by opening up the text and providing the reader with the chance – even forcing the reader – to answer back, produce and create meanings from the text. This blurs the distinction between readers and writers, undermining the authoritative position of the author:

> The goal of literary work … is to make the reader no longer a consumer, but a producer of the text … the writerly text is ourselves writing, before the infinite play of the world (the world as function) is traversed, intersected, stopped, plasticized by some singular system (ideology, genus, criticism) which reduced the plurality of entrances, the opening of networks, the infinity of languages. (Barthes, 1974: 4–5)

The similarities are clear, and lead Landow to merge information theory with critical theory of Barthes, Foucault and Derrida through a comprehensive description of hypertext and its potential from the point of view of active versus passive audiences, as well as from an ideological point of view in terms of the potential implications that hypertext and hypermedia structures have with regard to the subversion of hegemony and power.

Rivett casts a certain amount of caution on Landow's Barthes-inspired characterisation of hypertext, noting that the extent of 'hyper-reading' is likely to be influenced by the interpretative framework set up for the reader by the text, digital or not. The reader, when presented with a text, is not necessarily going to encounter the 'pure' theoretical freedom of hypertext, but the text as it is inflicted through the medium and conventions of the web site (Rivett, 2000: 36).

Manovich also qualifies this complete freedom of the writerly reader in hypertext by arguing that the relationship between producer and consumer is more complex. Readers are not necessarily creating 'new works' by navigating their own way through hypertexts. Instead, it is possible to see the 'complete work' of the text as the sum of all possible paths, and that a user, by choosing a particular path, only accesses a part of the total work (Manovich, 2001: 28).

Automated

Manovich (2001) can also be credited for suggesting that 'automation' is one of the key components of digital media. He proposes that the numerical constitution of digital media and communications means that such products can be easily manipulated through the use of automated templates and algorithms. This means that digital products and media can be automatically modified or even created through software and programs instead of being specifically created or modified by *people*. In short, much of what we experience as media objects in digital culture are created out of databases by machines as opposed to being the results of human endeavour.

The most prominent way in which this happens is through the increasing personalisation of media. When we consider that the internet and other forms of digital media base much of their commercial value on the ability to collect information in order to profile consumers and target them with advertising more efficiently, it seems clear that the automated processes of personalisation and profiling are fundamental to the digital media environment (see Chapter 5). Thus, when using a service like Google, personalised targeted advertising is automatically generated on our screens based on our web footprints and email content. My Amazon automatically generates an individual profile page with recommendations based on previous purchases and browsing. MyYahoo news automatically customises a user's news page in a way that selects news stories geared towards stated interests and preferences. Social networking web sites automatically configure profiles with friends, updates, actions and status reports. Lastly, iTunes, Last.fm and other music services recommend music to listeners based on their previous listening habits (see Chapter 3).

Automation also proves to be essential for our navigation through the vast amount of information present on the internet. Search engines are essentially vast automated database processors that present potentially relevant information to us based on some specific criteria. 'Buzz monitoring', a more recent tool of internet marketing, uses automated programs (web robots) to *troll* the internet looking for topics, trends and texts among blogs, discussion forums and social networks in an attempt to 'read' popular culture for marketing purposes.

Automation is also demonstrated in the form of modelling behaviours and environments. This occurs in a variety of ways, for example in the sorts of artificial life forms created in video and online games, such as non-player characters, which interact with players using behavioural algorithms to model the behaviour of a living being at some basic level. This also occurs in the construction of simulational environments such as 3-D software packages or point of view and first-person video games, which create immersive environments and the illusion of movement for their players.

In these brief examples, it becomes clear how automation, in part at least, removes human intentionality from the creative process within digital culture. A large amount of what we experience in digital media is 'unique' in the sense that it has been created specifically for us, but it is not 'original' in the sense that these unique creations are not composed of bespoke human-created material, but elements of already existing data residing in a database, and compiled by a machine using an algorithm.

Databased

When travelling by car, it is now fairly typical practice to consult either an onboard satellite navigation system or any one of the many online mapping services and route planners such as MapQuest, Multi-Map, Google Maps or the AA Route Planner. After submitting the starting point and destination, the user is given a map, a detailed list of directions, distances, landmarks, even the location of speed cameras. It is an impressive service, and provides us with a wealth of useful information with real practical benefits. The process that brings us this information is even more impressive, as these directions and maps are created from a complex maze of digitised databases of roads, cross-correlated with satellite images pulled from other databases, all of which are seamlessly put together to give the user a fairly simple picture of where to go, how to get there, and what to look for.

In the most general sense, a database can be defined as 'a structured collection of data' (Manovich, 2001: 218), or 'a container of information' (Paul, 2007). Outside of computing, archives, libraries, books and even (in pre-print days) elders, can to a certain extent be considered forms of database in that they store and organise information, so that it can pass down through the generations (Paul, 2007).

A database system is essentially composed of three components: the *storage* element (hardware storage in the case of computers), the means to *retrieve* and *filter* data (software which can sort information on the basis of certain parameters), and the means to turn that data into meaningful information (the user who creates meaning) (Paul, 2007).

What distinguishes such systems from libraries, archives and books are their flexibility. Digital databases can provide an almost infinite set of possibilities for the retrieval, filtering and organisation of data. Such databases consist of lists, tables and structures that have discrete units, objects or bits of information. These objects often have little or even no meaning on their own (and thus tend to possess the same significance as any other object), but have the potential to be related to other bits of information or objects and thus together can obtain a layer of meaning.

We tend to associate databases with computerised record-keeping systems or cumbersome workplace spreadsheets, but in actuality the spread of databases into everyday life and digital culture is pervasive, despite going relatively unnoticed. Online travel maps are one example, but it is the case that every web site, every online service, and the very internet itself, is a database. This leads Manovich (2001) to suggest that databases are becoming *a*, if not *the*, dominant cultural form of our times, and that 'almost every practical act involves choosing from some menu, catalogue, or database' (Manovich, 2001: 128).

This can be seen in lists of hyperlinks on a digital document or a web page: root menu lists on film DVDs (play movie, scene selection, languages, added features); personal characteristics on profiles; lists of pages on search engine hits. Indeed, the great commercial entities of the information age: Google, Yahoo!, Amazon.com, eBay and even Microsoft have made their billions by providing services that essentially build, use, and sort through, databases. Web pages themselves, although they appear to be a coherent visual artefact, are really assemblages of different elements: databases of text, images, moving images, sounds, all of which are separate files stored and then assembled together when viewed by a user (Manovich, 2001).

This illusion of coherence applies to the web as a whole. While surfing we perceive the web as a seamless set of visual and auditory experiences, but in fact it is a vast collection of files that is continually being sorted and assembled together to produce the visual artefacts we see on our screen (Featherstone, 2000; Manovich, 2001; Paul, 2007; Snyder, 2007). This may be experienced as a coherent totality, but much like the illusion used in filmmaking called 'persistence of vision', in which separate still images, moving at a rate of 24 frames per second creates the illusion of seamless movement, the aggregate space of collected files and databases brought together to create the web appears to us as a seamless 'space' which we navigate through.

CULTURAL FORMS

Every container of information, and every way of organising information, creates an information architecture of its own that has cultural implications. Storing information in archives or museums creates a particular form of power geometry, where access to information, and the way it is organised creates implicit hierarchies around who has a right to use information. Storing information in 'elders' creates another set of power geometries, and so does information stored in libraries and in books. The rise of a database culture as a response to a particular set of cultural and technological conditions therefore has the potential to create a significant cultural impact not only on how we organise and categorise the world around us, but also in terms of who has the ability to do the organising.

Narratives, as typified in modernity by the novel and the film, attempt to create order. They have beginnings, middles and endings: a plot or a story in which a sequence of meaningful events is in a contextual 'cause and effect' relationship (Manovich, 2001). Furthermore, narratives generally lend themselves to the notion of an author: a voice which speaks with a certain amount of authority with regard to the portrayal of the events being represented or described.

Databases are antithetical to this. They present the world as a list or a collection without any dominant order. They do order the world, but it is an ad-hoc ordering based on a particular user, and a particular set of parameters or relationships chosen at a given time. And because these are lists or collections, they are never complete. Stories end, novels have a last page, but lists (just like web pages, social networking profiles, or iPod playlists) can always be added to, and relationships can always be reconfigured.

Outside of media culture, one can see the effects of the shift towards a database logic in the fields of science (Hine, 2006), social work (Parton, 2008) and criminal justice (Aas, 2004). In social work and penal culture, for example, the impact of new communication technologies and databased record-keeping has led to a movement away from decision making on the basis of knowledgeable decision makers who are familiar with the narrative biographies of their clients, and towards the creation of de-contextualised subjects as 'database identities' who become categorised and then are acted upon on the basis of those categories. Aas (2004) calls this 'power without narrative' (the role of databases in surveillance and power is discussed in Chapter 5).

Networked, digital, hypertextual, databased environments tend to suppress narratives, and get rid of authors. As discussed in Chapter 3, such environments encourage the erosion of the distinction between producers and consumers of media. Two-way communication networks allow users to 'answer back', in addition to being able to contribute to the media environment through individual or collaborative efforts. Digitisation allows easy production of original works, or the easy copying or manipulation of already existing works. Hypertextual and hypermedia environments allow an autonomy to the user to select his or her own path through materials available, and databases allow users to retrieve and recombine existing objects, texts and data in an infinite number of ways. As a result, the power geometry in media has in many ways already begun to shift away from the hegemonic position of the producer (or author), towards the anti-hierarchical position of the consumer/producer, or 'prosumer' (see Chapter 3 on convergence).

Given these technological affordances, this section will discuss the unique cultural forms one can associate with digital media objects, specifically their lack of context, variability and rizomatic organisation. It will ultimately suggest that perhaps digital media objects may not be seen as 'objects' at all, but processes.

Context (or lack of it)

> Even the most perfect reproduction of a work of art is lacking in one element: its presence in time and space, its unique existence at the place where it happens to be. This unique existence of the work of art determined the history to which it was subject throughout the time of its existence. (Benjamin, 1936, from Frascina and Harris, 1992: 298)

Walter Benjamin's 'The work of art in the age of mechanical reproduction' (1936) is a highly influential work when it comes to discussions about digital culture. So much so that Hansen (2006) suggests that it has almost attained the status of cliché. Despite the clichés, it is, indeed, a seminal work which thoughtfully contextualises the changing visual culture within the early development of modernity.

Benjamin suggests that, with the advent of photography, film and phonographic recording, works of art, cultural objects and performances of music could for the first time be either copied on a large scale or mass-produced. Benjamin was interested in the implications of this. On the one hand, these technologies brought a democracy of culture, in that remarkable objects became more accessible as they were – in a sense – pulled out from the physical locations of the original or authentic works: the cathedrals, the private collections, the galleries, the archives, the opera houses, the museums and far flung locations, and into a more accessible everyday lifeworld of cinemas, photographic magazines, parlours and radio broadcasts. Mechanical reproduction upset the power geometry that existed when the work of art was only accessible in certain physical spaces and to which limited people had access.

This ability and determination to 'bring things closer', or make them more accessible to the masses in modernity certainly had its positives, but Benjamin also suggested that in doing this, something was being lost: aura. 'Aura' can be considered the feeling of awe or reverence created by being in the presence of unique or remarkable objects:

> We define the aura of the latter [natural objects] as the unique phenomenon of a distance, however close it may be. If, while resting on a summer afternoon, you follow with your eyes a mountain range on the horizon or a branch which casts its shadow over you, you experience the aura of those mountains, of that branch. (Benjamin, 1936, from Frascina and Harris, 1992: 300)

Distance, space, perspective, a horizon, historical and geographical specificity, all create context. One appreciates the mountain range because of the experience of 'natural distance' which allows us to appreciate the object in its uniqueness and in its relation to the others that surround it. Similarly, the work of art possesses aura as a result of its surrounding attributes: place in history, authenticity, ties to place of exhibition (and thus also ties to bourgeois structures of power). Technologies of reproduction including photography, film and sound recording, uproot objects of art and nature from their situational contexts. The camera, for example, through its ability to 'zoom in', or record in slow motion, alters how we perceive the object by transcending both the physical and perceptual distance between the object and the viewer, and therefore obliterates the contextual situation of the object:

> To pry an object from its shell, to destroy its aura, is to make of a perception whose 'sense of the universal equality of things' has increased to such a degree that it extracts it even from a unique object by means of reproduction. (Benjamin, 1936, from Frascina and Harris, 1992: 300)

Mass reproduction created the potential for any object to be seen anywhere, which inevitably has an effect on the meaning of things. Manovich (2001) cleverly updates Benjamin's seminal argument by likening it to Paul Virilio's (1992) notion of 'big optics' and 'small optics' in the age of real time communication technology. *Small optics* refers to viewpoints based on geometric perspective (distance), and *big optics* refers to the ability to communicate in real time on a global scale. Instantaneity creates a situation where distance and space no longer have meaning and thus a depthless and horizonless world is created. Dreyfus (2001) pulls at a similar thread in his discussion of nihilism in relation to internet culture. However, Dreyfus sees the contemporary subject (and not objects) as becoming de-situated. People in contemporary culture with a wealth of digital communication at their disposal are encouraged to take a disengaged 'God-like' view of the world, where all types of information, involving all manner of places, become levelled into an equivalence; a universal equality of information which makes no distinction in terms of importance or relevance to personal or geographical contexts.

Building on the previous discussion, databases too, contribute to the lack of context within digital culture: collections of discrete units which create meaning only when related to other discrete units by the ad-hoc ordering of a user and a particular set of relationships at a given time. Where a narrative would provide a context, a cause, a reason, or a story, a database provides a temporary relationship. The extent to which digitally databased media is able to mix and match all manner of text, sound, image, data demonstrates this horizonless, contextless world of Virillio, Manovich, Benjamin and Dreyfus. Time and space are absent on YouTube, where one can just as easily watch episodes of a favourite television programme from childhood as watch the latest news events, upsetting the experience of memory, time and narrative biography. Digital music sites and MP3 culture pulverise bands, albums and genres into semi-anonymous files of singles embedded into endlessly diverse playlists that almost unreasonably span musical genres and eras (see Chapter 3). Social networking profiles link friends from different periods of life, childhood, university, work, as well as family and brief acquaintances in a timeless and spaceless networked collection (see Chapter 7). In this environment, it seems quite reasonable to suggest that the accessibility created by the age of networked digital reproduction has accelerated the demise of the contextual link between cultural object, space and time.

Variability

In the previous section on *automation*, we discussed how a large amount of what we experience in digital media is 'unique', in the sense that it has been created specifically for individual users in the sense of personalisation and customisation, but not 'original', in the sense that these unique creations are not composed of bespoke human-created material. The uniqueness of digital media objects not only emerges from this ability to personalise, but from the fact that most digital media objects change over time. Manovich (2001) refers to this as the property of *variability*.

'Old media', Manovich suggests, tends to be finite in that narratives and authored works tend to have a set composition or sequence of events (narrative). In that respect, the media fit the times, as old media is associated with the methods of production associated with modern industrialism. Just like cars coming out of factories, old media objects were mass produced copies of the master or prototype, produced in large amounts to meet mass demand, each copy identical to the last, and unchangably fixed in materiality.

By contrast, digital media objects are produced under the rubric of post-industrial informational capitalism, a system of production that focuses on 'just in time' production methods, which cater more towards individual choice as opposed to mass demand and is less focussed on the production of physical goods (see Chapter 2). As a result, digital media objects tend to be characterised by variability. They are not finite or finished products (let alone mass produced material ones), but instead are objects that are continually updated, reassembled and recreated and exist in potentially infinite versions. This is the case for several reasons, and these reasons tie together all of the 'technical processes' discussed in the last section.

Because digital media is *digital* numeric code, and not a physical object, it is left open to all kinds of manipulation involving algorithms. In some ways the most obvious example of this is the very fact that when digital data is stored and transferred, it is almost always *compressed* using algorithms when it is stored or transferred, then decompressed using algorithms when it is used (see Chapter 3 on 'convergence'). In effect, the data is taken apart and reconstructed and, in that sense, digital media objects are continually reconstructed when used. This compression/decompression model is followed by any types of digitised media produced for mass consumption, including music files and digital television.

Because digital media tends to be *networked* and *interactive* it often gets altered by the efforts, needs and wants of the user. This is especially true when it comes to personalisation and customisation. Personalisation can be manifested in a number of ways, from targeted advertising, to customised viewing, through to the participation of users in communally produced media objects such as Wikipedia, Massively Multiplayer Online Role-Playing Games (MMORPG's), Alternate Reality Games, or open sourced software such as Linux (see Chapter 3). These objects are always changing because people are always adding to them, expanding them, or improving them.

Digital media is often *hypertextual* or *hypermediated* and is thus composed of a variety of linkages where the order of execution of those linkages can be determined by the user. These links usually change over time as they often either become out of date, or expand in number. This is especially the case with regard to social media (Web 2.0), where links or tags can often be added to an existing document or object quite easily. Social networking web sites and blogs provide a good example of this, where the content of a profile is continually changing through the addition of new updates, friends, links, pictures and comments.

As suggested above, much of new media is now *automated*, thus not created by a human author, but assembled on the fly through automated processes, algorithms and updates. Manovich (2001) makes the point that web sites in particular automatically configure and customise sites on the basis of the user's IP address (automatically changing language, or directing the user to a nation or region specific page such as yahoo.uk, or ebay.ca), or by altering presentation to the type of computer and web browser being used. Automated periodic updates change software and keep it up to date, as well as reconfigure social media profiles.

And finally, the form of the *database* itself, central to the way digital media is constructed, is amenable to variability because the whole purpose of a database is to be able to configure information in a variety of ways. Because databases are lists, conceptually, they tend not to be finite products. They are meant to be temporarily useful, flexible and expand. Thus, databases epitomise variability, whereas narratives tend to be static.

Rhizome

Several authors (such as Bell, 2001; Buchanan, 2007; Hamman, 1996; Hess, 2008; Stivale, 1998; Wise, 1997) have suggested that because the internet possesses features such as hypertext, networking and variability, the internet, and many parts of it, articulate the concept of the *rhizome* as characterised by Deleuze and Guattari (1988). Rhizome is a metaphor that Deleuze and Guattari use to describe a form of organisation that is not based on hierarchical structure, but a kind of horizontal network of relations. They contrast the botanical term rhizome with arboreal structures such as trees and their root systems, which they see as hierarchical, and associate with a particular way of thinking that involves tracing things back to centres or origins.

> A rhizome as a subterranean stem is absolutely different from roots and radicles. Bulbs and tubers are rhizomes. Plants with roots or radicles may be rhizomorphic in other respects altogether. Burrows are too, in all their functions of shelter, supply, movement, evasion, and breakout. The rhizome itself assumes very diverse forms, from ramified surface extension in all directions to concretion into bulbs and tubers ... The rhizome includes the best and the worst: potato and couchgrass, or the weed. (Deleuze and Guattari, 1988: 6–7)

Rhizome is a difficult concept, but for simplicity's sake most discussion of the internet as a rhizome will start with the six principles outlined in the introduction to *A Thousand Plateaus*:[4]

- 'The rhizome connects any point to any other point'. The connections are random in relation to each other and any point can be connected to any other (the principle of *connection*).

- 'The rhizome is reducible to neither the One nor the multiple'. In this respect it is neither a collection of individual things, nor one large thing. Instead it is composed of dimensions and lines of connection (the principle of *multiplicity*).

This also means that no point in the rhizome can be altered without altering the whole.

- 'The rhizome operates by variation, expansion, conquest, capture, offshoots'. In that sense, it does not 'reproduce', it transforms both itself and what it encounters (the principle of *decalcomania*).

- 'The rhizome pertains to a map that must be produced, constructed, a map that is always detachable, connectable, reversible, modifiable, and has multiple entryways and exits and its own lines of flight'. So in contrast to 'tracings' where one must follow a given path, a rhizome is akin to a map or a field in which one can enter at any point, and must construct their own path through (the principle of *cartography*).

- 'The rhizome is an acentered, nonhierarchical, nonsignifying system without a General and without an organizing memory or central automation'. This suggests that rhizomes have nothing akin to a 'centre' which is more important than other parts of the system (the principle of *heterogeneity*).

- 'The rhizome is made only of lines'. These lines can be severed or broken, but because it is acentred, such breakages do not impede its function but can instead create new lines for growth or transformation (the principle of *asignifying rupture*).

Typically, writers then discuss the internet, or some part of the internet such as a chat room or forum to demonstrate its rhizomatic principles. Within these parameters the principle of *connection* is fairly easy to establish, in that the architecture of the internet is one in which connectivity reigns supreme, and the fact that one can connect to the internet from just about any point, and traverse it freely from one hyperlink to the next in seemingly random ways, suggests that the internet follows the principle of *cartography*. For example, within five clicks on hyperlinks embedded in the Wikipedia entry for 'Germany' ('golden bull', 'indivisible', 'rain queen', 'meningitis') I can end up on the Wikipedia page for 'penicillin', an unexpected and novel pathway to say the least. The supposedly chaotic networked structure of the internet means that there is no real centre that is fundamentally important (heterogeneity), and the internet is fully able to sustain breakages without much effect on its function (asignifying rupture).

The last two principles, multiplicity and decalcomania, require more nuanced analysis. Multiplicity suggests that a rhizome is not a collection of units, not one unit, but a multiplication of dimensions. While many authors suggest that the continuing proliferation of computers and multiple other kinds of connections to the web, as well as the limitless number of web sites, are suggestive of multiplicity, Buchanan (2007) makes the reasonable point that what actually matters with regard to multiplicity is whether or not these new connections and web pages are dimensions, or units of the web, and whether or not subtracting them has any effect on the whole. He argues that one could remove several thousand web sites from the net without the whole being noticeably affected, and in that sense individual web sites can be seen as 'units' of the web, and not 'dimensions'. However, this is a tenuous argument, as one would think that Deleuze and Guattari's point here is one of connection and isolation. Since each web site or computer has multiple connections (both physically and in terms of hyperlinks) the whole is affected even by the severing of one, because connections are lost, altering the multiplicity of pathways.

Decalcomania is slightly more complex and refers to the idea of variation or trans- formation in expansion or encounter. This relates to Deleuze and Guattari's notion of 'becoming' (which is set in opposition with 'being' as a static form of existence) and sug- gests that rhizomes do not achieve growth through reproduction, but through continual transformation. In one of their more famous analogies, they turn to the relationship between 'the wasp and the orchid'. The petals and stamen of the orchid take on the patt- erning of a wasp in order to fool it into thinking that it is another wasp with which it can mate. The wasp is in turn attracted onto the orchid and thus collects pollen which it then distributes to other orchids. In this relationship, both have taken on aspects of the other. The wasp has become part of the orchid's reproductive system and the orchid has taken on the visual appearance of the wasp. They have been transformed, but not merged in their encounter (Bell, 2001).

One could speak on similar lines about the internet and its encounter with 'old media' in, for example, the encounter between newspapers and the internet. Newspapers have been transformed but not subsumed by the arrival of the internet (they still exist in print form, but also have been remediated in digital form on the internet), and the internet has been transformed in that newspaper sites are now popular destinations on the inter- net. Similar could be said about the encounter between the internet and the telephone, with the development of internet-enabled mobile phones and, conversely, internet- based phone companies such as Skype. More absurdly, the internet has encountered refrigerators. In 2001, LG Electronics introduced the Digital Internet Refrigerator:

> The refrigerator makes extensive use of touch screens, a simplified graphics user interface, electronic pen and voice messaging for a user-friendly experience. Using these tools, consumers can check real-time price information on grocer- ies; obtain tips on food, nutrition and recipes; be reminded of scheduled events; be informed when to change the refrig- erator's filter, and learn cooking methods for products stored inside. (Beststuff.com, 2001)

In this respect, it seems reasonable to suggest that the internet, and many of the things on it, follow rhizomatic principles insofar as it/they are in a continual state of 'becoming' or transformation in response to the surrounding environment. However, Hess (2008) argues that through the imperatives of commercialisation, search engines now follow a more hierarchical structure by returning commercially valuable sites higher up in results lists. In this sense, search engines end up ordering knowledge in such a way as to privilege mainstream voices, atrophying the internet's cartographic and heterogenic potential for resistance.

While one may see the internet as fulfilling many rhizomatic principles, it is problematic to suggest that the internet is a rhizome in the idealised form Deleuze and Guattari set out. As Hess suggests, dependence on commercial entities introduces arboreal structures, roots and hierarchies into the experience of the web and thus limits to an extent the degree to which the internet can be seen as truly rhizomic in terms of its epistemology and its potential for resistance. One only has to look at the compromises that Google has made with the government of China in order to get a Chinese-based Google page to see that, ultimately, commercial pressures will compromise rhizomatic principles (Buchanan, 2007). In that respect, we can see the internet existing in a kind of uneasy tension between rhizomic and arboreal forms of organisation and existence.

Process

Deleuze and Guattari's discussions of 'transformation' and 'becoming' bring us to the suggestion that the internet, and much on it, is in a continual state of transformation. This observation makes sense within the context of Manovich's claim that variability is one of the key principles of new media. As we recall from earlier, digital media is in continual transformation as it is always being updated, modified, compressed, decompressed, linked and databased, and in that sense has the potential to exist in infinite versions. Looking forward to Bruns (2008) (see Chapter 3), he lists 'unfinished artefacts, continuing process' as one of the key principles of 'produsage' in digital media:

> … as collectively prodused content is shared in an openly accessible information commons, the process of produsage must necessarily remain continually unfinished, and infinitely continuing …

> Such outcomes, produced through social processes, take on the same aspects of those processes themselves; they resemble cultural artefacts more than commercial products. (Bruns, 2008: 27)

These three concepts of becoming/transformation, variability and unfinished artefacts/ continuing processes all point towards the same key characteristic of digital media: constant change. When we consider much of what is found in the internet, very little of it is static: web pages acquire more links; databases continue to grow; software (especially open source software) continues to be improved and expanded; social networking profiles are continually being updated and add new friends; 'wiki's' of all kinds are always getting new entries or revising old ones; images and texts are repeatedly being copied and manipulated; online games, MMORPGs and ARGs are continually added to and enhanced by their players and participants.

In this respect, Bruns might be right to suggest that digital media are more like 'continuing processes' than 'objects'. Unfortunately, Bruns turns to calling digital media products 'artefacts', which is perhaps a misleading term in that 'artefacts' refer to tangible products in material culture. Manovich (2001) also seems inconsistent in this regard by continually using the term 'new media object', which also seems contradictory with what he is trying to achieve. However, this is somewhat unsurprising in that it is often difficult for us to conceive of 'processes' given that Western culture has tended to view the world from a substantist philosophical position (influenced by Aristotle), as opposed to a relational one:

> For Aristotelians, the primary categories of being are substance and accident, with all accidents inhering some particular substance …
>
> For relational metaphysics, relation or process becomes the primary reality in which substances function as movements. Clearly the world of advanced technological machines is to some extent more amenable to such a relational metaphysics. (Mitcham, 1994: 169)

But perhaps this is what we need to do when considering the 'stuff' of digital media. After all, it has no material form (although it is accessed through material objects and can be translated into material form), so it cannot be considered an 'artefact' or an 'object'. The fact that digital media tends to be in constant change only reinforces this view.

Given the characteristics of digital media such as variability and transformation brought up in this chapter thus far, and given the general shift in use of the internet from being a primarily informational source, to a social medium (Web 2.0), it is perhaps useful to see new media products being more akin to *conversations* than material objects. Conversations are social processes or experiences that may have an origin, but not necessarily an outcome (or at least an outcome directly related to their origins). This is cleverly illustrated by Stivale's (1998) examination of meandering threads of discussion in online discussion forums dedicated to Deleuze and Guattari.

Jenkins' (2006) 'Bert is evil' example is also illustrative of this. In the same way a conversation may have an original purpose but often takes diversions in unanticipated directions, and perhaps ending up in a place completely unimagined, Jenkins tracks how the image of Bert was grafted from *Sesame Street* episodes aimed at American children, placed ironically alongside Osama Bin Laden on the 'Bert is evil' web pages of a high school student (being transformed in the process), ending up, in the wake of September 11th, in an Osama Bin Laden image collage on Islamist anti-American placards in the Middle East (creating an entirely different and unexpected set of meanings and relationships), and finally ending up as a comical news item on *CNN* and a variety of blogs. The continual migration and transformation of the Bert image both in properties and meaning is an exemplar of how digital media products are both rhizomatic and in a constant state of 'becoming'.

IMMERSIVE EXPERIENCES

Once we start to consider digital media as producing processes, experiences, or conversations in continual flux more than they are producing finite 'objects', the more we are able to see how digital media has as much as, or perhaps more, in common with the tradition of the telephone and other telecommunications than with the aesthetic tradition of the novel or the painting. As Manovich points out:

> By foregrounding telecommunications, both real-time and asynchronous, as a fundamental cultural activity, the internet asks us to reconsider the very paradigm of an aesthetic object. (Manovich, 2001: 163–164)

The move to media *as process* entails within it new conceptions of the audience or user, as we have seen. However, the move also entails a transformation of the audience or consumer experience, from a static role of *viewer* to a role as *active, mobile user* or *participant* within the creation. This creates much more potential for digital media to provide a more immersive relationship between media and user. This new relationship is embodied in the features of *telepresence, virtuality* and *simulation*, which can be considered fundamental immersive elements of digital media.

Telepresence

One thing that communication technologies have the potential to do is alter our feelings of presence. The term presence itself can be considered 'the experience of one's physical environment' or more generally, 'the sense of being in an environment' (Steuer, 1992: 75). Presence is relatively unproblematic in unmediated situations, we *are* where we 'are', and that seems quite obvious and simple. However, when mediated communication or long distance interaction is introduced into the equation, things begin to change. In this situation we gain the ability to simultaneously exist in two different environments at the same time: the physical environment in which our body is located and the conceptual or interactional 'space' we are presented with through the use of the medium (Steuer, 1992). For example, getting a letter from someone far away may, if descriptive enough, transport our imaginations to a particular place or event being described. Well-written novels certainly do this.

This altered sense of presence becomes even more apparent when we are dealing with more advanced communication technologies. The telephone allows us, in real time, to be in two places at once. Where our bodies are and, also, in that 'space in between' where we are and where the other person is, not a physical space, but a conceptual one (Lister et al., 2009). This is the notion of *telepresence*: the experience of presence in an environment by means of a communication medium (Steuer, 1992: 77). In contemporary culture, the increasing blending of presence and telepresence manifests itself in the current ambiguities regarding mobile phone conversations and texting when in the company of others, particularly at the dinner table (see Rimer, 2009). Online, our perception of presence becomes even more complicated. Terms such as 'cyberspace', 'surfing' and being 'on' the internet are indicative of how our experience of the internet as an interactive, real-time media give us an enhanced sense of telepresence over, say, watching television. People 'watch' television.

This leads us to another feature of telepresence: that its experience varies between technologies as well as being influenced by social factors. Steuer (1992) suggests that technologically there are two things which determine the extent that telepresence is experienced. The first is *vividness*: the ability of a technology to produce a rich environment for the senses in terms of sensory *depth* and *breadth*. Sensory breadth refers to the number of senses engaged in the medium (sight, sound, smell, haptic, taste). Sensory depth refers to the quality or resolution the medium provides to a given sense. Superior sound, visual and other sensory qualities will create a much more immersive experience. The second factor is *interactivity*. As we discussed earlier, interactivity refers to the degree in which the user of a medium can influence the form and content of their mediated environment.

In addition to technological factors, it is important to note, as Steuer does, the importance of contextual or emotional factors in the experience of telepresence. The idea of *engagement* in the interaction underway is crucial in this. For example, exchanging work-related emails often does not engage one to a large degree, and thus creates very little sense of presence or immersion. However, the same might not be said using the exact same technologies to – for example – engage in cybersex discourse. More emotionally engaging interactions create a greater sense of 'first person-ness' (Laurel, 1991 cited in Steuer, 1992) that is the essence of vivid telepresence. The recent generations of video games, such as *Grand Theft Auto* and *Bully*, use the combination of telepresence, sensory depth and first person-ness to create a high degree of vividness and engagement for the player. This adds to the controversial nature which sometimes surrounds these games.

Virtuality

Any discussion of 'engagement' leads to another immersive aspect of digital media: virtuality. Rob Shields (2003) begins his discussion of *The Virtual* in 1556 with the execution of Archbishop Thomas Cranmer for heresy. The basis of this event was a debate in the early reformation period over the Christian Eucharist, and specifically the transubstantiation of bread and wine into the blood and body of Christ during the performance of the sacrament of the Eucharist. Within the Catholicism of the time, transubstantiation was (and still is) taken literally; the bread and wine *actually became* the body and blood of Christ. Protestants and reformers like Thomas Cranmer disagreed and suggested that this was not an *actual* transformation, but a *virtual* one. In 1556, that was enough to get one hanged.

Shields' excellent discussion demonstrates how the problem of the virtual is nothing new. Debates we have now about the worth or value of online communities (Chapter 8), or mobile phones in public places, or the 'danger' of cybersex (Chapter 7), are not very far off the sort of debate described above:

> The doctrine of virtualism raised questions concerning the way we understand presence – must it be concrete and embodied, or was 'essentially present' good enough? Was there anything there if it was virtual? (Shields, 2003: 6)

The merit (or lack) of virtual communities and the like is a topic for other chapters. Here what needs to be addressed is how 'virtuality' is an important aspect of digital media and how virtuality can be placed within a wider cultural context. In this respect, Shields is quite helpful in that he makes the distinction between 'the real', 'the actual' (or 'concrete') and 'the virtual'.

Within current discourses, the idea of the virtual is normally limited to discussions of digital technologies: ideas of 'virtual reality', 'virtual economies', or 'virtual worlds'. Within these discourses, there is a tendency to contrast such virtualities with 'the real'. Shields brings the discussions of the virtual back to a wider context, by defining virtuality as 'the nature of objects and activities which exist, but are not tangible or concrete' (Shields, 2003: 2). In many respects, Shields constructs a notion of the virtual which is inclusive of all sorts of social constructions and imaginings. Plays, for example, can be considered virtual in the sense that they create a world and a set of understandings and realities that are ephemeral, not concrete. It does not mean that plays or the worlds they depict are not 'real'. They do exist, but they exist as an abstraction.

Similarly, one could consider a digital file or document. They are virtual in the sense that they (up until being printed) are not material objects. But they are experienced, sent, viewed and can have a concrete impact in terms of their implications, depending on what the document was about and who was reading it. It would be silly to argue that a digital document is not 'real' just because it is not concrete.

Thus, the practice of contrasting the virtual with the real is problematic, as 'reality' is made up of both the concrete and the virtual in many ways, including the practices of religious rituals, abstract planning, and even in the imaginings of our own and other communities. We exist in both at the same time. This leads Shields to argue that the virtual is in opposition to the *concrete*, not in opposition to the *real*, and that reality in fact is always part virtual in everyday concrete, as well as electronic, instances. The virtual is real, but not actual.

Simulation

From a discussion of virtuality as a feature of digital objects, we can take Shields' insights and move forward to suggest that digital objects (or artefacts or processes) have an ephemeral as opposed to a concrete quality that makes them real but not actual. However, they can be represented in concrete form. This articulation of the relationship between the real and the virtual becomes useful because if we can see the virtual as a 'kind of' reality, we can start to address some of the fears that are involved in discussions of virtual communities, virtual worlds and virtual identities: i.e., that we are passing into some sort of fantasy world and losing touch with the real (Lister et al., 2009).

Any discussion of the virtual in digital culture almost inevitably leads onto a discussion of *simulations*. 'Virtual reality' or 'virtual worlds' are usually seen as simulations of 'reality', a kind of model of the real world. The simulational qualities of digital media can be considered in three different ways:

- As a technical or mathematical process often performed by computers.

- As a tradition in visual culture.

- As part of a historical progression away from 'the real' within media-laden contemporary culture.

In the first instance, simulation can be defined as 'a mathematical or algorithmic model, combined with a set of initial conditions, that allows prediction and visualisation as time unfolds' (Prensky, 2001: 211, cited in Lister et al., 2009: 41). Such simulations are not restricted to computers, but obviously come into their own in the computerised, information age. Within a wide variety of research, computer simulations are used to project into the future and to estimate the potential effects of a change in certain variables on a complex system or process. For example, climatologists will study the potential effects of a change in atmospheric CO2 levels on the global climate using computerised climate modelling, and economists would predict the potential effects of a change in oil prices on the stock market in a stock market simulation. Another popular encounter with computer simulations are video games of all kinds (see the case study in this chapter).

Manovich (2001) examines the simulative and representational as two different traditions within Western visual culture. The *representation* tradition is exemplified by the painting (or objects with frames and screens) and relies upon the immobility of the spectator. Representation allows for the creation of aesthetic objects that are fixed in space and time, and refer to something outside of themselves. In that sense, representations attempt to portray other things usually located in other places. By contrast, the tradition of *simulation* (epitomised in mosaics and frescoes) relies on a mobile spectator. The audience travels through the hall or church, encountering the frescoes in movement, so there is a blending of the virtual world of the created work and the physical space of the spectator or audience. Thus, simulations possess an immersive quality.

Digital culture tends to follow in the immersive simulational tradition by emphasising the mobility of the viewer, in a metaphorical sense through actions like hyperlinking, hypertext, the notion of 'surfing', and more literally with regard to the three-dimensional virtual worlds of first person or point of view video games and MMORPGs, in which the exploration of a virtual world is open to the user.

Within digital culture, immersive simulations obviously abound. Anyone can point to the virtual worlds of *Second Life* or *The Sims* as examples of simulated everyday life. Even more interesting perhaps are the next generation of virtual worlds which are overtly imitative of real offline environments. Here, efforts such as *Twinity* (http://www.twinity.com), a virtual reconstruction of Berlin, or *Near Global*'s (http://www.nearglobal.com/) current reconstruction of London immerse their users in accurate simulations of actual cities. Complete with the same shops and tourist sites that exist in the offline London and Berlin, *Near Global* and *Twinity* are pushing the simulation tradition into a merger between virtual simulations and physical spaces.

> Virtual worlds are simulations. Like a map they usually start out as reproducing actual worlds, real bodies, and real situations: but, like simulations, they end up taking on a life of their own …
>
> Virtual worlds become important when they diverge from the actual, or when the actual is ignored in favour of the virtual. (Shields, 2003: 4)

In the contrast between representation and simulation, the latter is usually viewed in the more negative light. Representation is generally seen as a genuine attempt to portray something 'real' or in a truthful manner. By contrast, simulation is often portrayed as deceptive, something which takes us *away* from the real or the truth. A brief perusal of any dictionary definitions for 'simulation' will pull up words such as 'imitation', 'likeness', 'enactment', 'feigning' 'a sham' or 'a false appearance', many of which are pejorative in nature.

This line of thinking is best represented by the work of Jean Baudrillard, especially in *Simulacra and Simulation* (1994). Baudrillard argued that there has been a historical progression in Western culture away from representation, where signs reflected something fundamentally real, to simulations, where signs no longer represent or refer to the real. He charts this movement in a series of stages which he refers to as the 'orders of the simulacra'.

In pre-Renaissance or feudal times, Baudrillard suggests, there was symbolic order. There was a fixed system of signs that reflected a basic certainty of life. Everyone knew their positions in a rigid social structure, therefore social positions and status could be read quite easily, for example, royals, nobles and aristocrats wore certain clothes and used certain symbols. People were intimately tied to the concrete realities of nature, signs and symbols were easily interpreted and in that manner, 'reality' itself could be seen as unproblematic. This certainty of meaning and the way things are was reflected in art and other forms of representation. Thus, medieval painting, for example, as much as possible strived for realistic depictions of what were seen to be real events. This can be seen in Figure 1.2, a medieval representation of the crucifixion of Christ. Art reflected a basic reality.

Historically, the beginnings of industrial society initiated a break of the intimate relationship between people and nature, and the political changes brought forth by the Enlightenment meant a break from the certainties of medieval feudalism, with less rigid social structures and challenges being made to the power and authority of Monarchy and the Church. From the Renaissance to the early part of the Industrial Revolution, Baudrillard argues that Western culture entered the 'first order of the simulacra'. In this context, the notion of the 'fake' or 'imitation' becomes important. Art, for example, starts to be viewed as imitative of life, rather than a representation of it. Baroque painting demonstrated a tendency towards idealisation (see Figure 1.3, a Baroque style painting of the ascension of Christ into heaven); classical architecture emerged as an imitation of styles of the past, aristocratic Victorian gardens were meticulously designed

Figure 1.2 Symbolic Order: 'Crucifixion' by Konrad Witz (circa 1444)

to look wild and natural. All these demonstrate the tendency at the time towards idealisation of nature, events and the past. Thus, in the first order, art imitated or perverted a basic reality.

Baudrillard suggests the time period from the early industrial revolution to the middle of the twentieth century, corresponds with the second order of the simulacra. This is the era of industrial mass production. The link between people and nature in the West became more distanced as, in the age of machines, nature is continually being modified into new, completely unnatural things. This manipulation of nature, combined with the seemingly limitless reproducibility possible under mass production (typified by the factory or the photograph), created a situation where copies became almost indistinguishable from originals, even to the point where the whole notion of an 'original' or an 'authentic' becomes problematic. Take, for example, the first mass produced automobile, the Model T Ford. Purchasing a Model T (or any other mass produced object) did (and still does) not mean that one has purchased a lesser imitation of some sort of 'original' Model T. The car itself did not refer to something authentic; after all, how can one have an 'authentic' machine? Instead, any Model T Ford referred not to an authentic or original, but to other Model T's as a series of signs (see Figure 1.4). Thus, in the second order, art and artifice masked the presence of a basic reality.

Figure 1.3 The First Order: 'Transfiguration' by Raphael (circa 1518)

From the mid-twentieth century to the present, Baudrillard argues that we have entered the third order of the simulacra or *hyper-reality*. This represents the transition from the machine age to the information age and the shift from a production to a consumption society. By this point, consumer culture has created such an uncertain social structure, and such a proliferation of signs, that their association to anything 'real' or 'authentic' has become lost. In that sense, a situation is created where we exist in hyper-reality, dealing with copies of copies to the point where we cannot tell the difference between copies and originals and, if anything, we prefer the copy to the original.

In this scenario, the real and the imaginary collapse into each other: politics becomes based on opinion polls (simulations of the public and their views): stockbrokers use computer models of the stock market for automated (or program) trading (accelerating the 'Black Monday' stock market crash of 1987); maps, tourist brochures and Google Street View, seen in advance, help to determine our experience of faraway places instead of the reverse.

Simulation of this kind is endemic to digital culture. Emails, in their ability to be endlessly reproduced, copied, responded to, forwarded and amended, embody hyper-reality in the sense that there is little attention paid to an 'original'. Music files, such as

Figure 1.4 The Second Order: The Ford factory, Manchester (circa 1911)

MP3s are not so much copies of songs as they are mathematical reproductions of songs compressed and decompressed by algorithmic software. Indeed, Poster (1990) makes the point that the majority of studio recordings in the contemporary music industry epitomise simulacra in the sense that songs are recorded one instrument at a time, often in different studios and over long periods of time. The listener is presented with what would seem to be a 'performance', but in fact it is a simulacrum of a performance: a copy of a performance which never really existed as an original (Poster, 1990 cited in Shields, 2003: 47). This can also be illustrated in Figure 1.5, where an avatar in *Second Life* was voted one of the top 100 most attractive women in the world in *Maxim* magazine's 'hot 100' of 2007.

Baudrillard's goal was to demonstrate how a shift to simulation from representation within contemporary culture was symptomatic of a historical drift away from nature and authenticity, or the real. For him, the danger of simulations lies in their ability to deceive, often through idealisation, so much so that simulations become preferable to the messiness and complications of 'the real'. In that respect, simulations have an ideological function: they work as distractions or alibis. His famous discussion of the first Gulf War (1995) is a fine example of how a simulacrum can serve to mask an ugly truth.

However, at this point we should refer back to the end of the previous section on virtuality, where Shields (2003) and Lister et al. (2009), informed by the insights of Deleuze,

2007 Hot 100 Photos
We proudly present you the 100 most astoundingly attractive specimens occupying this planet.

Digg This Story Facebook Yahoo! buzz

95. Second Life Girl

Second Life—a 3-D virtual world that's imagined, created, and owned by its online residents—was launched in 2003 and now boasts nearly five million inhabitants around the globe. Never taken part in the nerdfest? Isn't she reason enough?

Figure 1.5 The Third Order: 'Second Life Girl' as one of the 100 most attractive women in the world, according to *Maxim* magazine, 2007

suggest that the line between the actual and the virtual is continually being crossed, and both together make up the real as experienced in everyday life. So it may be that we are not, as Baudrillard suggests, losing touch with 'the real' but that what used to constitute 'the real' has undergone change.

Case Study: What Are Video Games? A Conundrum of Digital Culture

Culturally, video games are significant because they were the first form of mass digital media, as well as the first mass consumed interactive media (Newman, 2004), and have also been at the forefront of digital culture in terms of the creation of immersive environments and networking. Frasca (2003) boldly suggests that 'Video games imply an enormous paradigm shift for our culture because they represent the first complex simulational media for the masses' (Frasca, 2003: 224).

This bold assertion hides a larger debate regarding what video games actually *are* as a cultural object. Video games have elements of many different media: they have elements of a story and usually have characters, thus suggesting an affinity with narrative texts, they have visual, sonic and cinematic elements reminiscent of narrative film, they have rules and player agency associated with games and they have interactive and simulational elements that are most commonly viewed as fundamental to digital media. In many ways, video games defy categorisation.

Are video games 'narratives'?

In this chapter, one of the main arguments put forward is that in digital culture, the cultural form of the *database* is beginning to supersede narrative as the preeminent cultural form of contemporary times (Manovich, 2001). Increasingly, Manovich argues, media objects consist of separate elements arranged on an ad-hoc basic with no predetermined authorship or a structured sequence of events which move towards an ending. One of the main stumbling blocks to this generalisation is the video game, which Manovich himself recognises as the one bastion of narrative in digital culture. Indeed, most contemporary video games have a story, a setting and characters. For example, in the highly popular *Grand Theft Auto: San Andreas*, the game revolves around player/character 'CJ', as described in the promotional material for the game:

> Five years ago Carl Johnson escaped from the pressures of life in Los Santos, San Andreas ... a city tearing itself apart with gang trouble, drugs and corruption. Where filmstars and millionaires do their best to avoid the dealers and gangbangers.
>
> Now, it's the early 90s. Carl's got to go home. His mother has been murdered, his family has fallen apart and his childhood friends are all heading towards disaster.
>
> On his return to the neighborhood, a couple of corrupt cops frame him for homicide. CJ is forced on a journey that takes him across the entire state of San Andreas, to save his family and to take control of the streets.
> (http://www.rockstargames.com/sanandreas/)

It is argued that the narrative elements in a game promote structure, motivation, psychological depth and a context for the player's actions, adding to the immersive experience of the game and thus the quality of game play experience for the player (Mallon and Webb, 2005). In this light, video games have traditionally been seen as extensions of narrative, and have been analysed and conceived of as a form of interactive storytelling.

However, many video game scholars became increasingly frustrated with this approach, arguing that video games contain very few of the essential elements of 'narrative', that approaching them as narratives fundamentally misses the integral features of interactivity that is their core (Juul, 2001). In short, they argue:

- Narratives follow inevitable rules and predetermined sequences of action. Thus, video games are not a 'text' to be read because their outcomes depend directly on the action of the player (Frasca, 2003).

- The narrative components of video games tend to be non-interactive (for example, in the form of 'cut scenes' or instructions), and thus form only an incidental part of the player experience or motivation to play the game. Furthermore, the games themselves usually lack dramatic content (Crawford, 2003).

- Characterisation is weak or even non-existent in video games. At best, characters tend to be viewed in game play as sites for action. Indeed in many video games (such as *Tetris*, or *SimEarth*), there is no visible actor or character at all (Juul, 2001).

As a result, there is a large debate occurring within the small domains of video game scholarship in which many suggest that such objects would be better examined in light of their capacity as 'games' than as 'texts'.

Are video games 'games'?

Theorists such as Juul (2001) and Frasca (2003) suggest that video games should be studied from the standpoint of ludology (the study of games). The notion of a 'game' suggests two basic elements: rules and an objective (or a way to 'win' and 'lose'). These are the elements of what Callois (1961) refers to as *'ludus'*, essentially games with explicit rules that ultimately define a winner and loser (Frasca, 2003). This is of course common to all formalised games, not just video games. For example, football, as a game, has rules which include a field of play, a set time (90 minutes), an objective (to score more goals than the opposition in the set time) and strict rules about how this can be accomplished (not being able to touch the ball with your hands or arms).

Moving further with the work of Callois, Frasca (2003) suggests that *ludus* style game play occurs in three stages: learning the rules; playing the game; ending the game and deciding a winner. In this respect, Frasca argues that games and narratives are different. Games are rarely played only once (after all, one has to get used to the rules to play properly), whereas narratives are often consumed only once. In addition (also unlike narratives), one can never play the exact game twice, as the players and their actions will always be different.

Video games, especially earlier single-screen games such as *Space Invaders*, *Donkey Kong*, or *Asteroids*, have clear rules, a bounded sphere of action and a direct way to win. Any narrative elements ('save the earth from invaders', 'rescue the princess', 'save the ship from the asteroid field'), while they may exist, are ultimately subordinate to the main task as far as the player is concerned: to *win*, either by getting a high score, or living as long as possible. This seems clear and self-evident, but what about video games that don't end, or games which have no winners or losers?

Are video games 'simulations'?

In 1978, Atari released a new game for its 2600 console. Entitled *Adventure*, the game was based on the *Dungeons and Dragons* fantasy theme in which a knight must find a magic sword through a maze of rooms in order to slay dragons and recover a golden chalice. Essentially an exercise in problem solving, the game earned a place in video game history not for its graphics (which were basic in the extreme) but for its novel use of the cinematic convention of off-screen events (things in other parts of the labyrinth happened independently of the players actions) and the ability to freely move the character from one screen (room) to another (Robinett, 2003). What *Adventure* did was create a world beyond the screen: a world with a labyrinth of rooms and where things happened independently of the players actions.

Twenty years later, Aarseth (1997) argued that video games behaved much like cybernetic systems that incorporated feedback mechanisms to create an environment for game play (see Chapter 9). Frasca (2001, 2003) built upon this observation to argue that video games should not just be seen as narratives, or even just games, but simulations. Here, Frasca is working with a very specific definition of simulation:[5] 'to simulate is to model a (source) system through a different system which maintains to somebody some of the behaviors of the original system' (Frasca, 2003: 223).

Basically, Frasca sees simulation as a dynamic system that behaves in some manner and thus reacts to actions or events according to a set of conditions. Increasingly, as video games have moved away from single-screen action, the creation of simulational worlds has become a dominant part of video game culture, as evidenced in so called 'God games' such as *SimCity* or *Civilisation*, to social simulation games such as *The Sims*, sports simulations (*Football Manager*), to business, government, medical, flight and biological/ecological simulations. All of these games are thematic simulations or models of a particular system and as a game rely on the player interacting with complex feedback processes in order to transform the environment of the game into something the player desires.

In this respect, with these games there is often no specific goal which needs to be achieved to win the game. Players can merely 'tinker' or create their own goals to achieve (the ugliest life form, the most efficient city), and the game itself never really has to end. Thus, as Frasca (2003) suggests, video games as a genre not only incorporate the notion of *ludus*, but also what Callois refers to as *padia* or unstructured play. This is the form of play normally common with younger children who pretend (say, by modelling themselves on adult behaviour, playing 'soldier' or 'nurse') or tinker and experiment (with building blocks for example). Such play differs from (*ludus*) 'games' in the sense that rules are much less explicit, and there is no inherent purpose, winner or loser, or even a reason to end. If there are any goals, they are up to the player themselves and these efforts can be seen as a form of creativity.

Padia is more akin to simulation games, as these tend to be about exploration, experimentation and creativity. However, the popular first-person shooter game series, *Grand Theft Auto* (or similar games) incorporate both *ludus* and *padia* styles into its simulated world of urban crime. Players can choose to pursue the stated objectives associated with the plot of the game, or they can simply explore the world, start impromptu gun battles, or complete death-defying stunts. Indeed, there is a large amount of user generated content on *YouTube* in which people have created videos out of stunts and gun battles on *Grand Theft Auto* as well as other games.

Video games have also changed over time from being solitary activities played on isolated consoles or PCs to become social activities where users compete against, interact among and cooperate with, each other, through networked computers or games consoles. This has been accomplished by the online networking of console games and also through the growth of web-based MMORPGs such as *World of Warcraft* and *Second Life*. These games have changed the nature of video game playing online as they are not so much games as they are virtual social worlds. Many participants have even set up profitable businesses selling virtual goods in them. As many as 10 million people worldwide subscribe to *World of Warcraft* and perhaps 30 million people worldwide are involved in MMORPGs (Castranova, 2005).

There have been a number of recent large ethnographic studies of virtual worlds or MMORPGs (Boellstorff, 2008; Castranova, 2005; Meadows, 2008). Each of these have approached the phenomena from a different angle. Castranova (2005) sees MMORPG's as games, Meadows (2008) makes a distinction between 'game worlds' like *World of Warcraft*, in which there is some sort of competition among players (and the 'loss' of being killed and having to start over), and 'social worlds' in which there is no direct competition and no chance of being killed. Boellstorff (2008) makes a clear assertion that online worlds are not games, and thus are not video games. Certainly MMORPGs like *Second Life* are not games in the *ludic* sense, but one can argue that they demonstrate the *padia* quality of simulational play quite forcefully. Having no ending or no stated goal, *Second Life*, *Twinity* and other socially-based MMORPGs (and one could include the *World of Warcraft*) seem only to have the theme of 'existence', which can be subdivided into vague ambitions of exploration, creativity and a quest for increasing popularity or power within the world.

However, such ambitions will ultimately be manifest in different ways by different players: from exploring different virtual landscapes, to maintaining different forms of social relationships, to building structures and works of art, creating profitable businesses, acquiring skills and even amassing slaves. In this sense, the behaviour of players in MMORPGs is more akin to the creative exploration involved in *Grand Theft Auto* shootouts and stunting than any specific *ludic* objectives. 'Games', perhaps they are not, but they can be accurately described as relatively unstructured 'play' within simulations.

CONCLUSION

The purpose of this chapter has been to outline the basic elements of digital media as compared to traditional broadcast media (or 'old media') within wider technological and cultural contexts. This has been explored through the general themes of technical processes, cultural forms and immersive environments. Within these themes there have been several features which, in sum, constitute digital products as novel compared to previous media incarnations.

The various features within these themes were many and interconnected, but one general theme which has emerged throughout the chapter is the idea that digital media products are as much *process* as object. What I mean by this is that digital media or new media objects tend not to be things 'in and of themselves', finished and ready to be consumed as a finite product by the audience. Instead, digital media objects usually have just as much in common with (telecom) conversations as they do with media artefacts or objects. So where one views a traditional media object such as a film, a book, or a painting, these objects have a finite 'object-like' quality to them. Digital media objects, more often than not, break from this and are usually in continual production, being in constant dialogue and transformation with the audience and with other digital products and technologies.

FURTHER READING

As one would expect with such a long and diverse chapter, there are potentially many further texts that could be suggested. In terms of the broad scope of the chapter, I would suggest that Manovich (2001) is essential, and a highly influential book. Poster (1995) is also broadly useful and a seminal work. Landow (2006) provides an excellent discussion of the relationship between critical theory and technology. Jenkins (2006) and Bruns (2008) provide good discussions about participatory new media as 'process'. Shields (2003) is a good and comprehensive discussion of the idea of the virtual, with illuminating examples, and Baudrillard's (1994) classic work is the starting point for any critically-informed discussion of simulation.

To follow up on the discussion of video game culture, an excellent starting point is Wolf and Perron (2003) *The Video Game Theory Reader*, as well as Newman (2004). A good debate regarding simulation versus narrative is also held in the first issue of the online journal *Game Studies* (http://www.gamestudies.org/0101/). Meadows (2008) and Boellstorff (2008), both provide good in-depth ethnographic discussions of *Second Life* and other simulated worlds.

NOTES

1 Of course, there is an entire body of cultural studies and sociological work, from the mid 1970s onwards (and particularly throughout the 1980s), which would argue that these descriptions of the passive audience in broadcast media as extremely simplistic, especially in their description of audiences as some sort of undifferentiated mass that 'reacts' to media in a uniform way. See Abercrombie and Longhurst (1998) as a good summary.

2 Not to take anything from Manovich's excellent work, which is obviously highly influential in the making of this chapter, but no work is perfect, and *The Language of*

New Media fails to appropriately tackle 'interactivity', for example. Manovich is actually quite dismissive of the concept, suggesting it is 'a basic fact of computers' and therefore meaningless as a term. He gives ample discussion to the term 'algorithm', however, even though all software uses algorithms and in that sense, is also a basic fact about computers.

3   There are elements of hypertext within traditional print. For example, academic books are somewhat hypertextual in they often have footnotes and endnotes (like this), and references at the back of the book, all which are periodically referred to in the main body of the text. These allow the reader to break up the main narrative with other blocks of related content.

4   Here I note that I am following Buchanan (2007) in choosing to rely on Deleuze and Guattari's summary on page 21 of *A Thousand Plateaus*, as opposed to the earlier discussions of the six principles of Connection: Heterogeneity, Multiplicity, Asignifying Rupture, Cartography and Decalcomania. I feel that the way that the material was presented on page 21 was much more coherent and useful for this brief discussion.

5   It is important to note that Frasca's definition is heavily influenced by the computer science notion of simulation as a 'model' of a system. This contrasts Baudrillard's (and many other social philosophers') more pejorative notion of simulation as a deception away from reality, or even as a destruction of the real. Other online games are simulations more in the Baudrillard sense in that they aspire towards social realism, and replicate real life events. Military games such as *America's Army* (in which the player is put in the position of being a new recruit in the US armed forces) and their ideological counterpoints *Under Ash* and *Special Force* (both produced in the Middle East and which put the player in the position of Palestinian insurgency) depict real-life battles which have taken place within familiar geopolitical contexts (Galloway, 2004).

2

THE ECONOMIC
FOUNDATIONS OF THE
INFORMATION AGE

Whoever must be a creator always annihilates. (Nietzsche, 1968: 59, cited in Reinert and Reinert, 2006: 65))

In 1926, Nikolai Kondratieff published research which suggested that, since the beginnings of the industrial revolution in the mid-sixteenth century, the world capitalist economy had undergone a series of cycles of alternating prosperity and economic decline. These long-term cycles, or 'long waves', seemed to occur at intervals of between 50 and 60 years.

Kondratieff was not the first person to postulate long term economic cycles (nor cycles that lasted roughly 55 years), but it was Kondratieff who, by looking at price change data, supplied what at the time was seen to be reliable historical evidence of the phenomena. Furthermore, the timing of his publications (the mid 1920s) couldn't have been better, as his data seemed predictive of an upcoming major economic slowdown. By the time his work was published in English (1935), the world economy was in the midst of the Great Depression. As a result, Kondratieff sparked interest and debate over 'long wave' theories. Among his more interesting conclusions were:

- Major technical innovations were conceived in downswing periods, but were developed during upswing periods.

- Gold supplies increased and new markets were opened at the beginning of an upswing.

- The most disastrous and extensive wars occurred during periods of an upswing (Mager, 1987: 26–27).

Kondratieff and his followers saw four phases or 'seasons' in each long wave, these were:

- *Expansion* Profound changes in economic life, diffusion of technology, exploitation of discoveries and inventions, high investment, inclusion of new countries in the world economic system, social upheavals, including wars and revolutions.

- *The Peak* Maturity of industry created by the basic innovations of previous years. Affluence causes a shortage of goods, production becomes strained, inefficiencies develop and prices rise. Profits fall, causing inflationary recession.

- *First Adjustment and Plateau* A period of initial decline followed by a period of relative stability. This period is characterised by increasing government and consumer debt despite a general feeling of prosperity.

- *Panic and Decline* Debt accumulation, inefficiencies and corruption eventually lead to a crisis in public confidence and increasing business failures and foreclosures. Prices drop, and there is a rise in capital accumulation in banking. The period is characterised by an overall depression, but this depressed state leads to new means of cutting production costs and a search for inventions that will facilitate these. Thus, with this overall decline, there is an *accumulation* of invention.

Kondratieff made no real attempt to theorise his findings or explain the causes of these upswings and downswings – he merely charted their course. It was left to later economists, and in particular to Joseph Schumpeter (1939), to turn his observations into a theory.

Schumpeter provided the major support for Kondratieff's ideas empirically and expanded them theoretically. He was also largely responsible for bringing these ideas to America and the English speaking world. In his work, Schumpeter argued that innovation, and in particular entrepreneurial innovation, was a key influence on the economy. Classical economists, he felt, ignored the basic question of 'why does the capitalist economy change?' (Dahms, 1995: 5). He formulated a socio-historical theory that placed the entrepreneur-innovator at the forefront of major economic change. Innovators and entrepreneurs, he argued, were dynamic forces of creativity that had almost revolutionary capacities; what he coined as 'creative destruction' (Reinert and Reinert, 2006). Because of these forces, capitalism is in an almost continual state of ferment, with innovation destroying established enterprises, industries, infrastructures, business models, and creating new ones.

Within this context, Kondratieff's observation of clusters of innovations coinciding with economic downturn and upswings in long waves made perfect sense. Schumpeter took this further by elucidating a more comprehensive view of 'invention' to include entrepreneurial innovation in five ways:

1 The production of a new good.

2 The introduction of a new quality of a good or new use of an existing product.

3 A new method of production.

4 The opening up of a new market.

5 A change in the economic organisation (i.e., the creation of a firm or fund). (Dahms, 1995: 5)

Thus, Schumpeter theorised that each Kondratieff long wave reflected a cluster of radical innovations, many of which dealt with changes in the exploitation of primary energy sources.

Long wave theory itself went out of fashion for many decades after Schumpeter, but the economic recession of the 1970s and 1980s revived interest, with economists such as Mansch (1975), Mager (1987), Kleinknecht (1986 and 1987), Solomon (1987) and many others extending the work into contemporary measurements and putting the long wave theory back in debate. Most of this was around the question of whether or not the economic upheavals of the 1970s and 80s, and the rapidity with which so much innovation took place during these times, was indicative of a 'fifth long wave'.

Typical of this approach is Kleinknecht's expansion of Schumpeter's work, as seen in the table below:

Table 2.1 Schumpeter-Knleinknecht Scheme of Kondratieff Waves

K-Wave	Upswing	Downswing	Innovation
1st long wave: Industrial	1787–1813	1814–1842	Steam power (replacing water) Coal and iron (replacing wood) Textile industry
2nd long wave: Bourgeois	1843–1869	1870–1897	Petroleum industry Railroad and steamship industries Steel (replacing iron)
3rd wave: Neo-mercantilist	1898–1924	1925–1950	Electrical and chemical innovations Internal combustion engine Auto industry
4th wave	1951–1974	1975–1991	Natural gas, nuclear power (aborted) Plastics, aluminium Trucking (replacing rail) Air transport
5th wave	1992–2020(?)	?	Digital revolution?

Source: Ayres (2006)

The period from the early 1970s to the present has been one of considerable economic change worldwide. Many economists and sociologists of information technology (including Manuel Castells) have looked to long wave theory to provide a framework for discussion of those economic changes around innovations in production methods, information technology, economic organisation for firms and governments, as well as the new markets and realities opened up by globalisation.

Long wave theory is still very much debated. Most economists dispute its empirical foundations and methodology, and also point to historical inaccuracies regarding the current 'fifth wave', although some, such as Ayres (2006) make compelling arguments for why the fifth wave might have been 'delayed', 'lengthened', 'shortened' or 'aborted'. Furthermore, current economic circumstances of debt accumulation, stock market and real estate collapse, crisis in confidence all bear a stark resemblance to the 'panic and decline' phase of a 'K-wave'. And, much as predicted in the theory, this phase of economic decline has seen new investments and priorities given to technological innovation and research, as demonstrated in the policies of recently elected

US President Barack Obama, who has advocated huge investments into research of 'green technologies':

> The pursuit of discovery half a century ago fuelled our prosperity and our success as a nation in the half century that followed. The commitment I am making today will fuel our success for *another 50 years*. That's how we will ensure that our children and their children will look back on this generation's work as that which defined the progress and delivered the prosperity of the twenty-first century. (Obama, 2009: emphasis added)

This chapter's main ambition is to address the innovation argument and to examine how the current set of technological and economic innovations taking place might be a part of 'creative destruction', creating new conditions for capitalism to operate and even flourish. This will allow us to understand the negative effects of Amazon.com on traditional main street book retailers, or eBay's effect on collectors shops, second hand retailers and flea markets, or globalisation's effect on the working classes of (post-) industrial nations, as acts of creative destruction.

POST-INDUSTRIALISM

One of the first sets of discourses that related specifically to the idea of a knowledge or information driven economy was the concept of post-industrialism. This concept can be traced through a number of sociological thinkers like Daniel Bell (1973, 1979) and Alain Touraine (1971), and popular writers such as Alvin Toffler (1970, 1980) and Peter Drucker (1979).

The basic concept of post-industrialism involves an economic transition from a manufacturing-based economy towards an economy based on services. Service provision, and not the production of material goods, becomes the primary economic activity, and greatest source of wealth. Alongside this shift towards service industries would be the growth of technical and professional employment.

At the heart of this depiction of social change is a suggestion that society at large has gone through (and will continue to go through) a series of almost evolutionary stages which have revolutionary impacts on society as a whole. Daniel Bell (1973, 1979), the key thinker in this discourse, proposed three historical periods based on three 'revolutions' within the last 500 years:

- *Pre-industrial* (agricultural) society where agriculture is the primary activity: influenced by the agricultural revolution of scientific farming.
- *Industrial* society, where manufacturing of goods is the dominant activity: created through the industrial revolution in the sixteenth century.
- *Post-industrial* society, where knowledge, services and information are the dominant economic activity.

Table 2.2 Proportion of US employment in agriculture, industrial and service industries for selected years

Year	1870	1950	1978
Agriculture	47% (high)	12%	3%
Industry	27%	42% (high)	36%
Services	26%	46%	60% (high)

Source: Fuchs (1980)

This series of stages is congruent with Alvin Toffler's (1970) succession of first, second and third waves of social change. Bell suggests that this is in fact a revolutionary change, and that post-industrial society will ultimately transform the very basis of human society. This argument is premised on the basis that since the late 1950s, there has been a steady rise in the proportion of people employed in the services sector, and a steady decline in the proportion of those employed in either primary resources (mining and agriculture) or secondary industries (manufacturing and industry). This is a well-known and documented trend in all industrialised nations. For example, Fuchs (1980) demonstrates that in the United States between 1870 and 1978, the proportion of those employed in services has steadily risen, while those first in agriculture, then in manufacturing, declined (see Table 2.2).

Currently, all OECD countries with 'advanced economies' have more than half of their workforce in service industries, and several have over 70 per cent. It is important to note, however, that a decline in proportion does not necessarily mean a decline in raw numbers. In most cases, the actual numbers of people working in manufacturing has not declined (the UK is the notable exception to this), but have remained relatively stable or even increased slightly. Agriculture, however, has plummeted both in proportion and raw numbers.

So where one can imagine an industrial model of society, centred around the production of goods through mines and factories, powered by a workforce of proletarians living in urban areas near centres of production (the working class), Bell and others see a shift from this manufacturing of materials and the physical act of 'working' involving the use of machinery, to work becoming primarily *a social and intellectual act*. Work becomes a production and distribution of knowledge and information between persons and is epitomised by the service industries of retailing, education, finance, health services, transportation, government and research.

This change also results in shifts of power within society. In the industrial capitalist model, those who own the means of production (i.e., capitalists and those who own firms and factories) retain power, but in the post-industrial economy, those who control information and knowledge, such as researchers and technocrats, increase in power (Barney, 2004). Their power derives not from producing things or from their practical ability, but from the use of what Bell calls 'theoretical knowledge': where the power to change society comes from the power to innovate using known abstract theoretical principles, instead of empirical 'trial and error' in the material world.

For example, advances in computing science are achieved using mathematical principles and physics (Webster, 1995); in astronomy, 'black holes' were proven mathematically before being empirically 'observed' by astronomers; the 'greenhouse effect' is a hypothesis of climate change mostly proven through theory and models of climate change; work on the human genome project is producing new medicines through the theoretical principles of DNA being discovered (Barney, 2004); governments use known economic theories to manage inflation within their economies; parents use knowledge of psychological and sociological principles such as 'self-esteem', 'self-fulfilling prophesy', and 'stereotyping' as tools in raising their children.

Overall, Bell (1973) argues that the moves to a post-industrial society will entail:

- A decline in workers employed in industry.

- Increases in industrial output due to rationalisation and innovation in manufacturing processes.

- Increases in wealth and affluence.

- The expansion of service industries to fulfill the needs of a more affluent society.

- The preeminence of a professional and technical class.

- The heightened presence and significance of information.

- A shift from an emphasis on practical knowledge and empirical observation to theoretical knowledge and its emphasis on technical innovation.

- A rise of the individual, knowledge adept, social actor.

All three early proponents of the post-industrial society (Bell, Toffer, Drucker) pointed to the rise of individualism and consumerism as part of social changes brought about by this shift away from industrial society. Bell pointed to the rise of the 'knowledge adept social actor' whereas Drucker predicted a rise in individualism and a proliferation of lifestyles and subcultures (foreshadowed in the social turmoil of the late 1960s). In all cases, we see the relationship between the *mass production* of the industrial age with mass culture and consumerism standing in contrast to more *individualised consumerism* in the information age (see also van Dijk, 2006: 32). This will be explored further in the section on post-Fordism later on in this chapter.

Problems with the post-industrial thesis

Criticisms of the post-industrial society both as a theory and an accurate description of social trends were plentiful. For example, Kumar (1978) and Webster (1995) both suggested that the trend towards increasing employment in service industries has been a general trend spanning many decades, and not a fundamental 'break' in the kinds of work being done, as Bell and others suggested. They further argue that services have always played a large part in the economy (already 28 per cent of employment in the US in 1870,

Table 2.3 Persons employed in service, manufacturing and primary industries in selected countries (in thousands)

Year	Canada	Australia	Italy	US	UK	Germany	Japan
Service Industries							
1960	3264	2514	6696	38212	11642	10405	18190
1990	9083	5539	12357	84949	18544	16102	36550
Manufacturing Industries							
1960	1471	1207	4813	17149	8517	8901	9403
1990	2001	1204	4726	21184	5384	8843	15010
Agriculture and Primary Industries							
1960	795	448	6514	5572	1118	3567	12800
1990	531	438	1876	3355	568	966	4270

Source: Akyeanpong and Winters (1993)

as Fuchs' data shows), and that the growth of the service industries has largely come at the expense of a declining and rationalising agricultural sector. In addition, many suggest that manufacturing has never employed more than 50 per cent of workers even in the United Kingdom, and that apart from the UK, real numbers employed in manufacturing has usually remained stable, or even increased in the last few decades (see Table 2.3).

Furthermore, there is the question of what service workers actually 'do' (Webster, 1995). It is highly debatable to suggest that cleaners or retail workers working in check-out queues can be considered 'informational' or 'knowledge' workers. And certainly, in the case of the retail industry, this sector revolves ultimately around the provision of manufactured material goods. Thus, in many ways, there are clearly a lot of problems with post-industrial theory as formulated in the early 1970s.

THE INFORMATION SOCIETY

As Lyon (1988) notes, the concept of the information society inherits several features and symptoms of post-industrialism. The post-industrialists:

> Largely failed to justify the significance granted to trends such as the growth of theoretical knowledge and of services. A leisured society based on automated manufacture, a vast array of services and a culture of self-expression, political participation and an emphasis on the quality of life does not seem to have materialized. (Lyon, 1988: 10)

However, beginning in the late 1970s and largely with the help of Daniel Bell himself, the post-industrial society argument was reborn as the 'information society'. In its reincarnation, post-industrialism was more finely tuned and more focused around the transformative potential of the computer and high technology, rather than the occupational dominance of service industries (Barney, 2004).

The roots of the information society concept, and the focus on information, were planted decades before by Fritz Malchup, with his book *The Production and Distribution of Knowledge in the United States* (1962). In that text, Malchup made an attempt to chart the growth of the 'information industries'. He outlined five information industry groups:

1 Education.

2 Media and communication.

3 Information machines (e.g., computer equipment and musical instruments).

4 Information services (e.g., law, insurance, health and medicine).

5 Other information activities (such as research related and non-profit activities). (Webster, 1995:11)

Based on these categories, Malchup argued that by 1958, the information industries had expanded to 29 per cent of the gross national product of the United States. Several years later, Marc Porat (1977) continued in the Malchup tradition, but sought a more complete and detailed definition and measurement of the economic impact of the information economy in the US. His definition was broader than that of Malchup, and included both industries and activities that were specifically engaged in selling information as a primary product in established markets, such as media, education and research (what he called the 'primary information sector'), and activities where the primary product was not informational, but where knowledge application and manipulation was used to create the final material product. This would include, for example, the design, information manipulation, research and management that goes into manufacturing an automobile. He referred to this as the 'secondary' information sector.

Based on this expanded definition, Porat was able to argue that by 1978, 46 per cent of US GDP was accounted for in the information sector, and commanded 40 per cent of the labour force (Barney, 2005; Webster, 1995). Yoneji Masuda (1981) wrote from a similar position in Japan, touting the fundamental transformation towards an information society as a 'computopia' or a 'universal society of plenty that will occur by the twenty first century'. In the French context, Nora and Minc (1981) argued that the 'increasing interconnections between computers and telecommunications' would 'alter the entire nervous system of social organization' (Nora and Minc, 1981: 3–4; cited in Barney, 2005: 8).

The information society argument continues to receive strong challenges in the face of empirical research. Once again, the figures used as the foundation for the information society argument (as with the figures behind the post-industrial argument) were highly disputed by a number of academics including Webster (1995), Kumar (2005) and Rubin and Huber (1986). For example, Rubin and Huber (1986) suggest that there has not been a revolutionary upswing in information sector growth rates, but only modest rises. Furthermore, several authors (Kumar, 2005; Lyon, 1988; Robins and Webster, 1986; Schiller 1986, 1999; Webster, 1995) argue that there is an embedded ideology in these evolutionary, progressivist and fundamentally optimistic predictions about the future of the economy and society. Overall, these authors argue that capitalist industrial society is not being revolutionised or transcended, but simply extended, deepened and perfected (Kumar, 2005: 57).

Many also point out that the arguments about an 'information' or 'knowledge' economy rest on dubious conceptions of 'knowledge' and its relationship to economic processes. It can be argued that all economies are 'knowledge economies', in the sense that they need organisation and management. Once again, this leads us back to the assertion that these economies are not 'new', and that the use of such terms is not descriptive, but in fact ideological (Barney, 2005). It is with this view that those more critical of the information society concept turn to the concept of post-Fordism and flexible accumulation.

POST-FORDISM AND GLOBALISATION

In response to the somewhat optimistic, liberal view of production and work in post-industrial and information society theories, many who were critical of these views put forward accounts of the economic changes occurring since the 1970s as a transition from 'Fordism' to 'post-Fordism'

Fordism is a catch-all phrase that combines a particular way of producing goods, a particular construction of a market for those goods, and a particular type of relationship between the economy and the state (Barney, 2005: 10). In terms of the production process, the foundations of Fordism involve a number of characteristics:

- The use of scientific and rationalised labour processes inspired by the bureaucratic model of decision making, task completion and job specification (or Taylorism) and the adoption of technology.

- Mass production in large factories, by large corporations that dominate national domestic and colonial markets.

- Hierarchical management systems that concentrate decision making among management, and feature strict chains of command, job classifications and standard operating procedures in an almost military fashion.

- A highly disciplined mass of workers engaged in repetitive, specialised tasks involving little skill and minimal decision making.

- The intention of the state to keep equilibrium between production and consumption through welfare, unemployment insurance, regulation of the economy and public spending in times of recession (Barney, 2005). There was an attempt to maintain stability and a management of the economy within territorial units of the state under an economic regime often referred to as 'Keynesianism'.

- Collective bargaining (union membership) and institutionalisation through state regulation meant reasonable (and stable) wages, (often lifetime) employment and benefits. Despite the relatively low levels of skill/training needed to perform much mass production work, workers usually experienced comparatively good wages and the prospect of lifetime employment, creating a 'blue-collar' middle-class in industrial nations.

- Mass consumer markets engendered by the mass production of standardised goods at low cost. The consumer end of this relationship being encouraged by mass media and advertising.

The 'crisis' in Fordism began in the late 1960s. Social unrest in many industrialised countries and the rise of counter-cultural movements were the beginnings of a rejection of the 'mass society' model of production and consumption (Barney, 2005; Van Dijk, 2006). Furthermore, by the mid 1970s, profit margins in large corporations were shrinking rapidly due to the rise in oil prices and other commodities, as well as the saturation of domestic consumer markets brought about by earlier mass production (Harvey, 1989). In effect, corporations were having their profit margins eroded by decreasing demand for their goods on the one hand, and increasing material costs on the other.

The crisis in profit margins, from the corporate side, meant that solutions had to be found. First, the stable relationship between capital, government and labour needed to be broken. Labour costs had to be lowered so that production costs could be lowered and profits raised. As a result, the corporate sector pushed governments towards lower tax burdens and deregulation to allow them the freedom to increase their profit margins and compete effectively in growing and competitive international markets. This trend towards lower wages led to further unrest and increasing industrial action during the 1970s. This in turn resulted in the shutting down or relocation of many production facilities to areas of the world where labour was cheaper and less organised. States took on a more passive role, stepping back from welfare, deregulating the economy and decentralising power. In short, there was a move towards a *neo-liberal* approach to economic development: lower taxes and a friendly labour market.

Thus, there was a shift to a focus among firms towards an international outlook, because increasing global competition called for a more dynamic model of business that could better respond to changes in demand for goods and meant new international markets could be sought. The overall strategic planning and stability of the Fordist enterprise was being replaced by an emphasis on responsiveness to an ever changing external environment (Krahn et al., 2007).

One major response on the part of the corporate sector was to become more flexible (Barney 2005), and this adaptation is generally referred to in the literature as 'flexible specialisation' or 'flexible accumulation' (Harvey, 1989).

This essentially involved:

- Moving away from mass production runs to smaller batch production of an increasing variety of goods to suit more specialised markets, themselves encouraged by more advanced marketing techniques.

- A downsizing of large, vertically integrated corporations into more streamlined enterprises that either contract out manufacturing products to other companies, or create their own, more contingent workforce of part-time and contracted employees that could be called up when needed.

- Dismantling of rigid hierarchical management structures, in turn replaced by more decentralised networks of team work or networks of smaller subcontractors responsible for their own output and therefore decision making. This also entailed a shift from rigid job classifications to individual multi-tasking and adaptability on the part of workers.

The overall result, in terms of work arrangements, has been an increase of insecurity within the workforce of the major industrial nations. Employers increasingly use a business model that relies on a smaller core of highly trained workers for core activities, and either a contingent workforce in 'non-standard' employment relationships (i.e., temporary, part-time, contracted or sub-contracted work), or tasks subcontracted out to other firms entirely. Thus, currently in the US almost one in five workers is a part-time worker, seven per cent are 'independent contractors', six per cent 'self employed' and as many as five per cent contingently employed (Kalleberg, 2000). In Britain, only 75 per cent of the workforce works full-time, some 13 per cent are self employed, and just under six per cent are temporary workers (Office for National Statistics, 2007). Similarly, Canada had just over 18 per cent of its workforce working part-time, and over 15 per cent in self employment (Statistics Canada, 2008).

This gives large firms the flexibility to meet production demands without the costs of maintaining a large permanent workforce. This flexible strategy can be summarised by looking at three types of flexibility:

- *Functional flexibility* Creating more adaptable workers that are highly skilled and able to multi-task as needed, as opposed to fulfilling a rigid job specification.

- *Numerical flexibility* The ability to quickly alter the size of a workforce as needed.

- *Pay flexibility* The desire to reduce long term pay and benefit costs.

Thus, for many, work since 1975 has become more insecure and more based around a series of short-term contracts or projects.

The other major response to the Fordist economic crisis was for firms to take a more cosmopolitan outlook: to search beyond the state for new markets and new ways to take advantage of local conditions of labour and material costs during the production process. Fordism was essentially teritorrialised, focused around the nation state and its attempts to stabilise an economy in terms of production and consumption. However, post-Fordism also involved a scale shift of the operations of large capitalist enterprises from the national to the transnational or global scale. Thus, with large firms, we see the rise of the multinational corporation, which attempts to take advantage of the most prefer-able conditions for any industrial activity on a world wide scale. As Barney (2004) notes:

> It is not uncommon for raw resources from one country to be synthesized in a second into production materials, which are manufactured in a third into component, which are assembled into finished products in a fourth. (Barney, 2004: 40)

Nike is a good example of this process, relying on an ever changing global business network of suppliers and subcontractors around Asia, with more sophisticated high end products being manufactured in Korea, and lower end products being manufactured in China and Indonesia. Not one shoe is manufactured in the United States, Nike's corpo-rate home, where the financing and marketing strategies are coordinated. Indeed, Nike itself, like Reebok, Liz Claiborne and Ralph Lauren, does not actually engage in any manufacturing at all, but branding and marketing.

Overall, the garment and apparel industry is one of the most prominent industries in terms of globally outsourcing its production. For example, in the United States as early as 1992, 49 per cent of all apparel sold in that country was made within its borders. By 1999, that had dropped to 12 per cent (Rabon, 2001: 55).

This type of production has created a global division of labour where, increasingly, labour-intensive processes that require low skills are taking place in economically dis-advantaged parts of the world (where labour is cheapest). More highly paid activities, requiring more skill (research, marketing, more sophisticated manufacturing, financial services), are taking place among the developed nations and particularly in world cit-ies, where the head offices of multinationals tend to conglomerate. Thus, globalisation can be seen as a spatial extension of capitalist production regimes, but compared to the organisational simplicity of nationally-based Fordism, global, post-Fordist production methods are more complex and demands far more organization and coordination. This organisational complexity becomes a driving force in the development and use of ICTs.

INFORMATIONALISM AND THE NETWORK SOCIETY

One of the most ambitious and important descriptions of not only the information economy, but also social change more generally in the transformation to an 'informa-tion society' is provided by Manuel Castells in his information age trilogy (Castells, 1996/2000, 1997). It is a hugely ambitious body of work (which he continues to this day), which attempts to link discussions of economy, society, politics and globalisation within a meta-narrative of social change in the information age. In this section we will focus on the economic features of a network society as discussed by Castells and others.

The network society concept incorporates at least some elements of all of the preceding discussions of long wave theory, post-industrial society, information society, post-Fordism, and globalisation within its narrative. As such, many of the descriptions of the network society will seem similar to what has been discussed. But the network society thesis attempts to synthesise the relationships between these social, economic, political and cultural forces into a coherent theory by adding to it the increasing role played by networking and communications technology in all of these processes.

Castells (1996) contrasts two 'modes of development' (or how wealth is produced): industrialism and informationalism. Industrialism is fuelled by the exploitation of new forms of energy with the ultimate goal being maximum productive output and economic growth. Essentially, the economy utilises resources to produce an increasing amount of goods at a lower cost. By contrast, the goal of informationalism is the production of knowledge, which is achieved through technological development.

The difference between industrialism (and its reliance on new forms of energy) and informationalism (and its reliance on new forms of knowledge) is that industrialism is based on an economics of scarcity. That is, the cost/value of its products relies primarily on their rarity. The price of oil or gold, for example, is largely based on how difficult it is to find and buy at a particular moment. However, knowledge and innovation work on a different principle, because the accumulation and value of knowledge is not related to its scarcity. Instead, use of knowledge and innovation tend to lead to further knowledge and innovation. 'Madonna', is not a marketable product due to her rarity. On the contrary, in many ways, Madonna's value is related to her popularity. The more current value Madonna has, the more CDs, interviews, tabloid articles and merchandise there is of her to go around. Even if one can download her music for free, 'Madonna' as a product still has marketable value. Her decline or rise in value has more to do with cultural factors than her scarcity.

Thus, for Castells, informationalism is post-industrial. Like Daniel Bell, he sees this as the heightened presence and significance of information (and information holders) in society, and links this to the overall rejuvenation of capitalism. The platform for productivity in informationalism is the 'reflexive action of knowledge upon knowledge', and information replaces energy as the key to productivity and growth. Knowledge is of course heavily involved with the growth of IT industries that assist in the accumulation of knowledge to ever higher levels of information complexity and processing (i.e., computers help us to make more powerful computers). Lastly, Castells argues that the increasing importance of information and information processing creates a culture organised around electronic media and communication networks: a culture of 'real virtuality'.

This culture, and this economy, revolves around the communication of information: information to assist in the coordination of global economic enterprises (including the manufacture of material goods), electronic circuits of capital flow, intellectual property, foreign and transnational investment and currency speculation. As we have seen in the earlier discussion of globalisation, in many respects, virtual financial flows taking place over ICT networks dominates over trade of material goods.

With the advent of globalisation and the need for expansion and innovation in communications technology, many have argued that the rejuvenation of capitalism through the process of post-Fordism and flexible specialisation was inherently tied to the development of communications and networking technology, (Barney, 2004; Castells, 1996; Tonkiss, 2006; Van Dijk, 2006). This has been born out in a large literature that refers not so much to the 'information society' or 'information economy', but to a 'network society' and a 'network economy'.

For Castells, this rise of the network society has emerged from (and contributes to) a complex set of social processes, political events and technological advancements, beginning with the IT revolution (the rapid advancement of information and communication technologies from the early 1960s to the present day). Castells places these origins not only in the technology itself, but in the culture of innovation, experimentation, venture capital and risk-taking that grew up around the Silicon Valley IT industry from the 1960s. This culture, he felt, set the scene for the massive progress seen in computing and communication technology, and the rise of the computing, communication and information industries to become a powerful economic and social force in Western culture.

California, Castells argued, was the birthplace of the IT revolution because of the cultural/historical context of a willingness of the US Government to commit massive resources to military spending. This ultimately contributed to a thriving electronics and high technology industry. Ironically, he also said that the context of 'California campus culture', a culture of 'freedom', individual expression and innovation, entrepreneurialism and risk-taking, created an environment where established patterns of behaviour (for example, in investment and innovation) were broken, thereby ushering in the first stage of an information economy.

The crisis of the industrial economy in the 1960s and 1970s meant that advanced industrial economies had to become global and informational otherwise it would face collapse (Barney, 2004; Castells, 1996). Castells argued that this was one of the driving forces in the collapse of the Soviet Union, as Soviet statism did not encourage innovation, and was therefore unable to adapt to the IT and information age. So the network society is very much a species of capitalism and not a distinct break from it. It is essentially capitalism playing by a different set of rules.

The economic shift to globalised and flexible production methods meant that ICTs and communication networking became more important. Economic enterprises started to become de-territorialised networks of economic nodes and, in a sense, began to resemble the architecture of the advanced digital communication technologies that were making their global expansion possible (Tonkiss, 2007). Thus, social formations developed through the infrastructure of social and media networks, which enabled a mode of organization that is becoming dominant at all levels, individual, group/ organizational, societal/global (Van Dijk, 2006: 20), or within a network society.

The structure of networks

One can define a network in several ways, but essentially networks are comprised of three basic elements: more than two *nodes* (or points), multiple *ties* (or links) between them, and the *flows* between the nodes and along the ties which maintain the network.

In a culture that revolves around information and the communication of information through networks, Castells argues that the 'network' becomes the primary relationship in the information age. The 'network' starts to replace the 'hierarchy' as the social structure of informational culture. The network morphology sits in opposition to hierarchy, which Castells associates with industrialism. In a hierarchy, the flow of power and communication tends to be vertical in nature. Power flows from the top to the bottom, and communication tends to flow from the top to the bottom (in terms of directions or 'orders') and from bottom to top (in terms of incoming information, feedback, or reconnaissance). So, for example, if you were to imagine a business organisation in the hierarchical/industrial mode, you would have owners/CEOs giving orders to district managers, who give orders to supervisors, who give orders to shop floor workers. Information or feedback might flow back up the chain (in terms of say, productivity), but the directional flow of power is downward.

By contrast, networks are much more 'horizontal' in nature in that the flow of power and communication is much more evenly distributed among a series of interconnected 'nodes' or 'units' with multiple connections. Network architecture is more 'horizontal', dynamic and open-ended because any node will have multiple ties to other nodes (and therefore are not as dependent on one relationship or link). As a result, networks are usually expansive in nature, as opposed to self-contained and inward-looking.

So what is the difference? Networks have always occurred within society. One can speak of friendship networks, clan networks and trading networks, and these have always existed. In that sense, networks are nothing new. However, what is new is the relationship between networks and space. The key for Castells' network society thesis is that this network morphology is largely created and conducted through electronic media. What makes networks like this special is that they communicate (ideally) in 'real time'. In this respect, if one is 'inside' the network, space and time cease to become relevant, as communication or 'flows' have no distance and take no time. 'Outside' the network, distance and time are potentially infinite. Thus, the time and distance between nodes connected in a network will always be 'less' (no matter how far apart they may actually be in 'physical' space), than two nodes that are not in the same network (no matter how close they might be in physical space). In this respect, network connections are crucial in the network society and the primary discussion in a network society is who is and is not excluded from networks.

The network society emphasises a shift towards ties and flows and away from proximity and place: deterritorialised networks created through the use of global ICTs. In that respect, the networking logic substantially modifies the operation and outcomes in potentially all dominant societal processes: production, consumption, power, culture and experience (Castells, 1996: 489).

The space of flows and timeless time

Castells makes an explicit link between the morphology of the network and the process of globalisation and puts these two concepts together in what he calls *the space of flows*. Castells tries to build upon concepts of economic globalisation to assert that in the network society (of which the global economy is a part), the core activities (money, markets, production systems, information) are able to work as a unit in real time on a planetary scale or, as he defines the space of flows, 'the material arrangements that allow for simultaneity of social practices without territorial contiguity' (Castells, 1996/2000: 19).

Castells is referring to the globalised sphere consisting of communications, people and things with largely unrestricted mobility. Money and communication, of course, are the least restricted in terms of global flow and, as such, the space of flows is the space of free-flowing capital and real-time communication. This can be seen, for example, in international stock investment and trading with the ability of multinational corporations to coordinate production, investment and communication strategies on a global scale, and the ability of many to communicate and receive information through a number of information and communication technologies.

People, by contrast, tend to be far more restricted in terms of global movement. Some groups, for example international businesspeople, politicians, and the wealthy, have almost unrestricted movement across the globe, but this contrasts others, such as refugees, the unskilled, the poor, or the displaced, who tend to have quite restricted freedom to move about the Earth's surface.

In this respect, Castells contrasts the globalised nature of the *space of flows* with the localised nature of *the space of places*. For Castells, place is self-contained and rooted or fixed in geography, with limited connection beyond its own territory or place. It is the arena in which space and time *matter*, and the realm of experience for most – a place of geographically limited horizons.

To exist as a 'person' or as a 'place' in the space of flows is to be connected into networks that go beyond the local sphere and are not limited by it. With the network society, existence in the networks of the space of flows is crucial, as 'places' can be easily included or excluded (switched 'on' or 'off') by networks, and are therefore vulnerable. In terms of people, those who have the ability (through wealth, network connections and 'valuable' skills) to be mobile possess an inherent advantage over those that do not. In the same way, cities that do not have a presence in international flows of capital, people, labour and media are vulnerable. As a result, cities usually attempt to raise their international profile through building airports, hosting international events, or luring multinational corporations. Increasingly, people themselves attempt to raise their profile though increasing their social contacts, networking and a presence in online social and business environments (see Chapter 8).

In general, the space of flows can be seen to consist of several elements. First, the *communications infrastructure* and its associated electronic spaces, such as the internet and other forms of ICTs. Second, *networks of interactions* and the habitats of people who operate and belong to such networks. This can be manifested in the networks of international capital transfers, airline routes, relationships of individuals and firms, and operations of transnational actors. Third, the *nodes and hubs* within such networks. These are places where connections converge, such as global cities, major airports, stock markets. These are the spatial articulations of the space of flows.

Last, the space of flows is said to occur within an experience of *timeless time*: 'The desequencing of social action, either by the compression of time or by the random ordering of the moments of the sequence' (Castells et al., 2007: 171). This is the separation of time from physical context, the life cycle and the cycles of nature. Work, for example, in a post-Fordist and globalised context, becomes an activity not confined to certain times (say, the social convention of '9-to-5' in a particular place), but potentially an activity that can take place at any time. This can be seen in the activities of stock brokers, who can ply their trade in either London, New York, or Tokyo 24 hours a day from their laptop, or factory shift workers, who often work through the night or in other flexible working patterns to keep production going round the clock.

The rise of mobile technologies have helped to further blur this notion of set and segmented working hours. Workers do not have to be at 'the office' to work, but can now extend working hours to places where this was previously more difficult, such as the home, or while commuting or travelling. This is often referred to as the 'networked worker' (Madden and Jones, 2008) or the 'always on' worker, where the once normally separate spheres of 'work' and 'home/leisure' (and 'travel') have become increasingly blurred, with more and more people starting to spend more time working at home, either as unpaid over-time work, or as part of contracted work hours. The days of having prescribed work hours and a separate home life have, for many, disappeared (Anandarajan et al., 2006).

Network economy and network enterprise

Within an economic context, a network economy differs from an industrial economy in terms of scope, form and content (Castells, 1996). Where the scope of an industrially based economy is organised around nation-states, the scope of the network economy is global, using advantages of place globally to minimise costs in terms of production (particularly cost of labour), distribution and management. Where the form of an industrial economy or firm is structural and static (i.e., based on large firms with large standing workforces), the paradigmatic corporation of the information age, the *network enterprise*, is networked and flexible, using tactics like subcontracting, outsourcing and part-time workers in different locations around the world to expand, reduce or change production methods as needed.

Internally, the 'networked enterprise' can create more large scale, decentralised management structures through efficient worldwide internet communications. Castells (2001) refers to this as the 'management of flexibility': the ability to effectively manage the internal affairs of a large organisation even at long distances, through the use of communication technology. Between businesses, a firm can easily communicate its immediate needs to its suppliers, or its subcontractors. This management of flexibility leads to what Castells calls 'scalability', which refers to the ability of a network to be expanded or contracted on any scale as required for the efficient completion of a task at hand, or given a specific situation. For example, a globally networked organisation like Nike can expand its network of subcontracted manufacturers and increase shoe production when there is a large demand for its shoes, or shrink production by not employing as many subcontractors when it feels that demand for its product is low – all with very little impact on Nike itself in terms of job losses or having to hire workers. That is the scalability and flexibility of a networked firm. This strategy would be akin to a nation shifting from possessing a large standing army of full-time professional soldiers to employing mercenaries to accomplish specific military tasks or objectives.

Alongside this flexible workforce, the network enterprise economy evidences a change in how large firms deal with each other externally. This too becomes more fluid, where rival companies sometimes compete, and at other times find it advantageous to partner with their competitors in temporary or ad-hoc partnerships on certain projects. In the auto industry this has become particularly common, with separate manufacturers making components for other competing firms. For a number of years, Renault made engines for Rover, for example. More strikingly, Mazda manufactured the 'Probe' sports car for rival company Ford.

In that sense, economic relations between firms – and increasingly between firms and employees – has become increasingly based around specific projects or contracts as opposed to a long term, consistent set of stable production relationships.

Tonkiss (2006) describes the network economy and the behaviour of network enterprises as consisting of:

1 Decentralised networks of large firms.

2 Multi-locational, segmented production and distribution chains with firms in outsourced partnerships (i.e., globally subcontracted production chains).

3 Networks of small and medium sized firms linked to larger networks (larger companies relying on products produced by a network of smaller companies).

4 Project-driven and ad-hoc joint ventures between firms.

5 The growth of networks of synchronous activity between customers and firms (i.e., a more direct relationship between customers and firms based on feedback and data collection).

So the network economy (and society) differs from older industrial economic arrangements in that the network model is based on nodes, ties and flows on a potentially global scale. It is extensive, complex and integrated. This contrasts with industrial economies because industrial economies and Fordist firms tend to be based on more formal or institutional structures, which tend to be stable and organised in terms of hierarchy, segmentation and stratification. The network morphology stresses fluidity over stability and horizontal networked relations with other firms (and even consumers) over vertical, hierarchical, relations within firms.

WEIGHTLESS ECONOMIES, INTELLECTUAL PROPERTY AND THE COMMODIFICATION OF KNOWLEDGE

As suggested above, flexible and networked production methods on an international scale demand large amounts of coordination, research, the assembling and analysis of data, marketing, financial services, communication systems and many other operations which, on the surface, have little to do with the material products themselves. However, the kind of 'knowledge work' that is necessary to coordinate global production, distribution and marketing of goods is integral to the establishment and success of globalised post-Fordism and a network society.

So where the industrial economy concentrated on the increasingly efficient use of physical resources and more powerful and cheaper sources of energy, the informational economy is said to revolve increasingly around the principal of continuous innovation and the increasing deployment of weightless (intangible) knowledge resources (Coyle, 1997; Flew, 2005). As a result, where the content of an industrial economic enterprise is primarily *material* goods, the content of a post-Fordist, networked and globalised economy is increasingly *informational*, and increasingly maintained by communication networks in both production and consumption. Thus, the role of intangible, knowledge or 'weightless' goods (i.e., goods that are not material objects) increases to become a fundamental part of the networked post-Fordist economy. While on the one hand the role of IT in post-Fordism and globalisation is to assist in the coordination of flexible, globally dispersed production methods for the circulation of physical commodities, this at the same time creates a situation in which intangibles become more necessary to the success of the circulation of goods and the creation of profit.

Weightless money

The internationalisation of goods production associated with globalisation has run parallel to the internationalisation of finance and capital circulation. In 2007, foreign direct investment amounted to $1.3 trillion (UNCTAD, 2007). Developed countries were responsible for 84 per cent of these investments. Outstripping this by a long way is the volume of financial commodities exchanged daily on global currency and stock markets. Currency trading alone amounts to $3.2 trillion daily (Bank for International Settlements, 2007). That is 100 times more than the daily trade in material goods (Tonkiss, 2006: 45).

Banking, investment and other financial services associated with increased global trading and production has become a much larger share of GDP wealth in many advanced economic nations. For example, in the UK, the weightless financial sector has become the largest contributor to UK balance of payments, and banking has become the largest UK export (Swain, 2008). Swain goes on to suggest that in 2006, financial services made up 9.4 per cent of GDP (up from 5.5 per cent in 2004). If one adds professional services affiliated to the financial sector, such as accounting, legal services and management consulting (accounting for another 3.5 per cent), overall 12.9 per cent of Britain's GDP resides in the weightless financial sector alone.

From this it becomes worthwhile to note briefly how the virtualisation of money, and its transfer on the internet, has come to play a major part in financial practices and the virtualisation of money, particularly in banking and investing. At the individual level, the virtualisation of money and the moving of investment into the online sphere have allowed stock-trading and other forms of financial speculation to be participated in by a much larger section of society. Millions of people who previously would have never personally had much exposure to stock markets outside news reports have become online investors. The increasing virtual movement of money has also been aided through the increasing popularity of online banking for individuals.

Such weightless cash transfers have even spread to everyday transactions for people in developing countries where computers are comparatively rare, but where the virtualisation of money has manifested itself in the form of digital money transfers through mobile phones. This is a practice that has been widely adopted in Africa and in the Philippines, the most notable of which is the M-PESA system initiated by *Safaricom* in Kenya. Currently there are seven million users of the system (in a country of 38 million people), creating $2 million worth of cash transfers every day (the *Economist*, 2009). In effect, mobile phones have become wallets and bank accounts for many people, as the physical nature of cash is slowly dissipating.

Weightless services

The movement of money and investment is not the only component of the weightless economy. This also involves the services that revolve around accomplishing the global flows of investment and goods. Services such as accounting, legal services, insurance, management consulting, training, marketing, software development and the like constitute a whole sector of intangible producer services that are inherently linked to the rise of post-Fordist production methods, and constitute a rising share of economic wealth production.

For example, Belhocine (2008) suggests that corporate investment in intangibles in most advanced economies already parallels their investment in physical capital. In other words, businesses now spend as much on things that have a knowledge component, such as research and development, training, marketing, software, and organisational change as they do on materials and machinery for the production of tangible goods. This corporate spending on intangibles amounts to over 13 per cent of US GDP, just under 11 per cent in the UK, almost 10 per cent in Canada, over 8 per cent in Japan, and over 7 per cent in France. In terms of overall GDP produced through weightless goods, Cameron (1998) suggested that by 1994, 23 per cent of American GDP was produced through spending on software, financial products, telecommunications, the internet, entertainment and management consulting.

Weightless products

It is also important to note that weightless goods and services constitute an important and rising share of the leisure and media economy as well. In an era of media convergence (see Chapter 4), not only can weightless digital goods save distribution costs, but also material costs. Since the rise of the internet, the media and new media industries have increasingly shifted from providing 'weighted' material, i.e., tangible products (such as books, records, CDs, DVDs), to providing their products in weightless virtual form through internet downloads. For example, in 2008, 20 per cent of the total of legal worldwide music sales were digital (International Federation of the Phonographic Industry, 2009).

The rise in virtual provision of music, film and publishing means that there are few material costs in the manufacture of these products for the consumer (no CDs, jewelcases, packaging), and thus more profits for the producers. Even more strikingly, an estimated $5 billion was spent worldwide on 'virtual goods' such as avatars, virtual pets, virtual jewelry, virtual clothing and other activities related to online gaming (as well as virtual gifts in social networking) that have no application outside the internet (Mitra, 2009).

The advantages of a weightless economy

When compared to a tangible or weighted goods economy, Quah (1999) suggests that the weightless economy has several unique characteristics. First, because weightless goods have no material basis, they are not mutually exclusive. That is, use of or purchase by one person does not limit the use of others. Referring back to the example of oil, the price of oil is largely determined by the demand for oil and its scarcity at the time. The more rare oil supplies are, and the more people that are using oil, the less of it there is and thus the price goes up. This kind of logic involves all tangible goods, since their prices in the main will at least partially be set by the costs of the materials involved in their production. Thus, tangible objects revolve around an economics of scarcity. Weightless goods (particularly virtual ones) differ in that they have no materials involved in their production and, therefore, the use of them by one person does not limit the use of them by others. Certainly in the case of virtual goods, any number of copies of songs, books or software can be provided with no concerns about scarcity or elevating costs.

Second, because weightless goods use no material resources, they are less consuming of scarce natural resources, and their electronic distribution means that they use no oil or other fuels in their transportation. As such, they are seen as a much more environmentally friendly and sustainable source of economic growth.

Last, while their non-mutually exclusive nature in theory suggests a more equitable distribution of goods, at the same time, Quah (1999) argues that the global reach and electronic distributions of weightless goods contribute to what he calls 'superstar effects', in which more well-known and powerful brands or corporations have the potential to crowd out lesser-known brands and smaller (local) players. Theoretically, this has the potential to increase income polarisation by creating more access (and thus more profits) to larger and more well-known corporations, which would cut into the livelihoods of smaller players.

(Intellectual) property in a weightless economy

The rise in importance of the intangible or weightless aspect of the economy has profound implications for the idea of 'ownership' and the notion of 'property' in the information age. In the industrial age, power emerged most often from the ownership of tangible property: land, resources, machinery, commodities. In the information age, as both Daniel Bell and Manuel Castells suggested, power shifts to those who own, control and can utilise information.

Legal regimes tend to recognise two kinds of property: tangibles (material things, land, property, objects, resources) and intangibles (ideas, inventions, signs, information and expression). Intellectual property refers to the latter and comes in several forms (Yar, 2006):

- *Patents* grant exclusive control over the use of an innovation for a limited time period (normally 20 years). To gain a patent, one must demonstrate that the innovation is a new or improved process or device that has a commercial or industrial application or useful function.

- *Copyrights* are rights given to authors of original works or forms of expression. These include books, music, images, software code and database structures and contents.

- *Trademarks* are signs used to identify the source of a good or service, and trademark rights exist primarily to avoid misinterpretation and counterfeits. Marks such as brands and logos, as well as elements associated with them such as phrases, colours, sounds and even smells may be trademarked within industrial sectors.

- *Designs* are original ornamental or aesthetics aspects of an object.

- In addition, there are *trade secrets*, *moral rights* and '*rights to persona*' which allow ownership over intangibles.

Since the 'new economy' increasingly depends on buying and selling ideas, creations, processes and innovations (Marlin-Bennett, 2004), it seems inevitable that more stringent protection of such property is necessary to the functioning of a knowledge-based economy as a profitable enterprise. This realisation was not lost on American legislators during the 1980s when, in the face of increasing global competition (particularly from Asian economies), supremacy in knowledge-based goods and the creative industries

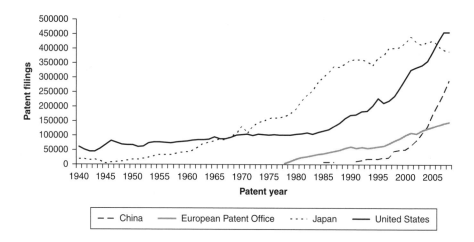

Figure 2.1 Trends in yearly patent applications at selected patent offices, 1940–2008
Source: World Intellectual Property Indicators 2009 edition, WIPO Statistics Database

were two of the few areas in which America was still seen as a world leader, and where its future economic success was seen to lay:

> In the next century, US economic growth and competitiveness will largely be determined by the extent to which the United States creates, owns, preserves and protects its intellectual property … (Lehman, 1996: 7)

As a result, the United States government instituted a series of actions to strengthen intellectual property laws, particularly in the international arena. This was achieved by linking strong commitments to the defence of intellectual property rights with bilateral trade deals with the United States (Lehman, 1996). These efforts culminated in the 1994 TRIPS (Trade-Related Aspects of Intellectual Property Agreement) and the establishment of the World Intellectual Property Organization (WIPO). These were multinational agreements, established to improve viability of intellectual property in international economies through increased legal rights of intellectual ownership and greater international enforcement of these rights through, for example, enforcing anti-piracy laws.

As a result of increased legal rights and enforcement, intellectual properties have, since the mid 1980s, become increasingly valued assets in the global marketplace. This can be demonstrated by the rising number of new patents registered every year (see Figure 2.1).

Proponents for such strict protection of intellectual property argue that these rules strike a balance between the interests of the public and the interests of creators and inventors by rewarding them for their efforts, time and work put into intellectual and creative innovations, and providing them with the incentive to engage in such tasks by making it possible to profit from creativity and innovation. Society as a whole, it is argued, benefits from the increase in human knowledge that results from the profitable pursuit of innovation and creativity (Marlin-Bennett, 2004).

On the other hand, many argue that if intellectual property rights are too stringent, that there is the potential endangerment of the right of the public to share freely in the cultural, scientific and technological heritage (or the 'intellectual commons') created by society as a whole. Some would argue that there is no such thing as an original idea in the sense that all ideas, innovations and expressions are built upon what went before (and manifested through the common resource of language and scientific expression), and that to sequester scientific and cultural knowledge into 'ownership' and thus limit its potential application is not only unjust, but also stifles innovation, the very lifeblood of the information economy. In this sense, strict intellectual property regimes can be seen as an antithesis to a knowledge-driven economy (Lessig, 2001).

Information feudalism

In addition, it is argued that the current emphasis on allowing knowledge to be strictly owned as a source of profit is deepening the current structures of inequality that already exist in capitalist society. *Information feudalism* (see Drahos and Brathwaite, 2002) represents the concern that the current emphasis on strong intellectual property rights could lead to a situation where ownership and knowledge of information and innovation is increasingly concentrated in the hands of the powerful.

At the corporate level, it is usually the case that firms own all the intellectual property rights to any creations of their employees (this includes students and staff of universities, and usually record companies' ownership of songs written by musicians under their contract as well). As such, it is not the creators, but the established owners of capital, who tend to benefit from intellectual property rewards. At the global level, information feudalism potentially operates by limiting the ability to use and profit from intellectual advancements to those people and companies coming from advanced industrial nations with an established history of intellectual property law. In both cases, the worry is that increased ownership of knowledge as a commodity centralises power though knowledge monopolies and restricts access to the benefits of knowledge to those who are willing and able to pay for it.

One way in which information feudalism is manifested is through *information colonialism*, or 'bio-piracy' (Shiva, 1997, 2001). This refers to a situation when profitable drugs or pharmaceuticals are developed using traditional indigenous or folk knowledge (often from developing countries) and then are patented by large corporations based in advanced economic nations. This creates a situation where powerful multinational corporations claim the right to profit from the knowledge of folk cultures, who not only don't profit from their knowledge, but may also be restricted by law or by market forces in using their traditional products.

A popular example of bio-piracy is the case of the *neem tree*. The neem tree is a shrub that grows in India (as well as Africa). It has traditionally been known to have many useful properties in terms of medicine, as well as agriculture, where its anti-fungal and pesticidal properties have been known for centuries (in India at least). In recent decades, the

American firm, W.R. Grace obtained American and European patents to process neem seeds into a commercial pesticide (India does not allow patents on medical or agricultural products). The patents were granted on the basis of being 'novel' or 'innovative', because the traditional Indian use of neem as a pesticide was not recognised, even though it had been used for centuries. W. R. Grace then established a neem seed processing plant in India and began commercially harvesting and processing large amounts of neem seeds for export to the United States. This increased demand created a shortage of supply and led to dramatic rises in the price of neem seeds, a resource that was previously free and in abundance to locals and farmers. The result was that many local farmers were in a position where they were no longer able to use their traditional free materials and knowledge, but had instead to buy the processed pesticide at high prices from Western companies.

Information feudalism also is having repercussions in the area of medicine, where research on genes and genomes, under the right circumstances, can be patented. Essentially this means that not only can life forms be 'owned', but also that the ability to build on medical advances, or to benefit from them, can be strictly controlled. In a classic example, Myriad Pharmaceuticals, an American bio-technology firm, patented the exclusive rights to the human BRCA1 and BRCA2 genes. Myriad discovered that mutations in these two genes create a high predisposition towards breast cancer in women. Under patent regulations, Myriad is the only company allowed to test or work with these genes for a period of 20 years. Worryingly, in terms of diagnosis, only Myriad is allowed to test for mutations in these two genes, and this test is only available at Myriad's US test centre in Utah, for a cost of several thousand dollars.

Both the neem and the Myriad cases demonstrate how new regimes of intellectual property rights – and the rush to treat ideas and knowledge as property and commercial commodities – has an inherent bias towards the already wealthy and established, and against the poor and developing, who not only benefit less from technological innovations than their more wealthy counterparts, but are also sometimes on the receiving end of yet another new form of exploitation.

CONCLUSION

> The bourgeoisie cannot exist without constantly revolutionising the instruments of production, and thereby the relations of production, and with them, the whole relations of society. (Marx, 1932: 324)

This chapter began with the suggestion that the capitalist economy moves in cycles, generated by acts of 'creative destruction', in which innovation paves the way for economic growth by destroying old economies, industries and ways of doing business. In that respect, the overarching suggestion in the chapter has been that the information age has emerged from a context of economic crises and restructuring, in which nationally-based Fordist industrial modes of production were transformed into globalised, post-Fordist forms of production.

In this way, Castells' network society thesis suggests that advances in communication technology made post-Fordism and globalisation possible, and encouraged economic forms of organisation increasingly based on widespread use of communication networks. Thus, business began to mimic the organisation of the infrastructure upon which it became dependent and adopted the network structure as a prevalent form of economic organisation. From this, the chapter went on to suggest that in a globalised, flexible and networked economy, the role of intangible or 'weightless' goods and intellectual property begins to rise in importance, thus epitomising the shift in advanced economic nations from a tangible, industrial economy to an intangible, informational economy.

FURTHER READING

For useful overviews of the post-industrial, post-Fordist, and information society arguments, see Barney (2005), Lyon (1988), and Webster (1995). For more detailed discussion and criticisms see Kumar (2005) and Schiller (1986). The best port of call for discussions about Castells and the network society thesis include Castells himself (1996/2000) and Marcuse (2002). For a discussion of intellectual property see Shiva (2001), and for an introduction to the idea of the weightless economy, Coyle (1997) is a reasonable starting point.

3
CONVERGENCE AND THE CONTEMPORARY MEDIA EXPERIENCE

> This pervasion of digital technology through our lives is part of a broader set of phenomena. The last 30 years have seen both the rise of globalization and the domination of free market capitalism, the increasing ubiquity of information and communication technologies, and the burgeoning power and influence of technoscience. Digital technology is an important and constitutive part of these developments, and has, to a certain extent, determined their form. (Gere, 2002: 10)

As Charlie Gere suggests in the passage above, globalisation, capitalism, communications technology, and digitisation are all phenomena that have become closely integrated. Globalisation, as we experience it today, would not be possible without the digital communication technologies that serve as its infrastructural backbone, as well as its informational lifeblood. At the same time, the imperatives of capitalism towards the expansion of markets and increasing profitability are fundamental to the development of all these.

This chapter will focus on a somewhat underrated, but extremely integral part of the information society and digital culture: the concept of *convergence*. Without convergence, the very notion of an information society would be difficult to comprehend, as it is because of convergence that we are able to send electronic money, or any other kind of information, around the planet in the blink of an eye. It is because of convergence that we are able to have near ubiquitous communication in our everyday lives. It is because of convergence that we have powerful computers. Indeed, it is because of convergence that we are able to move and store the vast amounts of data, information and communications necessary to keep our society going. In a way, convergence can be seen to ease the friction involved in creating global capitalism.

As a concept, convergence is easy to understand … to 'converge' is to *come together* or to *meet* … to *become similar*. In the context of new media, convergence is a term that has been used in a variety of ways: as a technological process associated with digitization; as a regulatory trend among governments; as a process among the media and telecommunications industry; and as the soon-to-be-dominant form of media culture. This chapter will discuss how these four forms of convergence are interlinked and are part of a historical trend that unites new forms of marketing and audience cultures with the media, telecommunications and computing industries under neo-liberal global capitalism. Finally, how these four forms of convergence operate in these contexts will be illustrated via the case study of the music industry.

TECHNOLOGICAL CONVERGENCE

The first form of convergence to consider is *technological convergence* (or what some call 'functional' convergence). Basically, technological convergence is the movement of almost all media and information to digital electronic formats, storage and transfer: the digitisation of all media, communications, texts, sound, images and even currency into a common digital format or language.

This process has involved a switch from (previously dominant) analogue forms of media to digital forms. Analogue forms of media refer to forms or devices in which data are represented by continuously variable physical properties or quantities. So, for example, a pressure gauge when one is getting their blood pressure taken at the hospital, or the grooves on a vinyl phonograph record that, when a needle is run across them, produce a sound. These are physical properties that are continuous in their representation of data.

By contrast, digital data is discontinuous representation of analogue or continuous physical properties. It portrays things in terms of discrete units, thus fingers and toes are referred to as 'digits'. Set numbers are also discrete units, and clocks that 'tick' between seconds (as opposed to a smooth, non-ticking second hand) are using discrete units and are therefore digital in the proper sense, as is Morse code. Computers use discrete binary digitisation: zeros and ones (or ON and OFF), to represent and store data and information. Thus, the letter 'A', for example, is 0100001 in binary digital representation. Other examples of binary digital communications include beacons (ON–OFF light signals) or Braille (raised or not raised dots arranged on a page).

Table 3.1 Media formats and delivery systems (circa 1975)

Media	Format	Decoder	Delivery
Print	Paper and Ink		Physical transport
Film	Celluloid Reels	Projector	Physical transport
Photography	Photographic Film		Physical transport
Music (album)	Vinyl Plates	Phonograph Player	Physical transport
Music (cassette)	Magnetic Tape	Tape Player	Physical transport
Television	Airwaves in allocated spectrum	Television Receiver	Air
Radio	Airwaves in allocated spectrum	Radio Receiver	Air
Telephone	Electronic Signals	Telephone Decoder	Telephone Lines

If we look historically at the different types of media and communication in the pre-convergence era (say, the 1970s), we have different types of mostly analogue media and different types of formats and delivery systems.

Since the early 1980s, there has been a steady conversion of all those types of media and communication to the 0–1 binary digital format of computers. It is the case now that text, sound, image and moving image (not to mention currency) can and is consumable by the same device, be it a computer, a digital television or a mobile phone. In addition, these items can be used across a number of devices, so a music CD will play in a DVD movie player, or in a computer or, obviously, in a CD player. This is the core of what is meant by technological convergence: all forms of media being increasingly stored and transferred on the same format and therefore becoming completely interchangeable.

This process involves a small trade-off of disadvantages and advantages. The one disadvantage is that the representation of phenomena in discrete units leads to a reduction in representative quality as variable phenomena are 'rounded off' into discrete units. So, for example, enlargement of a digital photograph results in pixilation as colours, lines and shapes are rounded off to the nearest discrete unit. This contrasts the enlargement of an analogue photograph, which results in fading or blurriness.

However, there are many advantages to digitisation. Among the most notable is that digital data can be stored and transferred much more easily and efficiently. Flew (2005) sums these up well by suggesting that digital information is:

1 *Networkable* It can be easily distributed through networks. Thus, any information can be shared and exchanged among large numbers of users simultaneously. There are few complications in terms of distance or distortion.

2 *Compressible* Uncompressed digital data is very large, and in its raw form would actually produce a larger signal (therefore be more difficult to transfer) than analogue data. However, digital data can be compressed. Compression essentially reduces the redundancy out of any given bit of information, so, for example, to compress the number '7.999999', one could represent the number as '7(6)', or as '8', depending on the type of compression used. Thus, in communication, compression reduces the amount of band-width space needed to send information (in the case of MPEG2 video compression that is a ratio of 55 to 1). So data can be compressed, sent and then decompressed at the site of consumption. This makes it possible to send much more information and results in, for example, digital television signals offering more room on the airwave spectrum for more television channels (5–6 in analogue versus over 100 in digital terrestrial), as well as opening up more room in the spectrum for emergency services and wireless applications.

3 *Dense* Another spin-off of compression is the density of digital data in the sense of how much information can be stored in a small space. Consider the amount of music stored on an MP3 player as compared to the storage of an equivalent number of physical CDs or phonograph records. The difference is, of course, astronomical. A typical MP3 player of today's technology can hold the equivalent of a small music shop worth of analogue albums.

4 *Manipulable* Digital information is easily changeable and adaptable, because all manner of text, sound and image are essentially the same. As a result, they are infinitely and easily combinable, whether it be combining text image and sound on a multimedia document or webpage, or the delivery of any form of media off any digital device. Digital data is infinitely malleable.

5 *Impartial* and/or *homogenous* What is meant by this is that no matter what the source, no matter what the content, no matter who or what the creator or the original intent of the content, all digital data is inherently the same thing ... zeros and ones. A good example of this is the 'Bert is evil' incident recounted by Jenkins (2006), in which a digital image of the famous *Sesame Street* character 'Bert' found its way onto a web site maintained by an American high school student who, among other things, 'Photoshopped' Bert's image alongside Osama Bin Laden (in accordance with the 'Bert is evil' theme). This image then found its way onto thousands of posters distributed across the Middle East for use in post September 11th anti-American protests. Thus, the 'Bert' data became used in a way not at all intended by the original creator (the *Children's Television Workshop*), nor even the student who altered the photo.

These kinds of advantages have pushed the consolidation of all different types of data onto the same format since the start of the 1980s. In that decade, digitisation expanded beyond computers and into communications through fax machines, early mobile phones and satellite television. But it was not until the 1990s that convergent media as we understand it today started to appear. With the explosion in popularity of home PCs and later the internet, distribution of text and image (if not sound and moving image quite by then) was becoming commonplace, and the concept of networking different media devices was certainly on its way. Post millennium we are now obviously well on our way: digital film, recording, publishing and photography are now the standard. The internet, computing and especially mobile telephony is increasingly associated with music, television, film as well as personal communication.

REGULATORY CONVERGENCE

Technological convergence created a new set of realities. Now that all forms of information and communication transfer were becoming digital, the previous differences between many industries, such as media, telecommunications and computing were starting to erode. These industries were beginning to come together in their reliance on trading the same basic commodity: the digital bit.

This posed a problem for governments who, because of these technological changes (along with economic imperatives under globalisation), needed to change the legislation that governed these separate industries. This led to a second kind of convergence sometimes referred to as *regulatory convergence,* which is a deregulatory strategy in the media and telecommunication industries adopted by the governments of many industrial economies since the mid-1990s. This set of regulatory changes has had a profound effect on the structure of the media, telecom and computing industries and a significant impact on our current media culture.

Traditionally, telecommunications was an industry dominated by regulated domestic monopolies (privately or publicly owned), with little internal and international competition. For example, AT&T, British Telecom, France Telecom, Deutsche Telecom and a series of provincial monopolies in Canada were all legislative telecom monopolies in their respective countries. These legislative monopolies were advocated on the logic that such an agreement was the best way to promote universal access to communications technology. Heavy restrictions to expansion outside the telecom sector were justified on the grounds that it would be undesirable for large corporations to be able to control several media and communications sources.

The result was large and powerful corporations that were severely restricted in what they could do outside their established markets and industries. Indeed, as Winseck (1998) argues, there were, within Canadian, British and American contexts, many legislative hurdles designed since the 1920s to prevent communications companies from doing business in other related sectors (such as media), lest they become too powerful across sectors and monopolise too much of the public sphere and culture in general. For example, in the 1920s and 1930s, American telecom giant AT&T was the second largest financial interest in Hollywood film production, but they were forced to give up these interests by the Federal Communications Commission in the 1930s. Similar legislation also later kept AT&T out of the computing industry (Winseck, 1998: 340).

A similar philosophy was applied to the media industry where, for example, in the United States, there were many restrictions on how many radio or television stations could be owned by one firm. This restrictive model preventing the concentration of private ownership of media content was commonplace throughout the democratic, free market economies of the world.

All of this began to change in the mid 1980s, when the US justice department filed an antitrust suit against AT&T and successfully broke up what was at the time the world's largest corporation by assets. This was a deregulatory move on the part of the US government. In exchange, the companies that emerged from AT&T were allowed to expand into hitherto forbidden industries, like computing and broadcasting. AT&T and the several smaller companies emerged into a deregulated, fully competitive telecommunications sector (Warf, 2003). Soon after, other countries such as Japan and the United Kingdom privatised and deregulated their state owned telecom monopolies.

Since the mid 1990s, there has been another, more profound state of deregulation due to the implementation of the 1996 Telecommunications Act in the United States. This act was an attempt to rationalise federal communications law to deal with the burgeoning telecommunications industry within the context of:

 Increasing competition of both domestic and international telecommunications markets, and the desire for American firms to remain powerful and competitive within that market.

The rapidly expanding internet, which blurred the distinction between media, computing and telecommunication industries.

 Technological convergence and the digitisation of all forms of communications, leading to a further blurring of the distinctions between media, telecom and computing industries.

By and large, this act was deregulatory in the sense that it abolished many of the cross-market barriers that had prohibited large corporations in one communications industry (such as the telephone industry) from providing services in another related industry (like cable or broadcasting). The act followed classic 'neo-liberal' principles in that its intent was to increase competition and innovation, stimulate investment and expansion of markets, and to provide greater access (and hopefully lower prices) for the consumer.

The Telecommunications Act was the precipitate for a larger trend in global regulation reform. The European Union passed a package of liberalised reforms of the telecom sector in 1998, as did many other countries around the same time. These regulatory reforms tended to follow three features:

1. To separate the regulation of infrastructure and content, with less regulation of infrastructure and often more regulations on content.

2. To simplify and minimise regulation and harmonise this regulation across media sectors.

3. To emphasise competition law over regulation in the media and telecom sectors. (Iosifidis, 2002 and see also UK Department of Trade and Industry, 1998 for an example)

Such regulatory reforms changed the environment in which media, telecommunications and computing companies operate. Where once, these industries were separate and often dominated by large firms or even monopolies, now regulatory reform and convergence has essentially allowed these three industries to merge into one large interactive multimedia and communications industry, with little to prevent the expansion of corporations into new industries and new parts of the world.

MEDIA INDUSTRY CONVERGENCE

Once the deregulatory groundwork had been laid, there followed a large number of mergers and acquisitions in the media and telecom industries (Chon et al., 2003; Iosifidis, 2002; Warf, 2003). These were driven by the combination of technological developments (digital convergence and increasingly powerful networking capabilities) and the overall climate of neo-liberal deregulation and globalisation. The word of the day was 'expansion', in the sense that it became clear that within the media and telecom sector, smaller corporations were going to be swallowed up by larger ones and that soon only a handful of very large multinational corporations would dominate the global media market.

Deregulation and digital networking technology paved the way for large scale cross-industry expansion or *horizontal integration*, in which a firm in one industry (for instance, telecommunications) expanded across to another industry (such as television broadcasting). The result was the blurring of the boundaries of the telecommunications, computer and media industries into something more or less approaching one giant industry of information production, communication and distribution, in which firms from all of these once separate sectors were now increasingly in competition or partnership on a global scale.

The second form of expansion was *vertical integration* in which a firm that is concentrated on one point in the production chain of a sector (for instance, film production) expands into another part of the production chain in the same industry, such as film distribution.

Both of these types of expansion drove a general strategy of industrial convergence within the media and telecom sector. From a business standpoint, the strategy of convergence had the potential to create a situation where a firm controlled both content production and content distribution across these sectors. Media industry convergence is the main reason that, for example, Apple (traditionally viewed as a computer firm) has become a major music distributer through its Ipod/Itunes service, or Sony (traditionally seen as a consumer electronics manufacturer) has become one of the biggest global concerns in the film and music industries, by virtue of owning Tri-Star Pictures and BMG Music.

The potential benefits of convergence strategies involving vertical integration and cross-sector expansion are numerous. Wirtz (2001) argues that cross-sector expansion is desirable because of the potential for price and service bundling, where one company is able to provide a number of separate services to a customer for one price and on one system (such as providing phone, internet and digital television services). Thus, the firm is able to effectively corral what might be a variety of consumer purchases from different companies into one bundled and highly profitable package. In addition, cross-sector mergers and acquisitions are an easy way to expand into new markets by taking on an established brand name, customer base and infrastructure. Expansion into new markets helps increase potential for profit and diversifies risk through having activities in several sectors, instead of just one.

Vertical integration within media convergence allows a corporation to potentially control the entire process (or value chain) of a product from raw materials and production, through to distribution, marketing and final sales. This, combined with horizontal expansion, has the potential to lead to what are often referred to as 'synergies', where products and profits can be controlled from inception to sales, and in marketing across sectors. This is particularly valuable in the media industry where marketing and promotion is vital to success and products are able to achieve profits in many ways.

For example, one can look at a large, vertically integrated, converged firm like Viacom. Viacom owns (among many other things) Paramount Films, a large Hollywood-based film production company. When Paramount Films creates a new film release, it has the benefit of the huge resources of Viacom to ensure its success. These films can be assured good distribution, as Viacom owns the Famous Players cinema chain. The film can also be rented or sold in Blockbuster Video, also owned by Viacom. In terms of marketing 'synergies', this Paramount film can be advertised (and reviewed) on any of the 20 major market television stations Viacom owns in the United States or on its cable and digital television channels such as MTV, VH1, Showtime, or Comedy Central. Of course, MTV and VH1 can also promote the soundtrack release to accompany the film. Perhaps an accompanying video game produced and sold by video games maker XFire (owned by Viacom) will generate spinoff revenues in the music and video game sectors for Viacom, as well as creating additional promotion for the film itself.

Apart from synergies, cross promotion and risk diversification, the other motivation behind expansion is survival. In the post 1996 media and telecom environment, mergers and acquisitions have been the order of the day. As McChesney and Shiller (2003) have documented, large media corporations are fully aware that they must either rapidly expand and acquire smaller firms, effectively becoming too big to purchase, or they will be acquired by other firms and cease to exist.

The result is a global media dominated by a 'first tier' of around ten very large global firms. McChesney and Shiller (2003) listed nine firms in this first tier (General Electric, Liberty Media, Disney, AOL/Time Warner, Sony, News Corporation, Viacom, Vivendi Universal and Bertelsmann). A more recent list would likely now include Google (worth $97 billion in 2009 and owning YouTube, Blogger and Deja) and Microsoft (worth $136 billion in 2009) and perhaps would exclude Vivendi out of the top tier. McChesney and Shiller (2003) argue that there is a further second tier of roughly 100 other large regional or national media corporations that dominate what is left of the global media market.

Concerns about media convergence

> Vertical integration was once looked upon with alarm by the government. It was understood that corporations which have control of a total process, from raw material to fabrication to sales, also have few motives for genuine innovation and the power to seize out anyone else who tries to compete. This situation distorts the economy with monopolistic control over prices. Today, government has become sympathetic to dominant vertical corporations that have merged into ever larger total systems. These corporations, including those in the media, have remained largely unrestrained. (Bagdikian, 2000: xvii)

The concern, for authors like McChesney and Shiller, is the inherent threats to democracy and accountability that follow when media and the public sphere become dominated by a small number of large corporations. In such a situation, it seems inevitable that the public sphere will be dominated by the political viewpoints of big business, and that there would be much less potential for criticism of large corporations or the avocation of policies which would harm their interests. As a result, the public are put in a position where they are only exposed to a narrow range of accounts or views of the world, thus providing these corporations with massive power and influence over the public, and over elected governments.

For example, Rupert Murdoch's *News Corporation* owns hundreds of newspapers worldwide including, in the UK, the *Sun*, the *News of the World* and *The Times*. News Corp also owns BSkyB, the UK's largest satellite and digital television broadcaster. Thus, Murdoch is said to have a large influence on UK national politics, including elections. The last three Prime Ministers (Blair, Major, Thatcher) have all elicited his support and, in the 1992 general election, the unexpected re-election of John Major and his Conservative Party was by many considered to be at least partly due to the support of Major by Murdoch's papers. This was even lionised in the famous headline 'It was the Sun wot won it'. In 1997, the *Sun* and *The Times* switched allegiance to Tony Blair and New Labour, arguably helping them to a landslide victory that year.

Similarly, and even more brashly, Italian media mogul Silvio Berlusconi has used his ownership of three terrestrial (and several digital) television channels, and his ownership of Italy's largest publishing house as a stepping stone to be elected Prime Minister on three separate occasions. He is famous for using his power over Italy's media to target political and judicial opposition.

But while mainstream media is said to be dwindling in diversity in the face of oligopoly, the internet has been held up as an infinite source of diverse voices. Many would suggest that the internet, because of its networked (or rhizomatic) nature and the ability of internet users to be both producers and consumers of media, can never be controlled to the same degree by large corporations, and in that sense is an antidote to the continued trend towards oligopoly in mainstream media. To a certain extent this is true, however internet firms are not immune from acquisition and convergence strategies. In fact, they are central to it. As early as 2001, research was suggesting that the total number of companies that controlled 60 per cent of viewer minutes spent online had already fallen from 110 in March 1999, to 14 in March 2001 (Jupiter Media Metrix, 2001):

> 'The Media Metrix data show an irrefutable trend towards online media consolidation and indicate that the playing field is anything but even,' said Aram Sinnreich, Jupiter senior analyst. 'The Internet may provide an opportunity for new players like Microsoft or Yahoo! to become serious media companies, but so far a major share of the market is being absorbed by a handful of companies, with those same companies continuing to direct traffic across their own networks of sites. Media companies competing for the attention of consumers must consider that while the key barrier to online entry and success used to be infrastructure, it has shifted dramatically to advertising and marketing.' (MediaPost, 2001)

This has arguably been the result of the increasing power of already established media and telecom companies to expand into the internet sector, as well as the creation and success of a small number of increasingly powerful 'pioneer enterprises', such as AOL, Google, Yahoo, Microsoft, which have emerged from the new media sector (Wirtz, 2001). For example, Facebook now claims to have over 300 million active users, and recent studies have demonstrated massive concentration of online video viewing within Google-owned sites (primarily YouTube), where almost 40 per cent of all online videos are watched (Comscore, 2009). At over 120 million viewers in the United States alone, YouTube is being watched by over one third of the American populace and further demonstrates the concentration of the online audience into a fewer number of sites.

CONVERGENCE CULTURE AND THE NEW MEDIA EXPERIENCE

This chapter has discussed how several types of convergence have integrated to produce two major trends within media:

- How *technological convergence* has led to a situation in which all forms of media, communication and information are made up of the same (digital) format, and thus have become interchangeable across a number of different devices and distribution systems.

- How deregulation of the media and telecommunications industries (*regulatory convergence*) has led to *media industry convergence,* in which large media corporations have expanded both vertically within their own industry and horizontally across other media sectors. This has created a concentration, of media resources in the hands of a small number of very large global media corporations, who can release and promote their products in many ways across several types of media.

In this section, we will examine how these two trends have manifested themselves from the point of view of the consumer. Jenkins (2004, 2006; Jenkins and Deuze, 2008) has argued that convergence has thrown media into a state of flux, in which media has moved away from somewhat static models of production and consumption of discrete media objects to become more participatory, and more akin to cross media 'experiences'. For Jenkins, 'convergence culture' is the result of the lowered production and distribution costs of media coupled with the expanded range of delivery or distribution channels available in digitised media environments, aided by the increasing oligopolisation of the media and telecom industry under corporate convergence strategies.

However, Jenkins chooses to move away from the arguments of Bagdikian, McChesney and Shiller, suggesting that convergence is an inherent 'threat' to a democratic society and media diversity, arguing that:

> Far too much media reform rhetoric rests on melodramatic discourse about victimization and vulnerability, seduction and manipulation, 'propaganda machines' and 'weapons of mass deception'. Again and again, this version of the media reform movement has ignored the complexity of the relationship to popular culture and sided with those opposed to a more diverse and participatory culture. (Jenkins, 2006: 247–248)

Jenkins instead argues that what is really happening is a complex process involving two trends. First, a concentration of media power, in the sense that ever larger media companies have sought to extend their reach, profitability and hold over the consumer by distributing and marketing their products and brands across a multitude of channels, creating larger revenues and more powerful access to consumers.

Second, Jenkins suggests that convergence has created a radical democratisation of media use which has loosened the control of media companies by allowing consumers to have more direct control over the media to which they are exposed, to help create new media themselves, and to interact with other users through media. Thus, Jenkins sees convergence culture as 'both a top-down corporate-driven process and a bottom-up consumer-driven process' (Jenkins and Deuze, 2008: 6; see also Jenkins, 2006).

Jenkins is emphasising the changing dynamic between producers and consumers in new media convergence culture. In order to tease out these dynamics, I suggest, based on the work of Jenkins and others, that there are three basic elements at play in the emerging convergence culture: cross-media experiences and consumption of cultural goods; a participatory media culture; collective or collaborative intelligence in the media experience.

The creation of cross-media experiences

A fundamental characteristic of convergence culture is the move towards cultural objects and information being increasingly consumed or experienced across several forms of media, and on a variety of devices. Henry Jenkins (2006) has perhaps been the most perceptive commentator in describing how images, moving images, sounds, stories, discussions, debates, brands and any other form of mediated information of expression are spreading themselves across a wide array of media devices: 'In the world of media convergence, every important story gets told, every brand gets sold, and every consumer gets courted across multiple media platforms' (Jenkins, 2004: 3).

Cross-media experiences are something that has been encouraged by media industry convergence on the production side. Jenkins (2006) uses the film *The Matrix* and its subsequent sequels as an archetypal example of corporate-driven trans-media, cross-media, or 'synergistic' storytelling. The core of *The Matrix* consists of three movies (*The Matrix*, *The Matrix Reloaded*, *The Matrix Revolutions*), but in addition to these, there is also *The Animatrix*, a series of short animated films made by a variety of well-known animators, a series of graphic novels and two video games (*Enter the Matrix* and the *Matrix Alternate Reality Game*). Each element is unique and designed to add something extra to the story and experience of *The Matrix*, which was conceived of by the producers (the Wachowski Brothers) to work together to create an overall experience. Even cheat codes for the game *Enter the Matrix* are hidden in billboards included in film shots in the *Matrix* trilogy (see Jenkins, 2006: 93–131 for full details about the *Matrix* trans-media strategy).

Similarly, the seminal film *The Blair Witch Project* used faux documentary web sites combined with pseudo-documentary films aired on a variety of broadcast television stations in the United States to create a pop culture mythology or fake legend of 'the

Burkettsville Witch' as much as a year before the actual release of the film. This created a 'buzz' and a sense of anticipation within popular culture prior to the release of the film, and added a sense of tension in the audience that the film itself could actually be 'real' victim-shot handi-cam footage of mass murder. In this respect, to simply turn up and see *The Blair Witch Project* in the cinema as a standalone film was really to miss out on the Blair Witch 'experience' as intended by the film-makers.

A similar spirit was present in the marketing strategy for Steven Spielberg's futuristic film *A.I*, which included the development of seminal alternate reality game *The Beast*. This game created a virtual world based around the world of the film, in which a murder mystery puzzle needed to be solved. Released alongside the film, it was intended to expand the life of the film on to the internet as opposed to through sequels. A fundamental characteristic of the game was that it should be experienced through as many different media as possible, including web sites, emails, phone calls, newspaper ads, faxes, SMS messages and television advertisements. The idea was to make the game more intriguing or more real by placing clues across several media sources (including hints in film trailers), thereby creating an alternate reality experience for the players and, ultimately, for the film (Stewert, 2001). A similar, more sophisticated alternate reality game, *I Love Bees*, where players had to collaborate to solve a cross-media puzzle involving alien invasion, was created to promote the release of the *Halo 2* video game (see McGonigal, 2008, for a detailed description of this fascinating project).

Now, to a certain extent, the cross-marketing of media commodities – films in particular – is nothing new. Film soundtracks that enhance the marketing and potential for profit for a film have been around for years. The merchandising of rock band KISS from albums, to figurines and t-shirts, comic books and even to the ill-conceived made-for-television movie *KISS Meets the Phantom of the Park* in the 1970s is an example of this kind of cross media merchandising, capitalised upon to great effect by the *Star Wars* series of films. However, the basic difference is that merchandising then operated more or less as a spin-off strategy, whereas contemporary cross-media strategies and experiences are seen as fundamental and integral to the product, which is conceived of from the beginning as a cross-media experience instead of a standalone, single media object. *The Blair Witch Project* and *The Matrix* are not intended to be watched as single isolated objects, but are meant to be one part of a multimedia story or world to which the audience is invited.

In this respect, the larger trends of digital and media industry convergence have made this possible, by encouraging the development of very large cross-sector global media companies that have the resources to create and market cultural commodities across several media platforms. But the ability to think in this manner is a consumer phenomenon as well, one in which consumers themselves generate cross-media experiences, in what Jenkins refers to as a 'participatory culture'.

Participatory media culture

If on the one hand, convergence can be seen as a producer-driven experience that crosses media sectors and conduits, the other hand can demonstrate that convergence is also a consumer-driven process, seen largely as an extension of fan culture. For a hypothetical example, one could use a popular and catchy television commercial. This commercial might be broadcast on a terrestrial television network first, and may, in turn be recorded and put onto YouTube for fun by a fan or a bored teenager. Perhaps this same person, or another person, creates a fan page on Facebook, drawing in more admirers among his or her friendship network. Other friends, checking up from mobile phones, PDAs laptops or computers, then watch the commercial on these devices. In this one simple example can be seen how the consumption of a media object has moved from broadcast television, to a computer, to a mobile phone or PDA.

Jenkins (2006) argues that convergence is more than just a technological process, but that the culture of convergence is a participatory one in which 'consumers are encouraged to seek out new information and make connections among dispersed media content' (Jenkins, 2006: 3). Thus, along with media or corporate convergence, there is also 'participatory' or 'grass-roots' convergence, where consumers are increasingly involved in seeking out information from a variety of sources, interacting with others who share interests, and even helping to produce their own experience of the product in isolation or in groups.

Jenkins uses the examples of internet 'spoil sites' for the American reality television programme *Survivor*, *Twin Peaks* chat rooms, and the relationship between the talent show *American Idol* and its gossip sites as prototypical cases of participatory culture in the age of convergence. In the case of *Survivor* spoil sites, fans extend their experiences of the programme by engaging in collaborative efforts online to solve key elements of the narrative puzzle (location, participants, winner) before the official broadcast on television. With *Twin Peaks*, fans engaged in similar online speculation about the central theme of the killing of Laura Palmer and often were quite critical of the overall writing of the series. In the case of *American Idol*, fans debate, gossip and criticise contestants (and the show itself) through a variety of web sites, including *YouTube*.

Dena (2008) examines the behaviour of consumers and producers in alternate reality games as characteristic of emerging participatory culture practices. She points out that ARG designers intentionally leave room or 'gaps' in their authorship of the games for players or audiences to contribute to the experience of the narrative. In that sense, they possess temporal, spatial and authorial distribution (Dena, 2008: 53). Within the design of games like *I Love Bees* or *The Beast*, participation is anticipated to be 'tiered' in the sense that it is fully expected that some players will play a very active role in contributing to solving the central problem and creating the overall experience of the game. These people form the core game players and have the largest input into the experience. A larger group will be expected to play a minor collaborative role, and the largest group will tend to play a more passive audience-type of role: essentially 'readers' who simply enjoy following the narrative of the game and the participation of other players (Dena, 2008).

In all of these cases, the experience of the object has spun out of the exclusive control of the producer. This is evident of how contemporary audiences seek to engage with media increasingly on their own terms and, as Jenkins suggests, will seek out new information, alone or in collaborative groups, in order to enhance their enjoyment of the product. Sometimes with – and often without – the cooperation of the producers themselves, who often encourage this kind of consumer-led participatory culture, and in other cases are more hostile and protective of what they see at their intellectual property.

Collective intelligence

A third facet of an emerging convergence culture, as a result of the interactivity and networking involved with converged media, is a new form of knowledge production and problem solving in which individuals collectively pool together their interests and expertise towards the solving of common problems, the creation of common resources or the pooling together of information for mutual benefit.

Several different authors, in their own way, have discussed the increasing significance of this kind of communal collaboration. Pierre Levy (1997) was one of the first, arguing that networking technology would 'mobilise and coordinate the intelligence, expertise, skills, wisdom and imagination of humanity' (Levy, 1997: xxiv) in ways that would ultimately transform the very production of knowledge itself. Similarly, Howard Rheingold (2002) later referred to 'smart mobs' as the self-structured application of human talents for cooperation through communication and computing technologies, which allow the 'mob' or 'swarm' to accomplish tasks that are beyond the talents of a lone individual. Essentially, he is referring to the practical application of 'collective intelligence'. Herz (2005) continues with the 'Bee' metaphor by referring to the 'hive mind' of collectivity present in online games, and Charles Leadbeater (2008) refers to such a collective pooling of knowledge and talents in innovative products as 'We-think'. However, no matter the term (and I will use the term 'collective intelligence' for the time being), the basic premise is the same: the spontaneous or self-organised pooling of talents, resources and information through networked communication technologies towards problem solving and collective creation that would not be achievable through individual effort.

It is widely acknowledged that one of the first, and still one of the best, examples of collective intelligence is the open source software movement. This came to maturity in 1991 with the release onto the internet of the Linux operating system by Linus Torvalds.

> Torvalds did not just put the program online but also its source code – its basic recipe – leaving it for software enthusiasts to take away and tamper with, to criticise and propose improvements. Open source software is software that nobody owns, everyone can use and anyone can improve, and open-source licensing is a way to hold ideas and information in common that under the right conditions can encourage mass collaborative innovation. That is what Torvalds eventually set off. (Leadbeater, 2008: 65)

The legacy of this foray into collaborative, collective intelligence is an extremely robust and reliable operating system that, by 2006, accounted for 80 per cent of the operating software on computer systems around the world (Leadbeater, 2008: 66). The collaborative nature of Linux has produced a product that is not only popular, but would have been impossible to coordinate at an individual or even corporate level. Leadbeater (2008) has noted that the Debian version of Linux released in 2005 had 229 million lines of source code, equivalent to 60,000 person-years of software coding. This compares to Microsoft Windows XP, which possesses roughly 40 million lines of code. Clearly, Linux has become a monumental collective endeavour which has helped to transform the operation of the internet and its culture.

Wikipedia, a common example of collective intelligence, operates in a similar, although slightly more managed, way. Wikipedia is a collaborative effort in the production of knowledge that is built up from a combination of anonymous contributors, thousands of registered users, several hundred 'administrators', bureaucrats and stewards, 51 'super-elites' (who can make major changes to the actual Wikipedia software and database), arbitration committees and, finally, founder Steve Wales. (for more explicit details, see Pink, 2005, or Bruns, 2008). While perhaps not the ideal in self-organised, non-hierarchical collaboration, the Wikipedia project is, ultimately, a collective effort of laypersons and specialists who contribute their knowledge towards a larger collaborative outcome that reflects the contributions of all, and is provided as a resource for all.

PRODUCERS, CONSUMERS AND 'PRODUSAGE'

It is common now within writings on new media to refer to the blurring of boundaries between 'producers' – those that produce content and cultural objects – and 'consumers', the audience or purchasers of such objects. Jenkins is right to propose that research on the media has been dominated by approaches that suggest a rather imbalanced power relationship, which over-favours the producers of media content over the users. Certainly the 'media effects' approach as demonstrated by much psychological work on media audiences is a gross exaggeration of this imbalance (see Gauntlett, 1998).

Abercrombie and Longhurst (1998) chart the changing view of audiences in sociological study from the simplistic 'effects' model, through to the 'cultivation approach', 'uses and gratifications' (all considered 'behavioural approaches'), through to 'encoding and decoding' models, the 'incorporation/resistance paradigm' and finally to the 'spectacle/performance' paradigm. The transition between these phases demonstrated an academic recognition of increasing power on the part of the user or consumer of media as an active agent using tools in identity construction, self creation and relationship formation. This contrasts the passive 'viewer' or 'victim' of media, represented as some sort of stimulus that is administered and provides a direct effect on the audience, or even the audience as an 'interpreter' of an intended and specific message within the media or text.

With the advent of convergent new media and the plethora of choice in sources for information, as well as the increased capacity for individuals to produce content themselves, this shift away from producer hegemony to audience or consumer power would seem to have accelerated, thus eroding the producer–consumer distinction.

Bruns (2008) sees this producer–consumer distinction as based on increasingly outdated conceptions of industrial production, where a finished and authored 'product' is produced or manufactured, distributed and then 'consumed' at the other end of the value chain. Bruns argues that such distinctions between producers and end users of content have become increasingly insignificant (Bruns, 2008: 2). Essentially, this blurring of distinctions is the result of five processes; the first being a more general marketing strategy which has been used increasingly since the 1970s and that encourages feedback processes between producers and consumers ('prosumers'), allowing for more consumer influence over the production of goods.

With the rise of the internet and other networking technologies, four other processes have been set into motion:

- Due to the increasing choice of information sources, access to information is increasingly organised on an 'information pull' basis, as opposed to a 'product push' basis associated with traditional broadcast media.

- The means of producing and distributing information has become much more widely available or *democratised*. Thus, the ability to produce information is no longer in the hands of a small minority or elite allied to specific interests. This means that those who used to be merely 'consumers' are now able to produce as well.

- Networking technology enables *collective* means of organisation and engagement where users, fans, or consumers can communicate directly with each other to form affinity groups around their interests.

- Digital content is easily produced, copied, modified, shared and distributed, thus digital information and goods have become *non-rival*, meaning that they can be endlessly used by all.

These changes suggest that what Jenkins (2006) refers to as *convergence culture* can basically be boiled down to new business models, new ways of marketing and product development that rely on information from, and engagement with, consumers as well as the use of new convergent networking technologies that make all of this possible.

This leads to what Bruns (2008) calls 'produsage', in which information and cultural products are 'prodused' in a networked, communal environment involving both traditional consumers and producers, and where such information or products are not finished products owned and controlled by an author, but communally owned, unfinished 'processes'. For Bruns, 'Produsage' has four key elements:

1. *Open participation/communal evaluation*, which allows diverse individuals to contribute to the product in question, if such contributions are deemed to be useful by the community of producers.

2) *Fluid hierarchy/ad-hoc meritocracy*, in which all participants, whether equal in skill or not, have equal ability to contribute. Usefulness becomes the key on both ends. On the side of contribution to the product, and on the side of interest in the product.

3) *Unfinished artefacts/continuing process*, which involves the move from conceptualising media products and objects not as finished or finalised 'products', but as 'artefacts' that are continually in construction.

4) *Common property/individual rewards*, where content is less seen as owned by an author or producer in a traditional sense, but has become more communal in nature, having been created by a produsage community, and providing rewards for that community.

Some of the best examples of produsage are well known, and have been discussed in this chapter, from the collective knowledge production that is Wikipedia (or the many other Wiki's in existence) to the collective photographic curation of Flickr, to the collective creation of an online world involved in online games such as MMORPGs, or alternate reality games like *I Love Bees*. Even social networking sites like Facebook, with its value dependent upon how many people use the network and how much user generated information is put on it, is a further example of produsage.

So we can see how the three elements of convergence culture, cross media experiences and products, participatory culture and collective intelligence, can be viewed from another perspective under the more economic label of 'produsage'. Bruns' term is useful in that it places these elements of convergence culture back within an economic context that emphasises the coming together of producers and consumers within interactive, converged, digital contexts. On the one hand this acknowledges, as Jenkins does, the increasing participation of consumers in the production process, but at the same recognises that many of these changes are the result of new and innovative business and marketing models. A beacon of participatory convergence culture such as the *I Love Bees* alternate reality game certainly gives a lot of scope to the consumer to help produce their own experience, but it can also be seen in simple economic terms as a successful and engaging marketing device for a video game.

Case Study: The Changing Culture Industry of Digital Music

Once music is 'dematerialized' from the physical entity of records and decentred from the 'tyranny' of television media, musical experience becomes increasingly fragmented and dispersed across different media and networks, but more enriched within different leisure and everyday contexts. (Lee, 2009: 15–16)

Fuck you, I won't do what you tell me. (Rage Against the Machine: 'Killing in the name')

On 20 December 2009, the expletive-ridden single 'Killing in the name' by California heavy rock band Rage Against the Machine was declared the official 'Christmas number one' in the UK singles charts, having sold 500,000 copies in the previous week. The Christmas number one is something of a UK institution, with betting agencies traditionally taking wagers up to a year in advance over what artist will gain the honour. The previous four Christmas number ones had all been claimed by winners of the highly successful television musical reality programme *The X-Factor*, a British version of *American Idol* and the now famous global 'idol' television franchise.

However, in this case, the *X-Factor* winner, Joe McElderry, was relegated to second place by 50,000 singles. What made this result particularly unusual was that 'Killing in the name' as a single was released in 1992, and was not marketed, nor released in physical form at all in 2009. Instead, the sales were driven by a Facebook and Twitter campaign started by part-time DJ Joe Morter as a satirical and political attempt to undermine the Christmas chart dominance of the mainstream media behemoth that is *The X-Factor*. Effectively, the Christmas number one was awarded to a song that was released 17 years previously, by a band that played no part in its promotion, and without selling a single physical copy.

This incident says much about the changes taking place as a result of the digitisation of music and the resulting convergence culture of music, the virtualisation of music sales, the decentralisation of power from mass media organisations into the hands of fans and music consumers, and the central role of networking and community within digital music culture.

The digitisation of music and its discontents

Within academic literature, the discussion of how digitisation and networking have affected music has primarily focussed on the ability to compress digital music files and distribute them easily and freely through digital networks. This has provided a serious challenge to the music industry proper (particularly publishers and record companies), as well as the current intellectual property regimes on which the cultural industries in general (not just music) are based.

As such, there has been a great deal of academic and legal discussion and debate around the notion of 'piracy', particularly as it relates to peer-to-peer file sharing networks such as Napster, Gnutella, Kazaa and the many others that became notorious in the late 1990s and the early 2000s. These sites were/are based on technology which allowed people to 'rip' (i.e., make a digitally compressed digital file such as an MP3) music they owned from their CDs onto their personal computers, then distribute or share these files with others within their network, essentially allowing everyone access to each other's digital music collections for free.

Such behaviour on the part of consumers was seen by record companies, publishers, some artists, and the recording industry in general as a massive threat, with the potential to undermine their rights to make a profit off the intellectual property they own. The response of the recording industry was to strictly enforce their legal rights, and many lawsuits and 'cease and desist' orders were targeted at, first, file sharing networks, then at many of the music consumers who used these networks to trade music files.

Many advocates and academics from a variety of disciplines (see, as a small selection, Alderman, 2001; Kusek and Leonhard, 2005; Yar, 2006) were, and remain, very critical of this approach, arguing that such measures:

- Were out of step with contemporary technology and cultural attitudes.

- Were an unfair restriction of culture (as a collective commons) and free speech.

- Were unfair in that music file sharers were not gaining commercially from file sharing (unlike commercial media pirates), but were merely following a practice of informal music sharing which has occurred for decades.

- Would be impossible to enforce.

In the minds of many, the litigious nature of the music industry was indicative of an archaic industrial motif and a general unwillingness on their part to adapt to inevitable change by adopting new business models. The prevailing argument among academics was that digital distribution of music and file sharing was potentially very good for both the music industry and music generally, because it would increase the market for music by allowing it to move and flow (Jones, 2002), making it more accessible to, and providing greater choice for, music consumers. If the music industry could embrace these developments instead of trying to suppress them, they would be better off in the long run.

Over the last half decade, the music industry has begun to experiment with and licence attempts to legally distribute and share music over the internet. One of the better known ventures is Apple's iTunes system, in which consumers can buy music files on a per-song basis. Other sites have used a subscription fee model in which a monthly fee is paid, which allows the user access to a musical database. Embracing the technology seems to have paid off, as 2009 has proven to be another record-breaking year for music sales, exceeding $1.5 billion in the United States alone, with digital music currently accounting for 40 per cent of all music purchases (and in particular, the vast majority of singles sales). Surprisingly, even more vinyl records were sold in 2009 than any other year since 1991 (Chancellor, 2010). Conversely, sales of music CDs have been declining throughout the post-millennial decade. What this suggests overall, however, is that even though free and illegal downloading is an option (and still a popular activity) for many people, the music industry continues to grow and profit, even in a mature and networked market like the United States.

'Mash-ups' and the crisis of authorship in digital culture

One particular digital culture phenomenon distinctly encapsulates many of the issues faced by record companies (as well as musicians): the culture and practice of musical 'mash-ups'. While 'mash-up' now refers to a variety of digital culture practices, a musical mash-up can be defined as the creation of music by the blending of two or more other musical recordings. This is most commonly achieved by combining the vocal track of one recording with the musical tracks of another recording.

While the mixing or blending of other recordings to create a new piece is not a fundamentally new practice (see McLeod, 2005), the mash-up musical genre is itself a child of the digital age. It depends on, first, the use of digital audio software such as ProTools and Ableton to manipulate music and vocal tracks from digital audio files to create the new work. Second, mash-ups are normally clandestinely distributed through networking technologies, particularly blogs and peer-to-peer file sharing (Howard-Spink, 2005).

The 2001 track 'A stroke of genie-us' by Freelance Hellraiser, in which pop diva Christina Aguilera's vocals are combined with the music of The Strokes is generally considered to be the beginning of the mash-up genre. However, its pinnacle was said to be reached in early 2004 when a hip-hop artist known as Danger Mouse produced a mash up that consisted of musical fragments from the Beatles 'White album' in combination with the recently released 'Black album' by hip-hop star Jay-Z. Despite a small pressing, 'The Grey Album' proved immensely popular and was shared prolifically on file sharing networks. Copyright holders EMI/Capitol Records issued Danger Mouse with a 'cease and desist' order, ordering all copies of the unlicensed product destroyed. This was responded to by a large online protest, known as 'Grey Tuesday', in which over 170 web sites broke the law by hosting the album for free distribution, resulting in over a million illegal downloads (McLeod, 2005).

What is significant about mash-ups, and what is perhaps symbolic about them in light of discussions about the music industry in digital culture, is that the genre by nature confounds notions of intellectual property and authorship. Legally, one must obtain permission (often by paying a fee or royalties) from the creator (or more properly, the copyright holder) to use or distribute any recorded music or selection of music. In mash-ups, this is almost never done, as mash-up artists generally view such recordings as part of a wider cultural or creative commons (Stark, 2006) to which all should have access and be able to use in creative activity (see also Chapter Two). The Danger Mouse 'Grey Album' is particularly prescient in this respect, as the Beatles back catalogue of recordings has never been licensed for use and is fiercely protected by its copyright holders (McLeod, 2005). It is a large, but tightly controlled, slice of popular culture.

The products of mash-ups are also problematic. They are in many senses original works of collage made up of other original works, but they complicate the notion of originality and authorship (the basis of the modern culture industries), as mash-up artists themselves cannot lay claim to any 'authorship' of their product as an intellectual property, and thus normally receive no direct income from their works. Thus, mash-ups blur many distinctions: those between producer and consumer, between amateur and professional, and between practitioner and distributor (Howard-Spink, 2005). In this way, mash-ups are symptomatic of the sort of 'produsage' practices associated with convergence culture (Bruns, 2008; Jenkins, 2006).

Digital music cultures and music consumption

> Within different everyday contexts, the experience of music is
> less about star identification than about socialization and per-
> sonal expression. Digital technologies have furthered the role
> of music in forming and refining interpersonal connections and
> expressing identities on the net. (Lee, 2009: 15)

Even with music sales booming, record companies have had to begin to adapt their role in a changing music culture. Some (for example Jones, 2002) have referred to the upcoming changes as 'disintermediation', in which the role of certain elements of the music value chain (artist – producer – manufacturer – marketer – distributor – retailer – consumer) are removed. So when MySpace became a phenomenon, it had the potential to seriously disrupt this value chain as the combination of cheap digital recording equipment and access to MySpace allowed artists to produce their own music, promote it themselves and distribute it directly to their audience. A value chain of seven links could be reduced to just two (artist–consumer).

In such a context, the challenge for the music industry becomes how to stay relevant in a digital environment that:

• Makes it easier for musicians to enter the marketplace by making available their own creations themselves.

• Where consumers of music now have access to almost infinitely large selections of content (much of it for free).

• Where consumers also have almost ubiquitous access to music through an increasing array of gadgets, both static (such as PCs) and mobile (such as phones and iPods).

• Where the social and economic arrangements surrounding intellectual property are breaking down. (Tepper and Hargittai, 2009)

In short, the music industry has to try to 'remediate' themselves in the music value chain to avoid being 'disintermediated' (Jones, 2002; Lee, 2009) . Remediation is the process by which control of some elements of the value chain could move to different players, or be given a new role (Jones, 2002). Two ways in which this is being done are in the related services of musical recommendation and community formation.

In an age of nearly infinite choice and ubiquitous accessibility for the consumer, many argue that one role that will become necessary and profitable is that of helping the consumer to navigate their way through the vast array of options available and steering consumers to (new) music they would enjoy (Kusek and Leonhard, 2005; Tepper and Hargittai, 2009; Voida et al., 2006). Internet radio stations such as Last.fm (owned by 'old media' firm CBS) and Pandora, for example, are built around their ability not only to provide customised streamed music content of chosen artists to their customers, but also their ability to recommend new music that is similar to the tastes of the user by constructing profiles based on listening habits (See Chapter 5 on profiling).

In addition, there is an increased role to play for intermediaries in the creation and maintenance of the social and relational end of music consumption through the formation and encouragement of musical niche communities and the social interaction of music fans (Lee, 2009). It is reasonable to suggest that music has always been part of the process of community formation, but in late modernity, musical tastes and affiliation have become central to the construction of social identities, especially among youth (Hebdige, 1979). Now, one of the key ways people relate to each other is through music.

With the dematerialisation of music in digital culture, such communities can increasingly form around tastes and be less tied to problems of access and geography. MySpace illustrates this point well. Fan communities form around established artists as well as new ones, despite where the band, or the fans, may be located (see Beer, 2008 for an example of MySpace community formation around musican Jarvis Cocker's site). Such groupings take place spontaneously on sites such as MySpace, as well as among discussion forums and blogging networks. From these interactions, people learn about new music from their peers. Within DJ culture, forums and blogs in particular have been crucial to the international spread of local 'house' mixing and hip hop styles such as 'Baltimore House' (Baltimore), 'Baile Funk' (Brazil), and Grime (East London), to international audiences (Devereaux, 2007; Stark, 2006), and even the formation of an a-spatial 'Blog House' style (Ilan, 2010).

At the same time, commercial enterprises have also stepped in to facilitate the relational consumption of music (Lee, 2009). Last.fm and Pandora, along with (News Corporation owned) MySpace, are music providers but double as social networking web sites where users can comment, send messages, create blogs and friend others, forming virtual networks based on shared musical affinities. In that sense, digital music cultures can be said to be the result of two simultaneous processes: decentralisation and the empowerment of consumers, alongside the potential enhancement of media corporations over the consumer experience (Lee, 2009; see also Poster, 2006; Jenkins, 2006).

CONCLUSION

This chapter opened with the suggestion that convergence can be seen to ease the friction involved in creating global capitalism. I have tried to illustrate how technological convergence eases this friction by allowing all manner of communication and cultural objects to be digitally deliverable across the planet, and across a wide range of media platforms, including phones. Regulatory convergence eases this friction by lifting many of the restrictions that media, telecom and information technology sectors have had to deal with in the past. Industry convergence plays upon technological and regulatory convergence, and eases this friction by erasing the distinctions between these sectors and creates large scale, cross-sector, global firms with a global reach and massive resources for innovative product creation and marketing.

All of these forms of convergence manifest themselves in an increasingly participatory and collective converged media culture which blurs the distinction between producer and consumer, and locates the media viewer more as an active user/collaborator in a diverse, cross-media, multi-site media experience. By creating a situation in which consumers and producers are in constant dialogue (to the point where they almost become indistinguishable), digital media becomes endlessly recyclable, endlessly transferable, endlessly adaptable and constantly available, resulting in a continual creation of new product and new experiences, which in themselves are often never completed.

FURTHER READING

In terms of regulatory convergence, McQuail and Suine (1998) is a well cited text. Media industry convergence and rising media oligopolies can be followed up in McChesney and Shiller (2003), and specific case studies of convergence strategies are demonstrated in Lawson-Borders (2006). A useful web site in this regard is the Columbia Journalism Review's 'Who owns what?' (http://www.cjr.org/resources/index.php).

With regard to convergence culture, Jenkins (2006) is essential, and for other takes on the notion of participatory culture in media, Bruns (2008) is very good, with excellent examples. Levy (1997) is theoretically interesting on the concept of 'collective intelligence'. Dena (2008) provides a good example with regard to alternate reality games and participatory culture, and McGonigal (2008) provides an extensive look at the example of *I Love Bees*.

Following the discussion of digital music cultures, Kusek and Leonhard (2005) provide a good overall discussion of the problem of digitised music and the challenges facing the music industry. O'Hara and Brown's *Consuming Music Together* (2006) provides an interesting collection of essays that discuss the relational elements of music consumption in online contexts, and for a current discussion of collaborative music fandom on MySpace, see Beer (2008). For critical discussions of intellectual property in the digital age more generally, see Lessig (2001) from a legal perspective or Yar (2006) from a criminological one.

4

DIGITAL INEQUALITY: SOCIAL, POLITICAL AND INFRASTRUCTURAL CONTEXTS

○ **Customer:** *'My modem is not working.'*
○ **Tech Support:** *'Ok. Let's start simply. Do you have a phone line running from the back of the computer to the wall?'*
○ **Customer:** *'I have no dial tone when I pick up the phone.'*
○ **Tech Support:** *'Do you have a phone line running from the back of the computer to the wall?'*
○ **Customer:** *'I bought this new computer, it's got (reads from store receipt) and 32 megs of RAM. But it won't work.'*
○ **Tech Support:** *'Ok. Tell me how you have it set up right now.'*
○ **Customer:** *'Well, I have it setting next to the phone, and the phone line is hooked into it.'*
○ **Tech Support:** *'Is anything running into the wall?'*
○ **Customer:** *'No.'*
○ **Tech Support:** *'So you have the computer sitting next to the phone, the phone line running into the computer, and that's it?'*
○ **Customer:** *'Yes. Am I supposed to plug the computer in?'*
○ **Tech Support:** *'Yes, it needs to be plugged in so the modem can dial.'*
○ **Customer:** *'What's a modem?'*

(Transcript of a technical support hotline conversation from http://www.rinkworks.com/stupid/cs_calls.shtml, accessed 15 August 2008)

As we saw in the previous chapter, ICTs are as increasingly central to economic prosperity in the twenty-first century. Globalisation abroad and economic restructuring at home are processes that have relied upon the increasing use of ICTs to enhance productive efficiency, lower production costs and stimulate consumer demand within contemporary global capitalism.

Few would argue with the statement that ICTs have become of increasing economic and social importance to the vast majority of us in advanced economies, and to many in developing economies as well. One of the conclusions of the last chapter was that the information age is not a fundamentally 'new' economic era, but that (whether an 'industrial' or 'informational' economy) the information society is still a capitalist society. That is, a society where some people work for wages and other people earn their living off either the waged labour of others, or investment capital.

This type of society, rightly or wrongly, creates economic and social inequalities. In this respect, the information society is no different from industrial society; there is a continuity of inequality and marginalisation between them both. But the notions of marginalisation and inequality are vague and can be considered in a variety of ways not simply limited to economic differences. For example, Selwyn (2004) outlines five broad ways in which people can be either marginalised or included in contemporary society:

1) *Production activity*   When people are engaging in socially or economically valued activities. Of course, this has a bearing on a person's economic status.

2) *Political activity*   Engaging in some sort of collective effort to enhance or maintain the social or physical environment.

3) *Social activity*   Engaging in meaningful activity with family, friends, communities or groups.

4) *Consumption activity*   The ability to consume a level of goods and services that are considered 'normal' within the society one inhabits.

5) *Savings activity*   Accumulating savings, pensions, or owning property, creating a sense of security.

In this regard, the main difference between industrial and informational society is that marginalisation in the information society revolves specifically around (unsurprisingly) information and communication: access to it, the ability to use it effectively and the rights to produce it. This affects the chances of a particular person to be marginalised in any of the above ways.

It is important to understand that the digital divide is a social and political problem, and not merely a technological one (Van Dijk, 2005). Digital inequality is merely another manifestation of the other inequalities that exist within our contemporary society. In many respects, it is no coincidence that the major categories of overall marginality on the domestic front – class, income, ethnicity, gender, rural/urban, age – are also the major categories that are suggested as influential in the formation of a digital divide. On a global scale, it is indeed no surprise, given the context of widening income and standard of living gaps between wealthy industrialised countries and developing nations, that most developing nations find themselves on the wrong side of the digital divide as well.

It is important to reiterate that technologies themselves do not determine society, but instead emerge from a context of socially constructed needs, wants and priorities, as does the way in which a technology is adopted. Thus, it takes more than just computers, broadband connections, modems and phone lines to make an information society, and more than simply a lack of technology to create inequalities within that society. In that sense, we need to take a more 'constructivist', rather than a technologically 'determinist' approach to the issue of divides and access (Henwood et al., 2000).

Van Dijk (2005: 15) is particularly enlightening on the social context of digital divides. His core argument is made in a series of points:

- Categorical inequalities in society produce an unequal distribution of resources.
- An unequal distribution of resources causes unequal access to digital technologies.
- Unequal access to digital technologies also depends on the characteristics of these technologies.
- Unequal access to digital technologies brings about unequal participation in society.
- Unequal participation in society reinforces categorical inequalities and unequal distribution of resources.

So, for Van Dijk, most research on digital divides takes on an individualist approach, looking at *individual* characteristics such as age, sex, race, ethnicity, personality and intelligence as causal factors in the non-adoption of technology. He argues that we should instead concentrate on *positional* factors, which set some groups in a comparatively disadvantaged situation to others to gain a more contextual insight into why some people are denied meaningful access to information technology.

He goes on to suggest that among digital inequalities, the most important positional factors are:

1. Position in the labour market: involving income, and access to ICTs at work.
2. Education: which has been profoundly affected by the influx of computers and internet into classrooms in the 1990s, helping older generations to gain access if they have school-age children.
3. Household composition: households with children tend to have the highest rates of access.
4. Residence in a particular nation or part of it: which involves the availability of technology, general levels of literacy, language skills (especially English), level of democracy, information society policies and a culture that is receptive or not to new technology.

Such a positional approach allows for reflection on the contextual circumstances that can lead to particular individuals or groups in society becoming marginalised in terms of information technology, and not be hindered by quantifiable measurements of theoretical access.

'DIGITAL DIVIDES' AND 'ACCESS'

When such inequalities are produced, they are usually referred to as 'the digital divide', a term which has been popularised in academic, policy and media discourses since the mid-1990s. There are, of course, many ways to define the digital divide, with the most common definition looking something like:

> The gap between those who do and those who do not have access to computers and the internet. (Van Dijk, 2005: 1)

Definitions exist to make understanding concepts simpler, more specific. However, in the above definition (a very common definition), we already find much that is vague, problematic and open for debate. We can start with Selwyn (2004), who sees the terms 'gap', 'access', and 'computers and the internet', as particularly problematic.

As Selwyn points out, research and rhetoric on digital divides tends to portray things in terms of binary oppositions (i.e., those who do and those who do not have access), and there are often references to 'the truly unconnected'. Such imposed binary oppositions do little to describe the real-life situation of people. There are fast, reliable, up to date computers, and there are slow, antiquated ones. There are people with internet connections, but some of these people (such as people living in China and Saudi Arabia), face massive restrictions on the kinds of content they can access. There are people who have no internet access or computer at home, yet have access and free use to good equipment and fast internet connections at work. There are also people who are very sophisticated in their skills and knowledge of software and the internet, and those with very limited skills who can only perform the most basic of internet and communication tasks. Given the complexities of actual 'use' and 'access', Selwyn suggests that we should be thinking more in terms of connectivity or an 'access rainbow', instead of 'haves and have-nots'.

Similarly, the concept of 'access' itself is very poorly defined and needs much refinement. Most notably, there is a difference between *theoretical* access and *effective* access, which can be complicated by a number of mitigating factors. Theoretical access is achieved when a person has physical access to a technology, for example having a networked computer in the home, or access to one at a local library. Theoretical access is the sort of thing that can be quantified through numbers and policy targets (such as can be seen in any of the following tables). Effective access refers to the ability, desire, or motivation to actually use a given technology and to be able to achieve benefit from it. Thus, there is a difference between access to computers and access to meaningful, useful and relevant content for the user.

Warschaur (2004) provides many interesting examples of how projects that encouraged theoretical (or physical) access to computer technologies failed because of lack of consideration towards effective access. In one example, he examines a project in New Delhi, India, which aimed to provide computing access to slum areas for the benefit of local children. Several 'hole in the wall' booths were set up in public areas with free access for children to the internet. However, the results did not go as anticipated, with little content in Hindi (the only language the children knew) available to the children at the time and, with little motivation given to the children to use the technology for academic or cultural pursuits, they began to use the booths as games terminals and for drawing. Ultimately the use of these booths impacted negatively on existing school work. This and other examples provided by Warschauer (such as the 'information age town' of Ennis, Ireland) demonstrate that merely dropping in technology is not the answer, but that an appropriate social context must exist as well. People need the skills, motivation and awareness of why a particular technology and its use might be beneficial to them in order to gain real and meaningful benefits.

To complicate the notion of 'access' further, Van Dijk (2005) refers in more detail to different kinds of access:

- *Motivational* access, in which people see a relevance or potential benefit for themselves in using ICTs.
- *Material* or physical access to the technology.
- *Skills* to effectively use the technology.
- *Usage* access in terms of the number and diversity of applications, and the amount of usage time, available to the person.

It is clear that access – and the barriers to access – are very complicated. It is important to consider that measurement of internet connections, household PCs or telephone lines per capita is by no means the only way to measure inclusion in the information society.

In addition, the standard definition of digital divide provided above is very 'internet-centric', in that there is the implicit assumption that it is 'computers and the internet' that define digital technology and access to information. Since one of the main premises of this book is that any examination of digital culture and the information society has to go beyond 'internet studies' to the wider context of everyday use of the plethora of digital technologies created though the convergence of almost all media to digital format, it is mandatory that I take exception to this assumption. Indeed, many researchers now include access to mobile phones and other digital technologies such as digital television and games consoles in their assessment of access or connectivity. With this in mind, Selwyn (2004) makes a very valid point that a focus on access to content, rather than on technological platforms, is a much more useful point of reference when discussing the digital divide (Selwyn, 2004: 34). To that end, the latter section of this chapter examines the use of mobile telephony in developing countries.

Domestic Digital Divides

Despite its vagaries, or perhaps because of them, the notion of the digital divide has caught the imagination of both academics and policy makers since the mid 1990s, a time when enthusiasm about digital technology and the internet in particular were reaching almost fever pitch. Investments in technology were booming, the internet was increasingly popularised and commercialised, and governments all over the world were bracing for – and usually encouraging – the shift to an information-based economy. Within this environment, the spectre of those who would be left out of the information age began to creep into public and academic discourse. In the words of Bill Clinton, President of the United States during this period, 'We challenged the nation to make sure that our children will never be separated by a digital divide'. (Clinton, 1996).

This was one of the first uses of the term within public discourse, and referred exclusively to what is now known as a domestic (or social) digital divide, defined as 'the gap between information rich and poor in each nation' (Norris, 2001: 4).

Within the very considerable pro-technology, post industrial rhetoric of the mid-1990s a social divide of information haves and have-nots was seen as a potential problem on the horizon from many different points of view (Cullen, 2001). From an individual perspective, in the same way being homeless (i.e., having no fixed address) creates a series of problems for an individual in terms of having a bank account, getting a job and collecting state benefits, a lack of access to information technology in an information society will have repercussive effects. It could result in not being able to participate in the economic and social benefits the information society has to offer in terms of education, business and consumer transactions, personal communication, information gathering, career opportunities and development.

- From a governmental perspective, a digital divide would affect the quality of life of its citizens, especially when considering the context of neo-liberal globalisation, in terms of economic competitiveness. In this respect, national (and local) governments have an interest in helping to provide communication infrastructure, training and incentives to reduce divides among their populations.

- From a business perspective it is in their interest to have as productive a workforce as possible to maximise profit in a globally competitive environment. The existence of stark digital divides would result in a large pool of labour whose skills would be either redundant or antiquated, creating a potential tax burden as well as an inefficient workforce.

- From a societal perspective, equality of opportunity is seen as ethically desirable. The existence of digital divides and the social and economic marginalisation that would result, is seen as undesirable.

In response to these concerns, the government of the United States set in motion a number of programmes and policies to deal with the digital divide problem. In 1995, the then Vice President Al Gore developed the National Information Infrastructure program, and in 2000 the US government provided $2.25 billion worth of initiatives to bridge the digital divide. This included the donation of computers and the sponsorship of community technology centres and training initiatives, in an effort to expand home and public access to computers and the internet for low-income families (Choemprayong,

2006: 204). Other initiatives, such as the Advanced Networking with Minority-Serving Institutions program of the National Science Foundation were designed to assist minority serving institutions, colleges and universities to help minority groups participate more fully in the information age (Choemprayong, 2006).

In particular, there was a plan to allocate $100 million to establish 1000 community technology centres, which was seen as quite successful in helping isolated and disadvantaged communities. And, as Cullen notes, this strategy was successfully adopted in other developed nations like Canada, which set up the 'Community Access Program' to give Canadians throughout the country affordable access to the internet, and the skills to use it (Cullen, 2001: 319).

The results of these sets of initiatives, and the general diffusion of access as ICT equipment has become cheaper, has meant that, by and large, domestic digital divides have been decreasing in industrial economies, with certain exceptions. The latest report from the PEW internet and Life Project in the United States examined broadband and dial-up access for Americans, which reflects the current trends in domestic digital divides in that country.

Once again, it is important to remember what has been suggested previously in the chapter, that broadband adoption (physical/theoretical access) does not necessarily translate into effective access or productive or beneficial use of the technology. But what Table 4.1 does reflect is the general difference in physical access to broadband among groups, thereby demonstrating the traditional individual categories where the digital divide is seen as significant: a small gender gap, a rather large gap based on age, some (widening) gaps based on race/ethnicity, rather large education gaps, a very large and widening gap based on income and a narrowing rural/urban divide. Similar findings have been suggested by van Dijk (2005), who argues that gender and disability divides have been narrowing across Europe, as have age divides (largely through the process of ageing), while racial/ethnic and income divides have been increasing.

GLOBAL DIGITAL DIVIDES

In the early 1990s there was a focus on the rhetoric of domestic divides, but by the mid-1990s there was increasing recognition that nations with the technological, social and economic resources to invest in ICT infrastructures and technologies, and whose citizens had the individual wealth to be able to access and own ICTs within these infrastructures, were at a comparative advantage to those who lived in poorer, developing nations without appropriate infrastructures or access to digital technologies. This disparity, based primarily on the geography of 'haves and have-nots' in the 'developed' versus the 'developing' world, is often referred to as the global digital divide, defined as 'the divergence of internet access between industrialised and developing societies' (Norris, 2001). This is illustrated in Table 4.2.

The main premise behind the global digital divide is the worry that developed industrialised nations are in a position to take full advantage of the information age, while developing countries are not. In that sense, information and communication technology

Table 4.1 Trends in broadband adoption by group (United States)

Percent in each group with broadband at home by year					
	2006	2007	2008	2009	% point change 08–09
Yearly adoption %					
All adults	42	47	55	63	+8
Gender					
Male	45	50	58	64	+8
Female	38	44	53	63	+6
Parents with minor children at home	51	60	69	77	+10
Age					
18–29	55	63	70	77	+7
30–49	50	59	69	72	+3
50–64	38	40	50	61	+11
65+	13	15	19	30	+11
Race/ethnicity					
White (not Hispanic)	42	48	57	65	+8
Black (not Hispanic)	31	40	43	46	+3
Hispanic (English speaking)	41	47	56	68	+12
Educational attainment					
Less than high school	17	21	28	30	+2
High school grad	31	34	40	52	+12
Some college	47	58	66	71	+5
College +	62	70	79	83	+4
Household income					
Under $20K	18	28	25	35	+10
$20K–$30K	27	34	42	53	+11
$30K–$40K	40	40	49	54	+5
$40k–$50K	47	52	60	71	+11
$50K–$75K	48	58	67	80	+13
$75K–$100K	67	70	82	82	+0
Over $100K	68	82	85	88	+8
Community type					
Non-rural	44	52	57	67	+8
Rural	25	31	38	46	+8

Source: Horrigan (2009)

Table 4.2 Worldwide internet use by region

Internet users per 100 persons by world region

Area	Internet users per 100 persons	High country	Low country
Africa	5.3	Seychelles 38.9	Liberia 0.0
Asia	14.0	South Korea 71.2	East Timor 0.1
Europe	48.0	Norway 88.0	Ukraine 12.0
Middle East	21.3	Israel 57.6	Iraq 0.1
North America	73.4	Greenland 92.3	Bermuda 63.5
Latin America/ Caribbean	23.8	Argentina 39.7	Cuba 2.1
Oceania	59.5	Australia 75.9	Solomon Islands 1.7
World	21.1		

Source: Internetworldstats.com (accessed 2 August 2008)

may be yet another way in which wealthy, industrialised countries can further enhance their already elevated position over developing nations, leading to further disparities between rich and poor nations, and even further imbalances of power.

This trend is seen as particularly unjust, since many believe that access to the internet, other digital communications technologies and the information they bring are particularly useful to developing nations. There are several reasons why this is the case. First, one of the major obstacles for developing nations is a lack of information available to the public. Access to information such as education, health, pricing and even weather prediction for rural communities are potentially even more useful in countries where there is little organised (or haphazard) distribution of such information to the general public. There is a real danger that the benefits of increased access to education, health, cheaper goods and the like will bypass those whose need is greatest.

Second, a lack of an efficient communication infrastructure means that most developing nations have a difficult time in communicating, organising and working together to solve common problems. It becomes very difficult to implement public works projects, utilise the human resources of a nation, or organise responses to natural and social disasters because the means to organise people's efforts, logistically, are hampered with inefficiency and confusion caused by poor infrastructure and communications. This is one of the major obstacles to the economic growth of developing countries.

Thus, the global digital divide has been the focus of many academic studies as well as public policy debates. The United Nations has held several high-level meetings on the topic since 2000, and actively promotes the notion of 'universal access' through a task force that has $500 million per year to spend (Cullen, 2001). Other UN programmes include the writing off of debt for developing countries that allocate funds to ICT development. UN agencies such as UNESCO and the FAO have also established global digital divide strategies. In addition, the World Bank and the International Telecommunications

Union have promoted policies to reduce digital divides between nations, and to monitor the progress made on connecting up developing nations.

Current trends show that proportionally, internet access is growing much faster in developing nations. However, this statistic hides the fact that while the proportional growth may be high, the growth in real numbers of persons gaining access to the internet is still very small in developing nations and is far outweighed by continued real number growth in advanced economies.

There have also been a number of private and charitable attempts to bridge global divides. Programmes such as the 'Simputer' and later the '$100 laptop' were both attempts to provide cheap, readily available and easy to use computers for access to the internet. The Simputer failed as it was considered too costly for the people it was designed to help. The $100 laptop has been more successful and has been used in a number of different developing countries, amid some success and some controversy.

Despite these attempts, it is clear that without some form of intervention, there is a real danger that the move to the digital age will greatly enhance the position of the advanced, industrialised economies over those of the developing world, allowing them to play by a fundamentally different set of economic rules (for example, the rules of a weightless economy as discussed in Chapter 2). Developed countries will potentially be able to use their increased access to knowledge, increased economic flexibility and increased communication efficiency, while developing nations could become ever more victimised and marginalised by these trends, mired in the *space of places* instead of participating in *the space of flows* (Castells, 1996; see Chapter 2).

MOBILE PHONES, ACCESS AND THE DEVELOPING WORLD

As mentioned throughout this book, any contemporary analysis of digital culture and the information society is lacking if it focuses exclusively on the use of computers and the internet. This is even more the case when it comes to the study of global digital divides.

If one was to equate 'access', 'use' or 'connectivity' only with access to the internet through personal computers with networked broadband connections, then the gap between industrialised countries and the developing world is indeed massive, and increasing in real terms. This is because most developing nations have very little fixed phone line infrastructure, especially in rural areas. For example, a country like Chad, one of the poorest nations in the world, still only has 0.13 fixed telephone lines per capita, where the United States has 53.35 fixed lines per capita (ITU 2006 data, available at www.itu.int). Many developing nations simply never have been in a position or had the resources to create a fixed line telecommunications infrastructure, which is a massive undertaking in terms of cost, logistics and maintenance. Indeed, many inhabitants of Africa have never made a fixed line telephone call.

Table 4.3 Mobile penetration by World Bank income categories

World Bank 2007 Categorisation (GNI per capital 2006)	Five largest countries	Median landlines per 100, 2006	Median mobiles per 100, 2006
Low income (<$905)	India Pakistan Bangladesh Nigeria Vietnam	0.9	7.5
Lower middle income ($906–$3595)	China Indonesia Philippines Egypt Iran	10.9	30.4
Upper middle income ($3596–$11115)	Brazil Russia Mexico Turkey South Africa	20.2	65.8
High income (>$11116)	United States Japan Germany France United Kingdom	44.3	100.8
World totals		13.2	50.8

Source: Adapted From Donner (2008: 141)

However, while the advancement of fixed line telephony has remained largely stalled in many parts of the developing world, mobile telephony has increased massively. So while Chad, at the extreme end of the scale, may have only 0.13 fixed phone lines and only 0.6 internet users for every 100 inhabitants, it has 8.52 mobile subscribers per hundred, and 24 per cent of the population is covered by a mobile signal (ITU, 2006). If one considered the amount of people who share mobile phones in Africa (a common practice), the user rate is likely to be much higher than the subscriber rate, so we could estimate that those with 'access' are much greater than that 8.52 per 100 persons.

Worldwide, as of 2007, there were 3.3 billion mobile phone subscribers, representing roughly 50 per cent of the world's population, and 80 per cent of the world's population has access to mobile phone coverage (Reuters, 2007). These figures alone suggest that, on the basis of numbers, the mobile phone is the most successful type of information technology so far and has made the most impact in terms of closing global digital divides. In Table 4.3, we can see that while high income countries have often achieved penetration rates of over 100 per cent (i.e., more mobile phone subscriptions than people), even the low income countries have already far outstripped the penetration rates of landlines in only a few years. This makes it clear that any discussion of digital divides must take into account the spread of, and use of, mobile telephony and communications. Currently, mobile telecoms seem to be the way forward for the developing world.

So why have mobile phones become ubiquitous, so quickly? Coyle (2005) provides a reasoned economically-based explanation for the massive growth of mobile phone use in the developing world. She argues that growth is the result of several factors, which for the sake of clarity, I will combine into economic, social and legislative categories.

[handwritten margin note: growth of phones]

Economic reasons

Economically speaking, one of the major reasons for the rapid spread of mobile telephony in the developing world is the shorter payback period on investment as compared to fixed line telephony. Basically, mobile telephony has lower installation costs, thus making it more immediately profitable for companies to invest in the infrastructure. Telecoms companies are able to achieve a return on their investment in comparably little time, making them more likely to invest in further infrastructure. Related to this, the mobile infrastructure is more adaptable to geographic hinterlands, making it more cost effective to provide access to remote or geographically challenging areas.

In addition, the variety of business model innovations surrounding mobile phones, such as 'pay as you go', or pre-paid SIM card arrangements complements the diverse economic situations of people in the developing world. James (2006) argues that the main strength of mobile telephony in developing countries is the versatility with which it can operate in terms of consumer models. Indeed, he argues that this is necessary in order for mobile telephony to have an impact on rural areas because the technology is still relatively expensive for people in such areas. James highlights several models of phone-sharing (the purchasing of time on someone else's phone, or the personal ownership of SIM cards while sharing a handset among many) as well as the use of intermediaries, as useful models to give mobile phone access to a numbers of people far beyond the number of subscribers. This versatility is one major reason that the use of the mobile phone has spread rapidly in developing countries, as it can be easily adapted to a variety of financial circumstances.

Social reasons

On the consumer end, lower social and income entry barriers for use and purchase are two major reasons why mobile phones have spread. Mobile phones can be purchased for low up-front costs in 'pay as you go' payment schemes or, as mentioned above, a variety of other models that lowers the entry barrier for those on low incomes.

Coyle (2005) also argues that mobile phones are complementary with use in developing countries as the technology is more user friendly. A lower level of skills is needed to operate a mobile phone as compared to the skills needed to effectively engage with computers and the internet.

Last, one can refer to the 'network effects' associated with the spread of mobile phones. The popularity of the devices has made them more desirable and necessary. As more people purchase them, it becomes more socially and economically necessary for those who don't have phones to obtain them.

Legislative reasons

In addition to economic and social conditions which have contributed to the spread of mobile phones throughout the developing world, there have been a number of policy-related reasons, usually argued from a neo-liberal point of view, to explain this dissemination. First, Coyle argues that governments have put obligations on companies to expand mobile phone infrastructure to certain minimum requirements as part of their 'Rollout' obligations for telecommunications licenses. Second, unlike many land-line sources that are operated on the basis of national monopolies, mobile services are in a fully competitive environment. In laissez-faire economic terms, more competition suggests lower prices for the consumer.

THE BENEFITS OF MOBILE TELEPHONY FOR THE DEVELOPING WORLD

One of the most oft-cited benefits of the spread of mobile phones to the developing world is that the development of mobile infrastructure will allow developing nations to 'leap-frog' over the fixed line stage of infrastructural development and, in that sense, allow developing nations to catch up to industrialised countries more quickly by avoiding an expensive and arduous stage in infrastructural development. Fixed line infrastructure is notoriously expensive to implement and maintain: even industrialised countries such as France did not achieve 'modern' levels of fixed line penetration until the 1970s. For developing nations, this has been next to impossible to achieve and has seriously hampered their ability to develop economically and to coordinate activities, especially in rural areas.

With mobile telephony infrastructure, the costs of development are much less, and therefore easier and faster for poor nations to implement. This means that essentially, these nations can achieve more parity with the West in their development. However, this argument is disputed by Castells et al. (2007), who point out that fixed line infrastructure often plays a large part in mobile service provision.

Waverman et al. (2005) and Thompson and Garbacz (2007) attempt to make an explicit link between mobile phones and economic development, which revolves around two propositions: first, that the spread of telecommunications creates 'growth dividends' by reducing the cost of interaction, expanding market boundaries and expanding information flows. That is, the network effects provided by expanding communications infrastructure means that there is more efficiency in interactions between people (for example, in organising businesses and services), more access to information, and the ability to market and provide one's goods and services in a larger geographic scale. This, in theory, results in more profits and less costs in terms of communication and transportation, and thus encourages economic growth.

This is an argument applied equally to any form of communications infrastructural development: roads, postal systems and fixed telephone lines. Second, Waverman et al. go further, to suggest that mobile telephony is doubly important to developing countries because industrialised countries already have the network effects of fixed telephony to which mobile telephony adds the benefit of mobility. For developing nations, mobile telephony acts both as a basic communication infrastructure providing network effects *and* a mobile system. Waverman et al. use the comparison of the Philippines, which has 27 per cent mobile penetration rates, with Indonesia, which has 8.7 per cent. They argue that the increased mobile phone penetration in the Philippines accounts for as much as one per cent in additional GDP that Indonesia does not enjoy.

In addition, mobile telephones are potentially empowering to farmers, fishermen and other people who produce market goods, in that it increases their knowledge of market prices in different locations, allowing them to achieve a maximum price for what they have to sell. Jensen (2007) argues, for example, that fishermen on the Kerala coast of India are able to use mobile phones to gain information on buyers in different ports, allowing them to land at ports where they could profitably sell their catch. This resulted in reduced price variability and a reduction of waste in the fishing system (Donner, 2008). Similar arguments could be made for those who have to buy commodities such as seeds, fertiliser, or farming equipment. More knowledge of options increases power and reduces inefficiency.

The undoing of the isolation that makes people the victims of captive markets also provides benefits in terms of interpersonal connections to friends and family, particularly when it comes to migrant populations. Maintenance of contact between distant relatives becomes more accessible, and this provides a real material benefit in the form of remittances: transfers of money from people who have emigrated to their families back home. This potentially has no small impact. Remittances to Africa currently run to about $12 billion per year. In the case of Lesotho, remittance payments total 37 per cent of that country's GDP, and up to 40 per cent of the income of poor households. Currently an average of 12 per cent of remittance income is being lost to transaction fees under the current money transfer system. For all developing countries, this amounts to $10 billion per year in lost revenues. Mobile based remittances could reduce this to four per cent (Scott et al., 2004) and have actually been successful in countries like Kenya with the M-PESA system (see Chapter 2).

Initiatives like the Grameen Village phone programme in Bangladesh demonstrate how the spread of mobile phones can also be linked to entrepreneurship and alternative forms of local income generation. In the programme, money is loaned to local women to set up a Grameen phone booth using mobile technology. Local people can then use the phone at prescribed rates, or through an intermediary, giving villagers telecommunications access and providing an income for a local entrepreneur. The Grameen phone is not the only example of this type of alternative provision model. There are a plethora of other programmes such as the e-charpal initiative in India, and several kinds of mobile phone kiosks in Africa (James, 2006; James and Versteeg, 2006).

Last, Williams (2005) suggests that the establishment of mobile networks in developing countries has a direct relation to foreign direct investment in those countries by adding needed foreign capital into their economies.

However, potential benefits can be countered by the potential problems that might accompany the spread of mobile phones. Much of the benefits listed above fall on economic analysis of efficiency and network effects, but such arguments falter when empirical research conducted by Donner (2005) and Souter et al. (2005) suggest that the vast majority of mobile use in the developing world is for personal as opposed to business uses. In addition, Donner (2008) makes the point that it is those with greater resources that are the most likely to take advantage of and use mobile phone technology. Thus, there is the potential for mobile telephony to enhance disparities within these countries, rather than reduce them.

CONCLUSION

In this chapter I have investigated the notion of digital inequality, or 'the digital divide' from a number of angles. The first, and perhaps most important point made was that digital inequality is as much a social and political problem as much as it is a problem of access to technology. Digital inequality merely reflects broader inequalities, both on a domestic and a worldwide scale. Lack of access to digital technology is merely one more way to be marginalised in contemporary culture.

Despite this, there have been a number of attempts to address both domestic and global divides, some with a reasonable amount of success. However, there is still a danger that the spread of digital communications technology will be a process that further enhances the position and wealth of those who already have the most advantages in our world, as opposed to assisting those populations that perhaps need help the most.

It is clear that digital divides are a complex problem, more than simply a case of 'access' and 'technology', but also a problem that involves skills, motivation and actual, constructive uses of technology. With regard to the developing world, the potential benefits of information technology are plenty, and could indeed help developing countries to overcome many of the problems that have interfered with their prosperity. But it is also clear that they will gain most not by mimicking what advanced economies have done thus far, but by taking advantage of the adaptable nature of digital technologies, such as mobile communications infrastructures, to engage with the information society in a way that meets their specific needs and circumstances. Most notably among these circumstances is the lack of a fixed line telecoms (as well as electrical grid) infrastructure. In this respect, when it comes to the developing world, we might have to revise our idea of the information society to include a shared mobile phone kiosk in Africa, powered by a car battery.

FURTHER READING

Many texts concerning the problem of the digital divide were written in the late 1990s and in the first few years of the 2000s. Norris (2001) is a good and widely cited choice from this period. Warschauer (2004) provides an excellent critique and commentary on commonplace digital divide policies with enlightening examples, and Selwyn (2004) is a good analysis of the concept of the digital divide. From a global divides perspective, Jones (2003) is a resource that includes the role of mobile technology in overcoming divides, and Donner (2008) provides a good overall discussion of research regarding the use of mobile phones in developing countries. The web site of the International Telecommunications Union (ITU) is also a good resource for research on global digital divides (http://www.itu.int).

5

'EVERYONE IS WATCHING': PRIVACY AND SURVEILLANCE IN DIGITAL LIFE

NEW PRODUCT for 2009!
Remote Monitoring Software for Mac OS X!

Monitor the online activity of your children or employees from anywhere: at work, in another room, at an internet kiosk, on vacation, on a business trip – even if you're thousands of miles away.

Automatically records every web site they visit, every keystroke they type, and every program they launch, plus sends copies of chats, instant messages and emails sent and received.

eBlaster recordings are organized into an easy-to-read Activity Report that is automatically sent to any email address you choose … as often as you like. eBlaster Activity Reports can be sent to another computer in your home, your office email address or any web-based email service like Google Gmail, Yahoo mail and others.

See inappropriate messages from strangers to your children or between employees right away! eBlaster Instant Notification keeps you 'in-the-know' by automatically sending you an exact copy of their emails, chats and instant messages as they occur.

(http://www.spectorsoft.com/index.html?UK=true&, accessed 3 October 2009)

The above advertisement for 'eBlaster' surveillance software in many respects epitomises one of the most important public issues related to the information age: the increased ability to gather data about others which, up until recently, would have been considered impossible and/or immoral. Thoughtful consideration of the above passage suggests this is a much more complex issue than it first appears. At first it seems repugnant … spying on the personal communications of one's children and one's employees … monitoring their every virtual manoeuvre … but upon second glance, it is easy to see the rationale behind such activity: the protection of one's children and the legitimate concern that employees do not misuse company equipment and instead get on with the activities they are paid to undertake. Who would argue with either of those two goals?

In previous times people, to a certain extent, would have had to trust their children not to behave inappropriately or endanger themselves, and employers would have to trust their employees to do their jobs and not take undue advantage of company property. Most of the time such trust was (and still is) well-placed, but not always. It is clear that the notion of trust involves a certain amount of risk for the person or organisation doing the trusting.

This applies to the larger contexts of nations and governments as well. Few would disagree that most advanced economic states are increasingly becoming surveillance societies. Perhaps at the more extreme end of this trend is the United Kingdom. Living through decades of terrorist threats and attacks from the IRA in the 1970s and 1980s, only to once again be put into a climate of fear during the post 9/11 'war on terror' and the target of yet further attacks, the UK has become one of the most surveilled societies in the world, with London at the epicentre of this trend. A typical London resident can now expect to be photographed 300 times a day by CCTV cameras, have their cars tracked through number plate recognition systems, their city movements tracked through the use of public transport (Oyster) cards, and potentially even their pedestrian movements located through the triangulation of their mobile phone signals (BBC, 2006). While on the extreme end, the case of the UK and London is not unique, as most countries have stepped up their surveillance procedures in the wake of the 9/11 attacks in order to minimise the risk posed by international terrorism.

Such scenarios of widespread CCTV and government surveillance conjure up fears of a 'big brother' society in which governments and law enforcement agencies amass huge amounts of data on individuals and continually monitor the movements of their citizens. This was the modus operandi of Fascist and Stalinist regimes of the recent past, and these are quite rightly legitimate concerns over which to be vigilant. However, this chapter will demonstrate that data collection and surveillance by governments is only one part of the overall picture of surveillance in the digital age. The opening passage suggests that surveillance and risk reduction is not only the occupation of *governments* looking to curb internal and external threats, but also *individuals* who want to protect their children, monitor their spouses, or invade others' privacy for personal gain, and *businesses* who want greater control over their employees, as well as gain insights into their customers.

This chapter will investigate the status of privacy and surveillance in the information age. It will start with a consideration of the changing nature of 'privacy' within Western culture and how current security and commercial concerns may be leading to further changes in our expectations of privacy. Then the context and amount of surveillance currently taking place in digital environments will be considered, followed by a discussion of the motivations behind the increases in surveillance currently taking place, with a particular emphasis on the political-economic dimension of surveillance strategies. The last section of the chapter will consider the potentially negative consequences of ubiquitous digital surveillance.

THE CHANGING CULTURAL CONTEXTS OF PRIVACY

The concept of privacy is complicated and hard to define. Much like the ideas of 'community' or 'identity' also discussed in this book, 'privacy' is generally considered to be an important part of life and yet its meaning is varied and contested. Spinello (2003) suggests that in general there are three elements to the notion of privacy: solitude, secrecy and anonymity.

Often, popular understandings of privacy are related to the concept of *solitude*: the ability to feel alone, isolated or cut-off from others, or colloquially, to be 'alone with one's thoughts'. Perri (1988) argues that this notion has its Western cultural roots in the idea of 'interiority' or the 'examined', 'contemplative' life as first articulated by the ancient Greeks, then rediscovered during the Enlightenment period. Those involved in the Romantic Movement in the eighteenth and nineteenth centuries later related this notion of interiority with the concept of 'solitude'. In solitude, away from others, one could find one's 'authentic' self by escaping from the self of sociability: an inauthentic self tainted by social interactions with others. In Western culture today, part of the idea of privacy and the demand for private space derives from this romantic notion of only being able to be oneself, by oneself.

The second major element in the cultural construction of privacy revolves around the concept of *secrecy*, as in being able to limit or have control over the amount of information others can know about oneself or 'The claim of individuals, groups or institutions to determine for themselves when, how and to what extent, information about them is communicated to others' (Perri, 1998 quoted in McGrath, 2004). This engages with the perceived right in Western culture to 'one's own business'. In personal matters that have no palpable effect on the rights of others, people are seen to have the right to a certain degree of autonomy over one's public face: the image one presents to the rest of the world. Thus, it is up to the individual to choose what information about one and one's life is available, and to whom.

Last, privacy has an element of *anonymity*. This can be seen as a peculiarly modern element of privacy. People are seen to be deserving of the right of protection from unwanted attention and scrutiny, or the right to simply be 'a face in the crowd' and go about one's business unhindered by the surveillance or attention of others.

It is important to remember that privacy is a concept with a culturally and historically contingent meaning. Western conceptions of privacy differ greatly from culture in other parts of the world. This is obviously the case as compared to tribal or Aboriginal cultures, but is also true of modern industrialised societies such as Japan (see Nakada and Tamura, 2005). Even within Western culture the importance of privacy has changed over time. In medieval times and up until industrialisation, the interdependency and small social scale of rural and village life, and the small family dwellings, provided very little in the way of what we now call privacy (and almost no anonymity). Contemporary conceptions of private life and personal space simply did not exist.

It was largely in the Victorian era and the period of industrial urbanisation during the late 1800s in which modern notions and expectations of privacy developed. The industrial period created a burgeoning middle class that had greater standards of material wealth, allowing for the creation of larger, multi-roomed houses. The capitalist economic structure of paid salaried work in factories and other forms of mass production developed at the time allowed for a complete separation of home and work life, where 'home' became associated with the private sphere and work with public life. Lyon (2001) argues that the modern division of public and private life emerged in this period. These new urban industrial landscapes, organised around the physical separation of home and work, combined to create rigid distinctions of public and private life articulated in the urban landscape through the creation of suburban areas of 'private' dwelling and central areas of 'public' work and leisure reproduced in the public and private areas of middle-class housing.

Thus, everyday life was divided by the public sphere of work and sociable leisure, and a home or family life which was seen as a secluded retreat from public life. The home was (and still is) seen as the bastion of privacy and private life. But the advent of mass media in the latter half of the twentieth century began to complicate these notions of private and public life. The mass media created public figures and celebrities to a degree previously unknown. For these public personalities, the idea of privacy (especially in terms of 'anonymity') started to erode as it began to be considered reasonable to invade the privacy of figures on the basis that the lives of such figures were of public interest. The rise of media celebrity in the twentieth century has helped to change our idea of privacy and the right to a private life.

Perri (1998) suggests that in the data-driven networked society, the cultural construction of privacy will once again change. In the face of a culture in which the spaces in our lives that are not surveilled are increasingly few and far between, 'solitude' and 'anonymity' will feature less prominently as a right, and the primary concern for privacy will shift emphasis towards the notion of confidentiality, particularly the confidentiality of (inevitably collected) personal information about individuals, and what can be done with that information (Perri, 1998; McGrath, 2004). This shift is likely to be driven by two cultural imperatives currently contributing towards the cultural and legal construction of privacy and the right to a private life: 'security' and 'commercial enterprise'.

Privacy as a legal construction: a contradiction?

Mills (2008) suggests that there are four broad categories of privacy related to different spheres of legal rights:

1   Freedom of personal autonomy, the most obvious being freedom of choice.

2   The right to control personal information, which relates to defamation, or the right not to have one's personal information disclosed to the public.

3   The right to control personal property, including one's name and likeness, as well as information about oneself.

4   The right to control and protect personal physical space, which suggests a freedom from unwarranted intrusion, surveillance and intimidation.

These rights are set in balance against societal demands for a certain amount of social control, security and conformity. The right to personal autonomy, for example, is not an unlimited right to do whatever one wants. It is clear that states have legal course to invade privacy in certain circumstances, especially when there is considered to be a threat to life or to state security. Today's political climate has seen a shift away from an emphasis on privacy and towards 'security'. The right to control personal physical space and the right to control many aspects of personal information and personal property (especially biological codes used in identification such as DNA and retinal scans) has taken a back seat to worries about crime and terrorism.

Passed in the wake of the September 11, 2001 attacks, the USA-PATRIOT Act was a landmark foray into increasing surveillance of populations. In particular, the Act expanded the ability of government agencies to use traditional forms of surveillance, as well as newer forms of digital communications and activity monitoring without needing to obtain search warrants and court orders. As a result, authorities in the US are now able to obtain a variety of information on individuals by, for example, conducting roving wiretapping on mobile and landline phones, monitoring the reading habits of users of public libraries, and obtaining information from private companies about customer web surfing habits and individual consumer profiles (Taylor et al., 2006).

In Europe, where there has been traditionally much more concern with enshrining and protecting rights to privacy legally (there is no legal 'right' to privacy in the US), most countries have devised their own legislation in response to terrorist attacks, which tend to follow the USA PATRIOT Act in the expansion of the surveillance powers of government, but to lesser extremes. These tend to focus on increased communications surveillance, increased identity requirements (especially for immigrants) and increased CCTV surveillance.

At the same time as the context of terrorism and crime have encouraged more data collection on the part of governments, the other impetus for the increasing collection of data has been the economic value of information about individuals. Trading in personal information databases has become big business and an ever more important part of the marketing and advertising of goods. This has spurred on a need for more privacy-enabling legislation to help prevent the widespread misuse of personal information by private organisations.

In terms of privacy-enabling legislation, the United States has tended to have a very fragmented approach to legislating the activities of private organisations. Overall, American legislation tends to concentrate on forbidding certain specific actions of intrusion and eavesdropping on communications, and has very little regulation over the distribution of processing of personal data (Van Dijk, 2006). Many loopholes exist with regard to the restriction of use of personal data in US contexts and this is largely due to the conflict between the demands of privacy legislation, and strong protection of freedom of speech within the American legal system (Mills, 2008). The selling of or distribution of personal information can be considered a form of commercial free speech, therefore American legislators are less likely to apply stringent laws that limit such actions.

By contrast, the European Union has tended to have a much more coherent approach, with much more emphasis on privacy protection and less on free speech. The EU directive on personal data protection is the most stringent in the world in terms of limiting the collection and distribution of information about individuals. In particular, Van Dijk (2006: 151–152) suggest that the directive:

- Is extremely broad in its definition of 'personal data'.

- Stresses the collection of data necessary only for specific or legitimate purposes, and that such data can only be collected and distributed with the express consent of the individual.

- Provides a list of categories of personal data that cannot be processed at all, including racial or ethnic origin, religious beliefs, political opinions, union memberships, health status or sexual behaviour.

Van Dijk argues that these benefits do not suggest that this legislation is ideal, but it does mean that, at present, Europe is at the leading edge in terms of privacy-enabling legislation. At the same time (as will be seen below) the European Union is somewhat contradictory in its ambitions to both enhance privacy legislation for personal data collected by private enterprise, while at the same time increasing the data retention requirements placed on private communications firms.

DIGITAL SURVEILLANCE: SPACES, TRACES AND TOOLS

David Lyon (2001) argued that there has been a change in the nature of surveillance as human interactions at long distances have become more common. In pre-modern contexts, relationships were primarily based on face-to-face interactions, in which both actors were co-present in the same space and time. However, as Giddens (1991) suggested in his concept of *time-space distanciation*, as modernity and capitalism progressed, human relationships (especially within economic spheres) were extended across longer distances of space and yet still had to be coordinated in time. The availability of long distance telecommunications and the general physical mobility of individuals in late modernity has only amplified this process, to the point where *telepresence* has begun to replace *co-presence* in human interactions.

This move from co-presence to telepresence has meant that surveillance has come to rely less on a watching, witnessing or policing of physical bodies based on physical proximity (embodied surveillance) towards the surveillance of what Lyon refers to as 'personal traces', or the metaphorical footsteps that people leave behind in the course of their activities. Within contemporary law enforcement this can be seen in the increasing use of CCTV cameras, as well as forensic – and particularly DNA – evidence. Within online contexts, this refers to the traces of internet activity left behind by an individual. Such online surveillance shows an increased concern for where people have been and what they have done and less concern with observations of current activities and the notion of catching someone 'in the act', as with embodied surveillance. How this is accomplished is considered below.

Key tools of digital surveillance

Within the online sphere of digital communications there are many tools that allow organisations and individuals to track, trace and monitor the actions of others. These tools run parallel to the well-known offline instruments of biometrics, RFID, CCTV, credit card transaction data, public record keeping and registers, loyalty shopping card schemes, public transportation travel cards and number plate recognition systems. The digital age has provided states, organisations and individuals with a number of new opportunities for the surveillance of populations.

State surveillance tools

In terms of direct state surveillance, one of the most powerful, although nebulous resources is a system called Echelon. Echelon is a secret data collection system run jointly by the governments of the United States, United Kingdom, Canada, Australia and New Zealand. Being a classified security system, details of how it operates are vague, but Echelon is said to screen all international communications (including phone and internet) for intelligence by sifting though communication texts for phrases, keywords and phone numbers that are deemed relevant for security purposes. In addition to Echelon, the United States also employs Carnivore, a kind of internet 'wiretap' system used by the FBI to monitor all incoming data into a particular IP address. To implement the use of Carnivore on US citizens, the FBI must justify its use to obtain a court order (see Marlin-Bennett, 2004).

Some countries are now using the internationally networked architecture of the internet to claim a right to surveil communications data that not only originates or terminates within their borders, but also information that passes through their infrastructure on the way to another country. In 2008 the US government passed the Foreign Intelligence Surveillance Act, which states that all internet communications going through the United States are now subject to government surveillance through various methods of 'wireless wiretapping'. Similarly, Sweden, an important northern European regional hub for internet traffic, passed the New Signal Surveillance Act in 2008, which permits Sweden's National Defence to access all internet and telephone conversations in and out of (and through) Sweden. This involves a large number of communications, which originate in Norway, Finland, Denmark and Russia (Irion, 2009).

At the same time, and in lieu of direct state surveillance, many governments are passing data retention legislation, which compels private telecommunications and internet companies to keep a record of all communications on their system for long periods of time, so that data can be accessed and used by governments in criminal and security investigations. For example, in 2006, the European Union passed the Data Retention Directive. This law was designed to assist in the coordination of criminal investigations within the EU. It demands that all providers of electronic communications services (such as mobile phone and internet service providers) must retain identifiable phone call and email data for at least six months and up to two years after the communication is made (the duration varies between countries). This data includes at minimum the originator and receiver of the communication, as well as the date, location and duration of the communication (Bigami, 2007). Many other countries have similar laws. In Russia, data must be kept for three years. However, in Australia there are no data retention requirements at present. In the United States, lax privacy laws has meant that most communications companies already retain customer communications data to use for marketing purposes (see below), but in 2009 legislation was put forward by the US Congress to ensure that this is the case. In its present form, this legislation would demand communications companies retain communications for a minimum of two years.

Commercial and private digital surveillance tools

One of the most popular forms of surveillance by commercial enterprises, and by now a fundamental part of web surfing, are internet or HTTP 'cookies'. A cookie is a small piece of text that is automatically downloaded onto a computer when its browser visits a web page. It then records one's internet activity and sends this information back to its home web site. The role of cookies is to provide authentication of a user and coherence within a browsing or surfing session. Cookies are fundamental to the interactive and personalised experience of the web as they record user preferences as well as web surfing activity. Web browsers normally have the facility to disable cookies to preserve privacy, but disabling cookies makes many web sites (especially those with a login or some sort of personalisation, such as MyAmazon or eBay) impossible to use.

In addition, free internet services such as search engines and email are used to collect data. Internet search engines such as Google, Bing and Yahoo! store the IP address and search terms of every search performed on their sites. These details are used to help direct targeted advertising at web surfers on the basis of an overall profile of search interests. Google currently keeps every search performed attached to your IP address for 13 months, Microsoft for eighteen and Yahoo! for nine, before the data is anonymised. Similarly, free online email providers such as Googlemail use automated data mining to scan messages and mailboxes for words and terms in order to gain insights into a user's interests for advertising purposes. In addition, in many workplaces, employee email is routinely monitored by employers. In 2001, it was suggested that 27 per cent of online workers worldwide already had their email monitored (Schulman, 2001).

Keylogging is a less popular, but perhaps a more clandestine form of digital surveillance. A keylogger is a software program that monitors keystrokes on a computer keyboard. In corporate use, keyloggers can be purposefully installed on employee computers to surveil employee activity (even words, phrases and messages, which are later deleted), or anyone else using company computers. Keyloggers can also be installed surreptitiously on personal or business computers through trojans downloaded during web surfing. Such malicious code can then send keystrokes associated with login and password data to a third party, creating opportunities for fraud, theft and invasions of privacy.

Last, interactive digital video recorders such as TiVo or SkyPlus record a viewer's television viewing and recording habits, which are then stored in a database and used to create a profile of them and their interests. This profile is used to personalise the television experience and draw insights into what kind of programmes an individual might want to record and even to record these automatically for that person. At the same time, this large amount of personal data is stored on company databanks and used in market profiling and targeted advertising research.

Mobile phone surveillance

As a last category of surveillance, one can set out the mobile phone as an extremely important mobile surveillance tool that not only captures digital communications, but also real-world locations and movements. Any mobile phone can have its position triangulated within a number of metres through its proximity to surrounding mobile phone masts, as long as the phone is switched on. This positional data is kept by mobile phone companies for between several months and several years and has already been used frequently in criminal investigations.

A new surveillance technique being used by the FBI under US wiretapping law is the roving bug. Roving bugs occur when the microphone of a mobile phone is remotely switched on using an installed piece of software downloaded without the knowledge of the phone user. The microphone can then be switched on without the holder knowing and nearby voice conversations can be monitored and recorded. The microphone can even be switched on when the phone is 'off'. The only way to completely disable the bug is to remove the mobile phone battery.

Last, for personal and business use, there are a number of mobile phone tracking software applications available such as Phonesitter or Mobilespy. These allow a third party to track and monitor the position of a mobile phone on the internet with GPS accuracy. Typical uses for these applications include parents and employers who wish to monitor the movements of their children and employees.

THE RISE OF SURVEILLANCE: CAUSES AND PROCESSES

What the previous section demonstrates is that surveillance is pervasive, and particularly so within online and digital contexts. At no point in the past have government agencies, private companies, or even lone individuals been able to collect so much information about others, in terms of their (virtual and physical) movements, their inter-actions and communications, or their interests and tastes. From this realisation, it is worth considering how this situation has arisen.

For Lyon (2001), there are four main strands of theory in which surveillance and its increasing pervasiveness in everyday life is discussed within the sociological literature: the rise of nation-state surveillance, the rise of bureaucratic structures, 'techno-logic' and the workings of capitalist political economy. More generally, one can see these themes relating to the overall imperatives of security, control, technology and commer-cial enterprise that provide major influences on the structure of society. The themes of security, control and technology will be discussed below. The discussion of commercial enterprise and political economy is sufficiently large to be taken up on its own in the next section.

Security imperatives: surveillance and the nation-state

Most people tend to think of surveillance and invasions of privacy as primarily resulting from an abuse of power of the nation-state. This is articulated in the general concern that we as a society are turning into a kind of 'big brother' state, in which large, all-seeing government organisations subjugate populations through excessive surveillance and record-keeping of its citizens. Fears of such a possibility are legitimated in the very real experiences of populations under Nazi dictatorship and Eastern-European Stalinist regimes, and are further ingrained into the Western cultural imagination through works such as George Orwell's classic *1984*.

Indeed, there is a substantial literature on surveillance within the social sciences which dwells upon the idea that, from their inception, nation-states have been worried about risks and threats to their security both from within and without their borders. As a result, nation-states have always had political imperatives to engage in surveillance. In the case of threats from outside, this involved espionage and the securing of borders. Inside these borders, it involved controlling and securing internal populations through surveillance. Much of this securing has been achieved by what Foucault referred to as 'biopower', or the systematic way in which states subjugate bodies and control/classify populations. In the nineteenth century, state initiatives such as public health legislation (including health documentation and record keeping), state education (involving the regulation and record keeping of the activities of juveniles) and the general collection of facts on populations through census data, employment and taxa-tion records, are all examples of biopower that came to prominence in the early days of the modern nation-state.

At the turn of the century, such biopower was enhanced though concerns for increased social control and law enforcement and led to further means of record keep-ing, classification and identification of populations associated with criminality through biometric identifiers such as fingerprinting (early 1900s) and eugenics (late 1800s). In a post 9/11 era, the use of biometric identifiers has been rekindled and emphasised through the use of DNA profiles, retinal scans, facial recognition technologies and other biometric identifiers that are increasingly seen as a central element in pushes towards increased security measures for passports and ID cards.

Of course, the increasing powers of surveillance by governments have not gone without criticism, even within a post 9/11 culture. One of the more interesting academic arguments has been provided by Georgio Agamben (1998, 2005), who argued that even before 9/11, governments had been increasingly operating under a 'state of exception', a situation in which governments, in the interests of 'security', were using extended powers associated with emergency legislation (such as martial law) in order to operate beyond the law. The war on terror intensified this process, and Agamben has noted how state practices of surveillance and biological 'tattooing' have spread from those who have been convicted (or suspected of committing) of criminal acts to the general populace. Fingerprinting, picture taking, face scanning and retinal scanning are the sorts of measures that were reserved for convicts and suspects, but now all of us are increasingly having our biometric data stored in databases and our actions monitored. All of us, in effect, are being treated as potential threats, suspected criminals, or terrorists.

Surveillance, control imperatives and bureaucratic structures

As a second theme in the literature on surveillance, Lyon (2001) suggests that the rise in surveillance can also be seen as resulting from the growing influence and intensity of bureaucratic structures, both state and private. Bureaucracy, in its ideal form, involves the rationalisation of large organisations and procedures to produce maximum efficiency. Behaviour in a bureaucracy is modelled on the most efficient means to produce a particular end. In this sense, sociologist Max Weber saw bureaucracy as the archetypal modern form of organisation: logical, rational and efficient.

Beninger (1986) argued that the rise of bureaucratic structures, and the roots of the information revolution more generally, lay in a 'crisis of control' brought about by the industrial revolution. He suggested that the increased scale of activity involving long distance travel and the increased speed of both travel and industrial production created the need for forms of control that went beyond the distributed control structures of the face-to-face social realm to the centralised, hierarchical, rationalised, bureaucratic realm. This centralisation of control was enforced by the advanced of communications technology and infrastructure of the time (telegraphy, telephone and mail).

In the post World War Two era, with the expansion of worldwide trade and globalisation, information technology, Beninger argued, began to supplement and replace the role of rationalised bureaucratic structures with automated coordination of activities centralised in information technology. Overall, Beninger suggests that the increasing prominence of information technology stems from a need to control and coordinate ever larger and faster processes of production across expanding spatial scales. Within this context, surveillance becomes just another means of securing efficiency and control among complexity and distance. Within market processes, surveillance of consumers helps make the consumption process that much more efficient by supplying, for example, targeted advertising or pre-approved credit cards. In the contexts of the state, the surveillance of all citizens as though they are under suspicion can be seen as the most efficient means to combat internal and external risks and threats.

Techno-logic

Lyon points to what he calls 'techno-logic', which is in effect an extension to the idea of surveillance as a consequence of rationalised bureaucracy. However, instead of resulting from an imperative of control and efficiency, in the theme of techno-logic, increased surveillance is a consequence of an increasing dependence on computers and machines. This approach is informed primarily by the work of Jacques Ellul (2001) and revolves around the idea that as computers become more integrated into society, the more society in its processes must reflect the demands of computerised ways of doing things. The central premise is that the use of technology, in this case surveillance technologies, creates a momentum of its own.

While such a suggestion can be seen as being somewhat technologically determinist, Lyon suggests the concept of 'function creep' as supporting the same premise. Function creep occurs when the use of a particular surveillance technology or method (such as CCTV being used to curb excessive vandalism at a school) begins to spread beyond its original (and reasonable) function and into other areas, or used in less reasonable ways. In this example, CCTV cameras used to prevent vandalism in one location might eventually spread into staff rooms and toilet facilities. Perhaps the introduction of cameras into all parts of the school paves the way for microphones to record conversations taking place within the school. Thus, the function creep progresses from a justifiable use of surveillance technology to one that is less justifiable and more invasive on personal freedoms.

COMMERCIAL IMPERATIVES AND THE POLITICAL ECONOMY OF SURVEILLANCE

The last strain of surveillance theory for Lyon is within the context of political economy. This set of discussions focusses on the economic imperatives of capitalism and the use of surveillance technologies in the workplace, but also more innovatively in the process of selling, marketing and consumption. In essence, the political-economic perspective brings in aspects of bureaucratic rationalisation as well as 'techno-logic', but adds to these the context of economic necessity built into capitalist structures.

Marketing and personal data collection

As suggested in Chapter 2, the main challenge within advanced industrial economies over the last few decades has been to expand stagnant markets and profit margins.

The strategy of globalisation has been followed to expand markets abroad, but there have also been efforts made to expand internally by getting people to buy more in domestic markets. One of the major strategies to encourage more individual consumption is to use marketing techniques that speak more directly to people's interests and personalities, thereby creating products, services and advertisements with greater appeal to individuals. Such strategies are often referred to as 'targeted', 'niche' or 'direct' marketing, in which a group of people (or 'market') are identified on the basis of any number of certain characteristics. These characteristics may be anything, but common categories are age, income or lifestyle. This market segment or niche is then targeted for marketing by creating certain products, services and advertisements that are more likely to speak to the circumstances, experiences or characteristics of that population, which:

- Allows marketers and advertising firms to create more effective advertisements.

- Creates efficiency in the advertising/marketing process, in that advertising money is spent directly on the more likely buyers of a product, instead of a larger, less interested mass of people.

This kind of marketing process is driven by information, particularly information about consumers. The more information available about consumers, the more 'understood' a consumer is and thus a more direct target they become for advertisers. In previous decades, such information about consumers was obtained with publically available data such as the census, surveys and mailing lists, which were cobbled together by direct marketing firms. Later on, as consumer culture became more automated through the prolific use of credit cards and 'loyalty cards', more information could be obtained, especially with regard to the purchasing habits of individuals. Not only was this information valuable to the organisation that collected it, in the sense that it gave them more insight into the habits and needs of their own customers, but increasingly this information became a valuable commodity in its own right, and was sold on to other firms and organisations.

This information-driven marketing strategy has undergone a revolution with the rise of the internet. Once the establishment of the web in the early 1990s made the internet a viable and usable environment for the average person, it was embraced by business as having massive potential to collect, store, analyse and exchange data on consumers (Zwick and Dholakia, 2004), as well as the potential to communicate more directly with them:

> There is no doubt that the main reason for corporate interest in the information highway lies in the fact that it is seen as opening up vast new markets, which also means expanding the range and effectiveness of targeting, motivation research, product management, and sales communication – that is, a total marketing strategy. (Dawson and Bellamy-Foster, 1998: 58)

The internet and the web have been so revolutionary in this regard because every action that takes place on the web, every purchase, every search, every web site viewed and every communication, leaves a trace, data trail, footprint or record of that action. This means that, effectively, all consumer and non-consumer activities can be monitored (Zwick and Knott, 2009).

If one looks at a company such as Google and its use of some of the digital surveillance tools mentioned earlier in this chapter, it is easy to see how much data one private organisation can obtain. Google provides many valuable services to the web population absolutely free of charge: searching, email, blogging facilities (through owning Blogger), language translation and many, many more useful services. Google makes 99 per cent of its revenue from selling directed advertising to consumers based on the multitude of information it collects from the people who use its free services.

How so? Google is obviously the most popular search engine in the world and, as it happens, using any search engine leaves a record of what a specific computer (ISP number) searched for and when. Google stores this information for 13 months to help in its marketing efforts. Furthermore, Google also installs cookies on the computer of each visitor to a Google site, which monitors what web sites are visited and when. In addition, people who use Google's unlimited email service, GoogleMail, are subject to having their mailboxes data-mined by automated search tools that collect information about what a user is talking about, their interests and the like. And if the same user also happens to use Blogger or Orkut, the blogging and social networking web sites owned by Google, all of the information provided by the user on those sites is monitored by Google as well, and becomes part of their database.

As one can imagine, Google is able to gain unprecedented amounts of information about the users of their services: what they are interested in, what they look at, who their friends are, what advertisements they have responded to in the past. From this information, they are able to present companies that have products and services to sell with a massive customer database and a way of targeting the specific type of person they imagine as receptive to their product. Google's massive value ($157 billion in 2009 (Yahoo! Finance, Nov. 25 2009)) is based on its growing database of information about consumers and the value of that to advertisers.

Databases, data-mining and discourses

The interactive nature of the web means that in many respects, it can be thought of as a large data-creating database. This data can be operated on to aid in the marketing process, or outside business uses, and be operated on for security and law enforcement ambitions. These 'operations' tend to be referred to by two terms: data *mining* – using computer programs to sift through large datasets according to some specified criteria (Marlin-Bennett, 2004), and Dataveillence – the systematic use of personal data systems in the investigation or monitoring of the actions of one or more persons (Clarke, 1993). For surveillance and security, that may involve an effort such as Echelon searching for terms such as 'bomb' or 'jihad' in email communications. For marketing agencies, it might involve any one of many demographic, income or lifestyle variables.

Whether data mining or dataveillence, the operations performed on digital information gleaned from web surfing and communications are achieved through the construction of databases. As discussed in Chapter 1, databases can be considered *the* cultural form of late modernity and the information age (Manovich 2001). In addition, Poster (1995) has argued that databases are also *discourses* in the Foucauldian sense of the term. That is, a way of thinking about and categorising an object or subject that is manifested through language and embodies power relations within society. Thus, discourses basically 'create' subjects or selves. Poster identified computerised databases as a form of discourse, in that they are a configuration of language that constitute an individual subject according to certain 'rules of formation' (Aas, 2004). Databases create social identities for people on the basis of certain parameters. In terms of crime and security, this may be 'suspicious/not suspicious', 'security risk' or 'potential tax dodger'. In marketing databases this may be a 'high value/low value/non-value' consumer, 'people interested in expensive cars', or 'people with credit problems'.

Thus, what the internet has been able to achieve for marketers and for security agencies is a means with which to create, collect and categorise information about individuals in a multitude of ways. This information is then used to sort or categorise individuals based on whatever information seems relevant to an organisation or institution at a particular time. In that respect, the potential identities for an individual are endless and constantly changing. Online life has basically become raw material for the production of consumer (and other) identities, as all behaviour is turned into data points that are organised, manipulated and transformed into a dematerialised identity to be targeted by those who have something to sell (Zwick and Knott, 2009), or those looking for threats.

The result is that the virtual identities produced from databases become virtual bodies upon which power can be enacted, with consequences for the 'real' bodies at the computer:

> As a meaningful text, the database is no-one's and everyone's,
> yet it 'belongs' to someone, to the social institution that owns
> it as property, to the corporation, the state, the military, the
> hospital, the library, the university. The database is a discourse
> of pure writing that directly amplifies the power of its owner/
> user. (Poster, 1995: 85)

The power of profiling

The production of identities through a collection of several bits of information is often alluded to by the concept of the profile. Profiling is defined by Clarke (1993: 403) as:

> A means of generating subjects or prospects from within a
> larger population, and involved inferring a set of characteris-
> tics of a particular class of person from past experience, then
> searching data-holdings for individuals with a close fit to that
> set of characteristics.

Within digital culture, we often think of profiles in terms of representations that we create of ourselves, say on a social networking site, on a blog, or on a dating web site. Indeed these are good examples of how individuals willingly give up personal information to marketing firms and help to themselves, in exchange for a free service. However, the state has a long history of profiling individuals, especially in relation to crime (criminal profiling) and health (diagnosis). The marketing information revolution of the past three decades has allowed consumer profiling to become a dominant activity in the commercial world, and provides a means by which to identify individuals who are likely to be interested in particular products and services. Profiles are the targets, or the means by which direct or targeted marketing attempts to achieve its goals. According to Clarke (1993), profiling procedure involves six steps:

1 Define a class of person.

2 Use existing knowledge to define a profile of that class of person (their demographics, their ambitions, their motivations).

3 Express the profile formally (a set of characteristics to look for).

4 Acquire data concerning relevant populations.

5 Search data for individuals whose characteristics comply with the profile.

6 Take action (i.e., market to them or investigate them).

On the web, such profiling is a continuous process, as there is a continual input of new data from browsing habits, purchasing and communication data, as well as a neverending amount of products and services to market. This continuous process is illustrated by Zwick and Dholakia (2004) using the example of Amazon.com and their personalised recommendation system. This system continually provides context-driven information (advertisements and recommendations) to their customers on the basis of running profiles. These profiles are maintained and authenticated by a series of features:

• A sign-in procedure authenticating the actual consumer, as opposed to just the computer being used.

• A record of purchase and browsing history on the Amazon.com site.

• Credit card information (including name, address).

• Cookies which keep track of online browsing behaviour.

Similarly to Google, this large amount of information collected by Amazon.com allows them to construct an image of their individual customers not only on the basis of what they purchase, but also where they live and what their overall interests would seem to be. This allows Amazon.com to then recommend books and items that may be more attractive and therefore easy to sell to a specific customer. One of the perceived benefits of this is an increased likelihood for impulse buying (Zwick and Dholakia, 2004).

Databases and profiling: pro's and con's

The point of creating databases and constructing profiles is to get closer to the individual: to make them measurable and thus ultimately predictable. While the tone of this section may seem quite critical, it should be pointed out that there are several benefits to profiling for business's consumers. First, consumer profiling provides customers with a more personalised experience and therefore information on goods in which they might be interested: profiles help people get what they might want. Second, profiling helps to avoid inundating a consumer with irrelevant information characteristic of mass advertising (junk mail and spam). Third, profiling improves the economic efficiency of marketing activities by making contact with good consumer prospects for a product and weeding out the poor ones. Last, it has to be noted that the vast majority of the operations performed on databases and profile creation are automated (see Chapter 1). So although personal information is collected in abundance, which creates a more personalised experience, the information is not normally subject to direct human surveillance.

At the same time, there are a number of real and potential downsides to the ubiquitous use of database and profile identities. First of all, one could make the point that databases and profiles, just like any form of discourse, do not *describe* or represent identities as much as they *create* identities that *make themselves true*. What I mean by this is that, as Clarke (1993) suggests, profiles attempt to predict future behaviours. At the same time, these profiles also prejudice future behaviours (of consumers) by limiting the exposure of certain individuals or groups to certain types of information deemed irrelevant or not suitable to them by the profiling process. This process limits choices and thus constrains future actions in a kind of feedback loop between profile construction and the narrow range of options then tailored to that profile (Zwick and Knott, 2009).

Second, the identities and classifications created are done so externally, by agencies outside the individual, and not internally, as a choice of the subject or individual. In that sense, a profile or database identity is an erosion of personal autonomy, where knowledge of individuals is instead used to label and control them without their consent and often without their knowledge (Poster, 1995). This is significant because, in the digital environment, these disembodied virtual identities are what stand in for the individual. As far as the profiling agencies and businesses are concerned, these profiles *are* the consumer. In that sense it is significant that individuals themselves have little say in how they are classified and are in general not aware of the information used to classify them, or even of the people and agencies involved in doing the classifying. Poster refers to this process of disembodied, largely anonymous surveillance and sorting as a superpanopticon.

Third, the information collected in databases and used in profiling in many respects breaks the distinction between public and private information. Poster (1996) contrasts the contemporary situation with the not too distant past, when most people made their purchases with cash, as opposed to with credit or debit cards (obviously necessary for online purchasing). In the age of cash, individual purchases and economic transactions were private and largely anonymous. What shops you visited and what you bought was between you and the proprietor. In the digital environment, all this has changed, 'the digital consumer is neither anonymous nor private' (Zwick and Dholakia, 2004: 30). Both this type of information, as well as information voluntarily supplied by consumers, now gets collected by firms who often sell it on to other companies, or is inherited by firms that purchase these companies. Even the databases of public or governmental agencies can end up in private hands if that service becomes privatised or outsourced to private companies. There is no real way of knowing where personal information will end up or how it will be used. As Poster suggests, information becomes 'everyone's and no one's', in that as personal (and often private) information has achieved commodity status, it can also be seen as a publically saleable item.

WHY CARE ABOUT A SURVEILLANCE SOCIETY?

What should be gathered from the previous sections is, first that privacy is a concept with many facets revolving around two very broad notions of 'solitude' on the one hand and 'autonomy' on the other. Second, that these 'rights' are not fixed or innate, but are culturally, historically and legally contingent. However, despite the contingent nature of privacy, it is important to note what the consequences might be of an increasing lack of privacy in an age of constant and uncontrolled surveillance.

Spinello (2003) suggests that a lack of privacy can lead to losses of freedom for individuals in two forms: *extrinsic* and *intrinsic*. An extrinsic loss of freedom can be considered a real, palpable loss of freedom by having one's behaviour or opportunities unjustly limited by others, and can come in many forms. An intrinsic loss of freedom has more to do with how people's perceptions help to curtail their freedoms. This last section will explore several ways in which negative or unjust consequences can emerge from too much surveillance (especially of the digital variety) and how both extrinsic and intrinsic losses of freedom can result.

People can potentially be affected by the use of information that they have not willingly supplied. The use of personal or sensitive information collected without a person's knowledge or permission can have all manner of potential personal or financial consequences for an individual. In a hypothetical example, a person may apply online for life insurance (say, as a compulsory condition of obtaining a mortgage on a house). Now, perhaps justifiably so, an insurance company will require information about current medical conditions, family medical histories, age, weight and the like in order to determine whether or not the applicant is worthy of a policy, or poses too great a risk for the company to insure. The applicant will willingly give up such information if they want a policy. However, suppose that the life insurance company also used cookies from its website to track the web surfing activities of the applicant as part of building a risk-assessment profile of the applicant. After examining cookie data and web activity, the insurance company comes to the conclusion that the applicant may engage in 'risky' sexual behaviour and refuses the policy. In this case, the applicant is judged on more information than he/she voluntarily submitted, and judged on data of which they are unaware.

This leads to the second point, that information collected about individuals can be used against them without their knowledge or knowledge of the data sources. Credit ratings, for example, are an important part of modern consumer society, which is founded on the idea that people need to borrow money to make large purchases, such as cars and houses. The lack of a good credit rating can severely hamper someone's ability to participate in consumer culture to a 'normal' degree, and even prevent them from finding a place to live. Yet credit ratings are a very secretive process about which most people know very little. They can be adversely affected by certain kinds of information, which circulate through financial institutions whenever a credit card, a mortgage, a loan, or even connecting to phone, power and other domestic utilities is applied for. When trying to organise these services in their daily life, most people are not aware of what information is being used to judge them as reliable applicants, or the variety of sources from which the information is coming. It is like being accused of being unreliable by an unknown accuser, using unknown data and without having the ability to answer back. Given its clandestine nature and the variety of sources, decisions based on such information can be very difficult to dispute.

Third, the information used may not be correct, taken out of context, or unfairly used. For example, in the above example of an individual applying for an insurance policy, the decision to deny the application might be based on web surfing data from cookies which suggest that the applicant engages in risky sexual behaviour. But there are many ways in which that assumption might be a false one. The individual might be sharing a computer with someone else, or they could also be concerned about a friend's health or behaviour and are looking up information with regard to these concerns. In either case, the decision to reject is based on mistaken assumptions (although they may be logical, or even reasonable assumptions) gleaned from cookie data.

To take a less hypothetical example from my own life, several years ago I purchased a self-help book online about Obsessive-Compulsive Disorder, through Amazon.com to give to a family member. To this day, whenever I log onto Amazon.com, it recommends books on OCD and displays this recommendation prominently on my personalised web page. In addition, I continue to get emails recommending OCD and other self-help books to me, with email subject headings like 'Get *Getting Over OCD* (Guilford Self-Help Workbook) (Guilford Self-help Workbook Series) by Jonathan S. Abramowitz for £12.83'. Amazon.com assumes that I suffer from OCD, and potentially anyone keeping track of my email communications or even walking into my office and noticing those emails on my computer can assume that I suffer from OCD as well. This seems like a reasonable assumption, but it is a wrong one because there is no context to the data in question (for a longer discussion about context and databases, see Chapter 1). Nonetheless, there is the temptation to make those inferences. Indeed, our previous discussion of 'profiling' suggested that surveillance for the purposes of monitoring crime and for gathering consumer data increasingly involves such inferences.

In addition, unlike analogue or 'hard copy' information, digital information about people has the potential for a permanent life span and can remain easily accessible indefinitely. In criticism of this trend, Blanchette and Johhnson (2002) provide a compelling argument for the necessity of 'social forgetfulness' in society. They suggest that in an analogue world of paper, file folders and filing cabinets, a certain amount of social forgetfulness was automatically built into any bureaucratic system, as it was only possible to keep detailed and readily accessible data on a large amount of people for a relatively short period of time before files and storage facilities became full. As a result, records for much behaviour, such as juvenile crime records, school records, financial problems, bankruptcies and the like would eventually be either destroyed or sealed away in archives after a number of years:

> In the paper-and-ink world, the sheer cumbersomeness of archiving and later finding information often promoted a form of institutional forgetfulness – a situation which parallels human memory. (Blanchette and Johnson, 2002: 34)

This forgetfulness corresponded with a general sense that it was necessary, especially in a democratic society, to allow people to eventually be forgiven (or at least forgotten) for past mistakes if their nature was not too serious and if the individual had reformed their ways. In a consumer society, such forgetfulness could be seen as vital. The need to overcome past mistakes in the form of personal bankruptcies or poor credit histories after a number of years of good financial behaviour is an example of how such forgetfulness can help to give people second chances to participate normally in society.

However, in the age of digitised record keeping and continuous collection of data, there are no physical or practical limitations to the duration that data about individuals can be kept, nor on the ease of access of such data. As a result, there is a danger that individuals will never be able to overcome their pasts. No transgression or misdemeanour will ever be forgotten, no second chances will ever be granted. In a networked and digitised surveillance society, mistakes made could conceivably haunt someone for the rest of their life, and continually interfere with financial and social well-being. The past will always be present, and the notion of 'reform' could very easily be replaced by 'exclusion' over perpetuity (Blanchette and Johnson, 2002).

Fifth, private data retained by commercial organisations is vulnerable to government seizure, especially under growing legal data retention requirements. Commercial data logging is always at risk of being turned over to government and law enforcement agencies for criminal cases as well as for private lawsuits. This has been recently demonstrated in court decisions in both the US and the UK, where the identities of anonymous bloggers and forum contributors have been subpoenaed by legal authorities and turned over by web administrators (Dyer, 2007; Gibb, 2009; Nasaw, 2009). Within security and personal defamation contexts, such measures seem to make sense, however, further incidents involving China and Yahoo! as well as India and Google have shown that such information can be demanded by governments when on the hunt to persecute political dissidents (Kahn, 2005; Snyder, 2008).

At the moment, such government manoeuvres seem far away from the reality of life under the relatively benign democratic governments of the West, but if that situation were to ever change, the sheer amount of personal information collected by commercial organisations would be a huge resource to an autocratic state, with consequences for all.

Also, the data collected by commercial and government organisations can never be fully secure, and leads to inevitable personal data breaches. Hardly a month goes by in any major post-industrial nation without some sort of scandal involving the leakage of personal information into public hands. Data can be left on trains, or in taxis, stolen from government or corporate computers during robberies, accidentally sent via email, or downloaded onto the internet. The examples are numerous:

- In September 2009, Demon internet, a UK ISP provider sent its customers a mass email regarding billing arrangements. Attached to this email was a file that contained the names, email addresses, telephone numbers and usernames/passwords of over 3,500 of its personal and business clients.

- Again in September 2009, the University of North Carolina School of Medicine was the victim of hacking, which compromised the personal information, including social security numbers, of 163,000 women.

- In June 2009, over 100,000 pension holders in the UK had their personal and banking details put at risk when a company contracted to develop software had one of their laptops, containing all this data unencrypted, stolen.

- In August 2009, the Rocky Mountain Bank of America accidentally sent a file with the names, addresses, tax identification numbers and bank loan information for 1,325 customers to an unknown Googlemail account.

Stories like these are commonplace, as suggested by the fact that these four incidents took place within four months of each other. Events such as these, as well as the rising number of cases of credit card fraud and identity theft, remind us of how much information about us is collected and held by corporate and public bodies on their computers and servers, and how vulnerable such databases are to human error as well as criminal intent. But past the headlines of data leaks and security breaches that make us feel concerned and vulnerable, there is a larger question about not only the security of personal data, but the sheer amount of it which needs to be protected.

Last, but by no means least importantly, are the *intrinsic* consequences of over-surveillance. Intrinsically, the effect of hypersurveillance, or digital panopticism is to *create a state of consciousness in which one is aware of permanent visibility*. The effect of this awareness is that it leads to a change of behaviour in the face of the inherent threat of surveillance. In other words, people limit their actions and behave differently when they feel as though they are being watched. When taken to extremes, this produces a sense of being continually oppressed under a regime of power. People become fearful not of doing wrong, but of being seen as wrong. Furthermore, as Blanchette and Johnson (2002) suggest, anxiety from the repercussions of making a mistake or doing something one may later regret is not conducive to a free or democratic way of life:

> Privacy is not just something individuals want because it makes
> them feel good or is good for them; rather, privacy is good for
> society insofar as it promotes the development of the kinds

of individuals who are essential for democracy … a world in which everything one does is recorded and never forgotten is not a world conducive to the development of democratic citizens. It is a world in which one must hesitate over every act because every act has permanence, may be recalled and come back to haunt one, so to speak. (Blanchette and Johnson, 2002: 36)

CONCLUSION

The growing density of surveillance practices in everyday life is not the product of some capitalist conspiracy or the evil effects of a plutocratic urge. No, it is the outcome of the complex ways in which we structure our political and economic relationships in societies that value mobility, speed, security and consumer freedom. (Lyon, 2001: 2)

This chapter has provided a general overview of many of the main issues regarding privacy and surveillance in the digital age. When considering such a discussion, it is important at the outset to realise that privacy as a concept is historically, culturally, and legally contingent. Thus, it is reasonable to expect that just as our expectations of privacy have changed in the past, they might very well change in the future.

Our increasing use of, and dependence on, digital communication technologies in everyday life, through work, shopping, entertainment and social interaction has led to the point where movements (both virtual and real), communications, tastes, financial situations and even (to a degree), our thoughts, interests and opinions can be monitored and recorded to an unprecedented degree. One of the key perceived advantages of these digital technologies is that they can (hopefully) help to reduce risks through the continual collection of data about individuals and their actions. However, the reduction of risk is inherently tied to an increase in the amount of control that pervades society. This is a current tension within a contemporary society that has, on the one hand, an unprecedented ability to monitor the actions of individuals and, on the other, has an implicit cultural and explicit legal value for individual rights and freedoms. Here the phrase 'knowledge is power' (in this case, knowledge of other people) certainly springs to mind and points us towards the increasing amount of state surveillance (as well as by individuals interested in gaining power over others) that is possible in the digital age.

At the same time, it must be recognised that the lion's share of surveillance data is not collected by governments, but by private corporations operating under the central principle at work in the information age: that information itself has attained the status of a commodity. It could also be suggested that 'knowledge is revenue'. In this respect, personal data collection has become an ordinary and often lucrative part of the web and other digital communication technologies where such information is solicited, collected, sold and used to aid in marketing and advertising strategies. The sheer variety of organisations collecting and distributing information, combined with the sheer mass of information being collected, makes this kind of information potentially much more vulnerable than the classic fears of a 'big brother' society.

FURTHER READING

For an overall discussion of the surveillance society, Lyon (2001) is very comprehensive and interesting, and Spinello (2003) is useful as well. Garfinkel (2001) is an accessible overall discussion concentrating on the American context. For an early, but excellent discussion of digital panopticism and profiling, see Poster (1995). Elmer (2004), Aas (2004) and Zwick and Knott (2009) provide good discussions about the use of databases and profiling in everyday life, and Marlin-Bennett (2004) is a useful overall discussion of the legal dimensions of privacy and data collection.

6

INFORMATION POLITICS, SUBVERSION AND WARFARE

In 2001, internet rumours of a new revolutionary transportation technology began to circulate. Known as 'IT', the vague comments of many inventors and scientists fuelled speculation that this top secret new invention was going to change personal transportation forever, revolutionise our cities, change the way we live and stop global warming. In 2002, the secret was out ... 'IT' was the Segway, a two wheeled personal transportation device with an ingenious gyroscopic balancing system that allowed individuals to travel at 12.5 miles per hour with very little chance of crash or injury. However, in the six years since Segways have been available for purchase by the general public, the total sales have only been around 50,000 units. Their use has been banned on many pavements and sidewalks in the United States and elsewhere, and their impact upon urban life has been insignificant.

It is almost inevitable that any significant new technology will be predicted to transform society, or at least to embody huge potential to transform society, for better or worse. It is often said, especially in the initial stages of the adoption of a particular technology, that the technology will generate social change based upon the implicit values, virtues, or vices possessed by that technology. The early days of the internet and the web were filled with writings of the promise that this new communication technology, by its networked nature, embodied the values of freedom, community, altruism, democracy and citizenship (Chadwick, 2006; Poster, 1995). This line of thinking is akin to the sort of technological determinism discussed in the Introduction and such a view can be seen in internet pioneer John Perry Barlow's famous '*Declaration of Independence of Cyberspace*', intended to be a caution against government regulation of the internet:

> I declare the global space that we are building to be *naturally* independent of the tyrannies that you seek to impose upon us.
> (Barlow, 1996: paragraph 2 [my italics])

Barlow was merely reflecting the enthusiasm among many at the time that the internet would, by its very nature, lead to a transformation in politics and the relationships of power between people and their governments in civil society. The frontier-less, globally networked, decentralised, interactive architecture of the internet was seen as enabling new freedoms of speech and association (Hague and Loader, 1999). It would create an environment in which:

- There would be unfettered construction and dissemination of information that would release the stranglehold of mainstream corporate media on public life, thereby providing more awareness of and perspectives on issues and information suppressed by mainstream media. In other words, an environment of *information democracy*.

- There would be more direct participation of citizens in government and in the political process. This would be achieved through increased information availability, as well as increased facility for consultation between governments and publics. Even the replacement of representational politics with direct democracy in which citizens themselves (as opposed to elected representatives) could vote on government legislation (or 'e-democracy') was forecast (Coleman, 1999). This can be seen as a *democratisation of decision-making power*.

- Access to more information and more decision-making power would create *more engaged citizens* able to express their voice in an environment of free speech and association. This would revitalise the political public sphere and create a more *deliberative democracy* and a more expressive politics.

This chapter will examine the accuracy of these claims after two decades of the web. As Chadwick (2006) suggests, with the near ubiquity of the internet and other forms of ICT, the issue is no longer whether politics *is*, or *will be* online, but in what forms it is already present online and with what consequences. Politics is clearly online, but the shape it has taken is in many respects surprising and suggests that, like the Segway, the technology itself is only one part of the equation. The social context of technological change plays a vital part in politics in the information age.

THE POLITICAL CONTEXT OF INFORMATION POLITICS

For the last two decades, many political writers have suggested that the Western liberal democratic tradition has been stagnating, as the fundamental institutions of that model (political parties, the established political class, national representative structures) have been largely ineffectual in dealing with the major changes and challenges posed to late-modern nation-states. In particular, the challenge of globalisation has undermined the perceived relevance of politics at the national level as globally-integrated economies, supra-national political bodies, and economic neo-liberalism has eroded the ability of nation-states to manage their own affairs with any significant autonomy (Dahlgren, 2004). One has only to look at the recent global financial crisis, its seemingly local origins in the US mortgage market and its transformation into a worldwide economic calamity, to see that the economic integration of nation-states has limited their financial autonomy. In such a context, faith in the relevance of a national political system is difficult to maintain.

This crisis is manifest in a number of ways (Chadwick, 2006):

- A steady decline in voter turnout for elections at all levels (national, regional, local) but particularly at the national level, since the early 1960s.

- A decline in membership of mainstream political parties.

- A trend towards single issue politics and away from ideologically-based discussion and voting, leading to much more unpredictable voting behaviour.

- A drift from mass mainstream parties largely based on class lines to 'catch-all' parties that prioritise electoral success over coherent strategies or ideological beliefs.

- The professionalisation and mediatisation of politics, in which rational political discussion has been replaced by highly mediatised campaigns and elections based on scandals, sound bites and 'dumbed-down' media-friendly marketing and advertising.

- Changes in party funding, in which party financing has been increasingly dominated by large corporate donors and wealthy private individuals, and less from grassroots members, leading to cynicism and suspicion of mainstream party politics.

In response, political theorists have argued that a 'new politics' has emerged (especially among younger people), often described in terms of 'new social movements' (or NSMs). The phrase refers to a wide variety of entities, including social interest organisations, non-governmental organisations (NGOs), activist groups, single-issue campaigns and coalitions, and civic networks. Classic examples of new social movements include the environmental/ ecological, women's, gay rights, anti-globalisation, 'fair trade', global human rights and 'fight global poverty' movements. New social movements in general are seen to have a number of features that differ from established political organisations and parties of the past.

NSMs tend to be less economically or class-oriented and more focused on social changes in lifestyle, cultural or identity-related issues. Traditional politics associated with industrial modernism focused on material or economic issues such as how economic resources were distributed in society. As such, there was generally assumed to be a relationship between a particular group or class and the economic interests of the group or class with regard to socio-economic status or power in that society. For example, labour movements and their associated 'labour' parties pushed for greater worker rights and the redistribution of wealth between rich and poor. But rather than a politics driven by the economic interests or grievances of a particular group, new social movement politics tends to be driven by expressions of individual identity, choices, rights, or inter-ests, as can be seen in – for example – the gay rights movements, or ethnic separatist movements (Johnston, 1994). This can be seen in a way as a privatisation, individualisa-tion or even a consumerisation of the political sphere.

Relatedly, NSMs are often issue-oriented and ad-hoc as opposed to ideological. Until the late 1960s, politics in the modern nation state was dominated by ideological concerns. Mass political movements revolved around particular all-encompassing worldviews such as liberalism, communism, socialism, conservatism and fascism which had grand visions about how society should be organised as a whole. New social movements eschew these meta-narratives of society and instead focus on specific issues, for example, 'third world debt' or 'the environment'. Thus, membership in a new social movement is less demanding and can be considered a reflection of personal choice on a particular issue and not an ideological statement or commitment. As a result, an individual can belong to or identify with several social movements or organisations. At the organisational level, activist groups and organisations often act in coalition with other groups, uniting on a specific issue they may have in common. A good example would be the protests and action involved in the anti-globalisation movement, which the Canadian Security Intelligence Service described thus:

> Protesters represent a broad spectrum of causes and goals-environmentalists, animal-rights supporters, union members, human-rights activists, anarchists, even the White supremacist milieu. But with the exception of large and prominent organi-zations, e.g., Greenpeace, the names or titles of groups are not significant. Many groups are merely splinters, have few mem-bers, are formed briefly for the need of the moment, change their names frequently, or are located in a specific region; in many cases, individuals are members of several groups at the same time or espouse various causes. (CSIS, 2000: Paragraph 19)

NSMs tend to be decentralised, diffused, networked organisations with considerable local autonomy. They are more akin to Castells' (1996) *networked enterprise* (see Chapter 2) than they are to the kind of centralised hierarchical bureaucratic structures and large bodies of fee-paying members associated with traditional political parties and mass social movements. Membership in NSMs tends to be more fluid, with a small group of core members and a much larger but more casual group of people who may be mobi-lised as activists for specific campaigns. This is reminiscent of a casual pool of labour for a networked business enterprise (see Chapter 2).

These decentralised organisations are much more likely to pool their memberships and resources together and cooperate or coordinate in an ad-hoc manner with other organisations to increase the awareness or impact of specific campaigns or protests. For example, the CSIS again describes those involved:

> Diversity is a major characteristic of anti-globalization protests and demonstrations, which are often described as 'multi-generational, multi-class, and multi-issue'. Participants represent a variety of issues and not all are pursuing globalization as their pri-mary target. For some protesters, anti-globalization is a prin-cipal concern, but for others it is merely a shared goal, with the demonstrations simply a means to an end. (CSIS, 2000: Paragraph 17)

NSMs tend to move away from nationally based issues and political structures and are often more transnational in focus, as many of the issues they deal with have transnational or global consequences and solutions. As a result, their focus of political action is rarely the political institutions of the nation state. Where the tradition of mass politics was squarely focussed on national political structures (either through the ballot box, or through 'revolution'), the methods of NSMs tend to differ. In attempting to accomplish their goals NSMs have an ambiguous relationship with formal political institutions. Sometimes they operate with or alongside governments, and other times they operate in coalition with other NGOs or independently to achieve their aims. In addition, NSMs tend to use methods more associated with civil disobedience, non-violence, or dramatic display, often referred to as *direct action* (Johnston, 1994). In that sense, they tend to focus their method on using recognisable brand images and the media to insert their message into popular consciousness. Sometimes, such use of mainstream media and corporate images for the purpose of protest or subversive social comment is referred to as 'culture jamming' (Lasn, 2000).

ICT-ENABLED POLITICS

Castells (1996) included many of the concerns of social movement theory into his grand narrative of the information age and argued that the crisis in contemporary politics was one side effect of the rise of the network society, resulting from:

- The economic basis and labour structure of the network society (in the form of post-industrial flexible production) undermining traditional ideological or class-based economic structures by devaluing manual labour and instilling a sense of uncertainty and individualism in working life (see Chapter 9 on community). As a result, class-based politics (associated with traditional political parties) is replaced with identity politics.

- The increasing significance of media in politics and everyday life has reduced politics to a media savvy use of symbols. Politics and campaigning has become professionalised and akin to a marketing exercise.

- Because ICT-enabled communication is instantaneous and largely uncontrollable, it becomes impossible to control information. Thus, politics in the information age tends to be negative, scandal-ridden and prone to the use of misinformation. This devalues the political process and stifles political debate, leading to cynicism towards established forms of politics and politicians.

It is not surprising that many writers suggest that the infrastructure of the internet and other digital ICTs can be considered a good fit with the methods and organisational needs of NSMs (Van de Donk et al., 2003). In many respects, the advent of digital networking can be considered as a boon to the ambitions of NSMs or what some call more loosely 'alternative' or 'sub-politics': a politics that works outside mainstream formal politics (Beck, 1997). This type of political action can take advantage of the internet and other networked communication technologies in several ways.

Visibility

> 'We Zapatistas have extended a bridge to other social and political organizations, and to thousands of persons without a political party, and we have received respect from all of them, and we have corresponded with them all. And we have also, together with others, extended bridges to the entire world and we have contributed to the creation (alongside men and women of the 5 continents) of a great network which struggles through peaceful means against neoliberalism, and resists by fighting for a new and better world. We have also contributed something to the birth of a new and fresh cultural movement which struggles for a "new man" and new worlds.
>
> ... Today, July 19, 1998, the Zapatista Army of National Liberation endorses this Fifth Declaration of the Lacandon Jungle. We invite everyone to know it, to disseminate it, and to join in the efforts and the tasks which it demands.
>
> DEMOCRACY!
>
> LIBERTY!
>
> JUSTICE!'
>
> (ELZN, 1998)

On January 1, 1994, the first day of NAFTA (the North American Free Trade Agreement involving the United States, Canada and Mexico in a common free trade market), the ELZN or 'Zapatistas' captured seven cities and town in the province of Chiapas, Mexico. This was in part a protest against the neo-liberal policies of the Mexican government and the oppression of the indigenous peoples and peasants of the resource-rich Chiapas region, and in part a protest against the wider concept of neo-liberal globalisation. Poorly armed, these rebels were soon beaten back into the jungle by the Mexican army.

In normal circumstances, what could be expected was a continued military campaign and, following inevitable victory by government forces, the bloody suppression of the insurgents. However, the Zapatistas were very tactical in their use of the media – and particularly new media. News of their struggle and their plight was spread around the fledgling world wide web. The communiqués, speeches and images of their charismatic leader, Subcommandante Marcos, struck a chord with internet audiences. Soon the Chiapas rebellion had turned into a 'war of ink and internet' (Froehling, 1997), which mobilised support around the world. This led to several protests within and outside Mexico and ultimately mainstream mass media coverage. Facing a public relations disaster, the Mexican government was forced into negotiations to meet the concerns of the Zapatistas and the indigenous peoples of the area.

The Chiapas rebellion was arguably the first major political event in which the internet became a decisive factor. In pre-internet circumstances, the chances that the world would have known about the plight of a rag-tag group of indigenous rebels in a remote corner of Mexico would have been minimal. Such news would usually be suppressed by nationally-based, government-sympathetic media. However, the internet gave the Zapatistas message *visibility*.

The web can be seen as a giant publication outlet (Hill and Hughes, 1998), in which the costs of production and publication are minimal and the costs of distribution are nil. Thus, where marginal or small groups, movements and political outsiders of the past faced the many *barriers of cost* in getting their message out through independently printing and distribution information about their cause, or by buying expensive time on traditional mass media outlets such as television and radio, digital technology has allowed even the smallest organisation, or a lone individual the ability to get their message out to a potentially worldwide audience with very few barriers of cost.

The other major obstacle to visibility has been the hegemonic *barrier of access* to mass media. Large private media organisations, as economic entities driven by an economic agenda and owned by the wealthy, tend to support more conservative views, and often ignore (if not actually suppress) stories or issues that may show them, their sponsors, or the liberal-economic status quo in a bad light. Similarly, state-owned media corporations will often not publicise views or stories that are overly critical of their own government or those of their allies (see, for example, Herman and Chomsky, 1988).

By its decentralised nature and ease of access, digital networking technologies allow the hegemony of mass media organisations to be challenged, providing publicity for countless events, incidents and stories from multiple perspectives, which might not normally be available to the general public. Mitra (2005), building upon Watts (2001), looks at how the internet enables groups who have been traditionally powerless, or deemed unworthy, to have a 'voice' within the public sphere. For Watts, the gaining of voice (i.e., the ability to insert your own perspective within societal discourse), is fundamental to attaining the role of a powerful agent in society, whereas lack of voice implies powerlessness. Use of the internet and other ICTs helps to overcome the economic, cultural and technological barriers to the establishment of a voice for minority or marginalised groups.

Many authors, such as Mitra (2005), see such developments as a positive step for minority groups. However, the lack of barriers means that any political view can be and is represented somewhere on the web: from the voices of the marginalised, to extremists at all ends of the political spectrum. This includes less desirable racist and far-right organisations that would run afoul of anti-hate laws in many countries if their material was physically printed, but can achieve a voice on the web (see Atton, 2006; Back, 2002).

Internal organisation and mobilisation

New social movements in general have much in common with Castells' (1996) notion of the *networked enterprise*. Networked enterprises take advantage of communication technology to create a situation where the core enterprise can expand or contract production in relation to market demand for their goods. This is done through affiliation with a network of subcontractors and a flexible labour force that is employed on a project or contract basis instead of being permanent employees.

Similarly, new social movements and other political groups have adapted to the availability of communication technology and made their structures more internally flexible, in that they are able to use these technologies to do more with less. For example, the increased visibility which is afforded to political groups by digital technologies means that there is an increased arena for fundraising and less need for an army of 'on the street' canvassers to raise funds. The use of email lists, text messages, social networking sites, microblogging and other forms of networked communication also mean that organisations are able to speak directly to both fee-paying core members as well as more casual non-members, who may be motivated into action or contribution by a specific issue or an event in their local area. In other words, such movements and organisations have used the advantages of networking technology to transform from centralised bureaucratic structures dependent on large bodies of fee-paying members into a more fluid model of organisation.

External collaboration and coordination

On November 30, 1999, the World Trade Organization (WTO), an international body made up of the representatives of 153 countries and responsible for regulation (and liberalising) 95 per cent of the world's trade, held a ministerial conference in Seattle, USA. To protest what was seen by many as the WTO's global, neo-liberal economic agenda, diverse groups of environmentalists, labour organisations, religious groups, student groups and anarchists (among many others) decided to travel to Seattle to participate in a large-scale demonstration, with the aim of which would disrupting the meeting, making the mainstream news and convey an anti-globalisation, anti-WTO message to the world.

Planned months in advance through web sites, chat rooms and online bulletin boards, and organised on the day through wireless computers and mobile phones, the sophisticated organisation of the demonstrations and the sheer numbers of protesters achieved these aims by blocking downtown streets and tactically outmaneuvering police attempts to break protest lines. Apart from some incidents of vandalism, the protests were largely non-violent and consisted of street parties, rallies, teach-ins and other forms of awareness-raising. However, confusion and a general feeling of being overwhelmed meant that police in many cases used heavy handed tactics, such as pepper spray, rubber bullets and arresting people indiscriminately. The so called 'Battle in Seattle' is still seen as the pinnacle act of the anti-globalisation movement and brought the idea of network-enabled protesting and organisation into mainstream public view. Furthermore, the protest in Seattle was not the only protest on that day. Several other protests were orchestrated on the same day in other cities around the world.

The kind of coordination that took place in the WTO protests and in similar anti-globalisation demonstrations (such as the 'J18' 'carnival against capitalism' a year earlier) provide good examples of how collaboration and coordination of political activities between different groups is enhanced through the internet and other digital communication technologies. Again, much like Castells' networked enterprise, new social movements and activist groups are able to use communication technology to help them come together in an ad-hoc manner to achieve a specific goal or raise awareness of a specific issue:

> Creating the foundation for dramatic change, the internet has had a profound impact – in part by enabling organizers to quickly and easily arrange demonstrations and protests, worldwide if necessary. Individuals and groups now are able to establish dates, share experiences, accept responsibilities, arrange logistics, and initiate a myriad of other tasks that would have been impossible to manage readily and rapidly in the past. International protests and demonstrations can be organized for the same date and time, so that a series of protests take place in concert.
>
> [...] The methodology has been remarkable in terms of organization, especially because a central 'director' is not evident and, in part, the resulting lack of infighting has been the secret of success. Like the internet itself, the anti-globalist movement is a body that manages to survive and even thrive without a head. (CSIS, 2000: Paragraph 23–25)

This kind of networked collaboration through email, forums, chat rooms, bulletin boards and mobile phones has allowed disparate groups to productively work together to stage protests and raise awareness of issues. Despite being made up of autonomous organisations – often with different agendas and political perspectives – these groups are able to coordinate their efforts to protest for a common cause of concern.

In cases of direct action, such as the Seattle protests, online-enhanced coordination allows different groups to take on specific organisational roles to cope with logistical requirements such as the provision of food, communication, training in protest tactics, and legal advice. In effect, digital communication allowed groups and organisations from all over the world to share expertise and experiences so that the protest would have maximum impact (Chadwick, 2006; CSIS, 2000). In the case of Seattle, a working group called the Direct Action Network was established to oversee the construction of a temporary communication network comprised of mobile phones, wireless computers, radio devices, police scanners and laptops, which was used as a common resource for communication and organisation between groups. This included the monitoring of police activities and the live broadcast of unfolding events over the internet to aid publicity

(Chadwick, 2006: 127). This network proved to be essential to the outmanoeuvring of the police and creating maximum impact.

Flexible organisation and 'smart mobs'

> the combination of groups and participants coming together creates a powerful impression and an impact out of all proportion with their individual strengths. The melding of the various groups into one large body implies power, and attracts attention and publicity, which, in turn, draws more and more participants.
> (CSIS, 2000: paragraph 17)

The Seattle demonstration and other similar anti-globalisation protests in the late 1990s and early 2000s made an impact because those 'on the ground' were able to achieve a heightened level of awareness of their surroundings and coordination with others by being in constant communication with each other. As a result, they were able to operate with the same sort of coordination that one may see in a swarm of bees or a flock of birds. Rheingold (2002) refers to such group behaviour as 'smart mobs', where communication with others in mobile contexts allows individual actors to achieve tasks and awareness that are beyond their capacities as individuals, a sort of collective intelligence (see Chapter 3).

For Rheingold, the best example of the smart mob behaviour was the 'people power II' protests in the Philippines in January of 2001. This protest was in response to the collapse of an impeachment trial of the then president of the country, Joseph Estrada. In reaction to the collapse of the trial, as many as a million people, receiving instructions and forwarding messages through text messages on mobile phones, gathered in the main square of the capital, Manila. Such a large scale display of antipathy towards the president was one reason that he resigned four days later. In a somewhat similar mobile phone-based collaboration, in September 2000 an ad-hoc coalition of road hauliers, farmers, taxi drivers and other special interest groups organised a series of blockages of fuel depots around England to protest the high price and taxation of fuel. The blockades starved the country of fuel to the point where 90 per cent of petrol stations ran dry, and rolling blockades disrupted traffic flow in cities around the country (Dilley, 2000; Robinson, 2002).

Both actions created a massive impact for the public, and a crisis for governments. Such mobs or swarms have become more commonplace since 2001, with spontaneous political protests based on similar lines taking place in France, Chile and several former soviet republics (see Hermans, 2008), and most recently in the 2009 election protests in Iran.

Permanent political campaigns: linear collaboration

One potential criticism of single-issue politics aimed at media awareness is that such movements can create flashpoints of awareness around certain issues, which then fizzle out as publicity inevitably moves onto other media-friendly issues. In this respect, one could criticise ICT-enabled social movements as operating like marketing campaigns for consumer goods: simply creating a short-term 'buzz' around an issue in order to maximise a short-term gain when many political issues actually require long-term commitment and attention.

However, collaboration among movements and organisations on single issues has also led to the creation of permanent campaign networks (Bennett, 2004; Chadwick, 2006). In such networks, online collaboration and information gathering among groups is taken in turn to ensure the long term action is maintained after public awareness of the issue fades. This is achieved by the acceptance and handing over of responsibility for a campaign or issue to different groups at different stages of a particular campaign. For example, most campaigns will go through a series of stages, including defining and legitimising the issue, raising awareness, negotiating solutions and monitoring or institutionalising solutions.

In permanent political campaigns, organisations which have expertise or specialist knowledge related to certain stages may get involved until that stage of the campaign is completed, then hand over responsibility to another organisation to complete the next stage. As a result, a kind of linear collaboration among groups is achieved.

Bennet's (2004) and Carty's (2002) accounts of the anti-sweatshop movement's targeting of Nike provides a good example of this kind of linear collaboration. In the 1980s, Nike, among other corporations, stood accused by a number of NGOs and labour activists of using subcontractors in Asia who routinely abused rights and paid extremely low wages to workers. However, it was not until the mid 1990s when a group called *Global Exchange*, which had expertise in public relations and a large activist network, joined the anti-sweatshop movement that public awareness of the issue was raised. Global Exchange used their skills in awareness-raising to turn the anti-sweatshop movement into an issue of popular concern. Global Exchange ran a media savvy campaign using both old and new media and created enough adverse publicity for Nike that they eventually agreed to alter their subcontracting practices and open themselves up to independent monitoring of their labour relations. Global Exchange then moved on to other issues and new organisations stepped in to fulfil the monitoring role in making sure that Nike continues to honour its labour commitments.

An internet public sphere?

Another way in which digital technologies can be seen to potentially engage people with political matters is through the creation of a digital public sphere. The concept of the public sphere within contemporary social thought revolves primarily around Jürgen Habermas' work in *The Structural Transformation of the Public Sphere* (1989). A public sphere is that part of the social where citizens can exchange views on matters of importance to the common good, with the view that something approaching 'public opinion' can be formed with regard to issues, problems or political matters of the day. Habermas suggested that in the eighteenth century, with newly available mass printing techniques, a proliferation of newspapers and other forms of popular press and an unprecedented freedom of the press, the salons and coffee houses frequented by the bourgeois classes of northern Europe (particularly Great Britain) became the loci for a culture of reasoned critical debate of the political issues of the day. These debates were independent of state influence and fed into the privately owned popular press of the time. Thus, a 'public voice' was created that served as a foil to government, and a means of popular engagement for citizens on political matters.

For Habermas, the rules of a successful public sphere involved:

- A focus on rational and critical debate and the avoidance of emotion or emotive language in such debate.

- A focus on the content of statements, not the position or standing of the speaker.

- Equality of all participants so that status does not play a part in the debate.

- Freedom in matters of discussion in that any subject should be open for debate and any issue should be eligible for discussion.

- Freedom of assembly.

- Freedom of speech, expression and publication on matters of general interest.

- The intention to reach consensus within debate.

Habermas argued that the public sphere reached its zenith during the mid-nineteenth century. After this point, increasing government censorship of the press, the increasing commercialisation of media and the growth of private media oligopolies meant that by the mid-twentieth century the public sphere was tamed by large media corporations and the state (Chadwick, 2006). The lack of an inclusive and engaging public sphere is seen as one of the major symptoms of the current crisis of politics in liberal democracies today.

In this respect, ICTs and particularly the internet are seen as potentially contributing to the revitalisation of a political public sphere because of:

1 Increased access to political information to be used in rational debate and deliberation.

2 Increased accessibility and ease of publication, allowing people to not only consume, but also to produce, political discussion.

3 The potential for anonymity and thus equality of status among participants.

4 The almost complete freedom of speech and association, once again, aided by a degree of anonymity.

These features of internet technology together fill almost all of the conditions of a successful public sphere (apart from the requirements of 'reason over emotion' and 'intent towards consensus'). Indeed, there has been an explosion of political discourse on the internet through web pages, online forums and chat rooms, online news organisations and newspaper comments sections and political blogging. Together these create what Dakroury and Birdsall (2008) call a 'spaceless public sphere'.

Blogging in particular is seen by many writers as potentially a major contributor to the public sphere both in terms of political comment, but also as an alternative source of news and political information (Gunter et al., 2009; Wright, 2009). Such a public sphere has minimal censorship or restrictions on freedom of speech. As of 2007, there were an estimated 113 million internet blogs in existence, with 175,000 new ones being created every day (Dakroury and Birdsall, 2008). Within blogging alone this suggests unprecedented opportunity for individuals to contribute to the public sphere. This has become particularly important with regard to those under 40 – and younger people in particular – who tend to be the most disenfranchised from the mainstream political process and press. On the internet, younger people can use blogs and other forms of online 'DIY culture' as spaces for personal and political expression about social issues (Harris, 2008).

However, there are several important caveats. First, with the move away from mainstream media as a primary source of exposure to news and political debate and a move towards the multiplicity of the internet with its endless sources of news and different perspectives on events, there is a danger of what is termed 'selective exposure', in which information outlets are selected on the basis that they match the beliefs and predispositions of the audience member (Stroud, 2008). In other words, with the massive amount of choice on the internet, people are able to selectively expose themselves to a narrow range of information and ideas, chosen on the basis that they confirm or reinforce prejudices or beliefs. Sunstein (2001) refers to this practice within online forums as the 'echo chamber effect' in which one's views are simply mirrored and repeated back to oneself, meaning that no real discussion of contrasting ideas ever really takes place. Thus, the internet may be helping to create many 'publics' that have little engagement with, or exposure to, each other, as opposed to creating constructive debate.

Second, many would note that online discussion in many cases hardly follows the ideal of 'rational debate' (Chadwick, 2006; Poster, 2001). Instead, anonymity seems to afford more leeway for abusive language and bullying (flaming), pointless messages or intentionally provocative comments ('trolling' or 'thread jacking'), gossip and misinformation. This scenario is obviously not conducive to productive dialogue, nor the achievement of consensus (Norris, 2001; Van Dijk, 2006).

Third, it is important to point out that the web, by and large, is not a public resource or common, but is made up of the services that private companies provide to the public largely for free. Many of the politically-oriented blogs, forums and web pages are hosted on servers and sites that are owned and run by private corporations who provide these services in order to gain advertising revenue (for example, the service Blogger is owned by Google). Such companies have an implicit economic interest in providing facilities for more popular or mainstream groups and communities (to maximise advertising revenue) as opposed to marginalised or economically less valuable groups of people (Chadwick, 2006). They also have an interest in not offending their advertisers and, as such, may prefer to avoid or censor controversial points of view. So while in many respects the web provides unprecedented freedom as a public sphere, this freedom is tenuous and tied to the interests of the commercial organisations that provide the infrastructure for publication, debate and voice. It is, essentially, a public sphere in private hands that exists for the purposes of profit.

DIGITAL DISOBEDIENCE: ICT-BASED ACTIVISM

The Seattle WTO demonstrations did not only take place on the streets of Seattle and the other cities involved in the protest. On the day, all manner of internet attacks were directed against WTO web sites. A group called the *Electro-hippies Collective* launched a series of attacks to disable the WTO web site (Chadwick, 2006: 132) and a group called *RTMark* created a number of spoof WTO web sites which redirected traffic intended for the WTO to sites that critically parodied their mission and their objectives (Eagleton-Pierce, 2001). Similarly, in 1998 during the Zapatista conflict, a group called the *Electronic Disturbance Theatre* organised a protest in which roughly 10,000 people participated in a disabling virtual 'sit-in' of the web sites of the President of Mexico and the US 'Pentagon' (Eagleton-Pierce, 2001).

Traditional forms of civil disobedience and activism tended to target the physical structure of society through acts such as sit-ins in offices and public institutions, or the blocking of roadways (Wray, 1999). Indeed, one can think here of the famous photo of the blocking of the Tiananmen Square tank column by a lone protestor. The point of civil disobedience is to voice disapproval by interrupting the normal flow of operations of an organisation: to interfere with the status quo.

Being the principal infrastructure of the information age, it seems inevitable that the internet has and will become the means by which protests will be delivered and politically-minded disturbances will be created. Chadwick (2006: 130) has compiled a list of the types of electronic civil disobedience, or 'hacktivism', which are currently used:

- *Defacement*   Defacing web sites and changing their content. Essentially, this is cyber vandalism of an organisation or individual web page for political purposes.

- *Distributed denial of service (DDOS) attacks*   Action in an attempt is made to flood a network with requests for data from many computers at the same time, disabling the network of the target organisation. The group *Electronic Disturbance Theatre* created and released free online software called 'tactical floodnet', which performs this function.

- *Ping storms*   Similar to DDOS attacks, but a network is inundated with 'ping' requests that disable the system.

- *Email bombing*   Flooding an organisation's email system with thousands of messages, usually using some sort of automated system. The intent is to cripple an organisation's email system and shut down its internal communications.

- *Malicious code attacks*   Disabling an organisation's computers by releasing a virus or worm into the system.

- *Redirects*   Intercepting web traffic intended for a particular site by various methods in order to redirect the traffic to another site created by the demonstrator. A group called *The Yes Men* created and released the 'Reamweaver' software, which allows for the easy creation of spoof web sites. In fact, their spoof WTO web site was successful enough to fool some organisations into inviting members of *The Yes Men* to speak on behalf of the WTO at conferences around the world, thinking they were sending emails and invitations to the real WTO web site.

One could also add to this list the practice of 'Google-bombing', where search engine algorithms are taken advantage of in order to raise the ranking of a particular web page in conjunction with a particular search term or phrase. So, for example, the most famous Google-bomb was the 'miserable failure' bomb in which, when those terms were typed into Google, the web page of the biography of former US President George W. Bush was brought up as the most relevant hit. In 2007, Google changed its search algorithm to avoid Google-bombing but new techniques have since been found to continue the practice.

The above list can be boiled down to two broad categories of online civil disobedience or hacktivism in terms of intention and focus. First, there are infrastructural attacks in which the intention is the *targeting of the infrastructure* or communications of an organisation to disrupt their normal flow of activities. This is typified by DDOS attacks, ping storms, email bombs and malicious code attacks. Second, there are actions that focus on spreading a message, making a point or criticism through the *manipulation of an organisation's information or public face*. Defacement or vandalism is the most crude and obvious tactic, whereas redirecting, spoofing and parody are slightly more subtle forms of political comment.

Electronic civil disobedience actions thus far can be seen as minor inconveniences to the organisations involved. However, internet-based forms of protest may be potentially significant for future political action, given that the internet is quickly becoming the locus for the majority of mediated communication and culture. Thus, it is important to consider digital activism or hacktivism as a form of political action that may increase in importance in the information age. Indeed, this chapter will later discuss the notion of 'cyber warfare' from the perspective of infrastructural attack by state enemies.

ICTS AND MAINSTREAM POLITICS

Aside from the influence of ICTs on new social movements and sub-politics, potential innovations that have occured in mainstream electoral processes must also be considered.

In this arena, Chadwick (2006) suggests that there are three areas in which there is potential transformation:

1 Increasing party competition, notably by giving a higher profile to smaller or outsider parties in elections.

2 Increasing power diffusion through an increasing emphasis on, and engagement with, grassroots support.

3 Institutional adaptation, in which the democratic potential of the internet is tamed by its engagement with mainstream politics.

This section will consider these points briefly through the examples of the Dean and Obama presidential campaigns in the United States in 2004 and 2008.

One of the more powerful forces in mainstream party politics of liberal democracies is known as the *incumbency effect*. The incumbency effect is a situation in which the current elected official in office has an implicit advantage over any challenger, especially one from a smaller party or an independent candidate. As a result, the incumbency effect tends to reinforce the status quo in mainstream politics. Interestingly, since the proliferation of mass media and particularly television, the incumbency effect has increased substantially (Ansolabehere et al., 2005). As such, there is the general belief that mainstream mass media coverage of elections tends to pay more attention to those already in office (or at least candidates from established front-running parties), giving them a distinct advantage.

As a result, one of the potential advantages of the internet may be that it will aid in diluting the incumbency effect by increasing the media exposure and therefore the chances of smaller parties and outsider candidates in the political process. The last two American presidential elections provide some suggestive evidence that there may be some basis to these suggestions. The first case was the campaign of Democratic Party leadership candidate Howard Dean in 2004. Dean was a little-known politician who at one point had been the Governor of the small state of Vermont, and therefore entered the race to be Democratic Party presidential candidate as a rank outsider. Trippi (2004), Wolf (2004), Hindman (2005) and Chadwick (2006) all document how the Dean campaign's innovative use of the internet managed to turn around his fortunes and make him the frontrunner for most of the campaign, only losing out to John Kerry in the final stages.

The Dean campaign used blogging to establish a personal connection between Dean and voters. Feedback on the blog in turn influenced the candidate's policy stances, further solidifying this intimate link between Dean and would-be voters, helping to mobilise supporters to convince others to join the Dean campaign. In addition, the campaign strategy utilised social networking (an application based on meetup.com) to encourage supporters to hold meetings, events and parties in locations throughout America, adding a real sense of excitement and involvement in the campaign. These strategies succeeded in mobilising and gaining supporters and generated $40 million in fundraising for the Dean campaign, far more than other rivals who initially were seen to have substantially more support.

In the 2008 US presidential election Barack Obama entered the race for the Democratic Party presidential nominees not so much as a rank outsider, but as one of two potential rivals to front-runner Hilary Clinton. Aided considerably by a large internet campaign, Obama not only won the race to be the Democratic nominee, but then became the first major party presidential candidate in history to opt out of public funds for the financing of his campaign. At one point in January 2008, Obama raised $35 million over the internet in 36 hours, mostly from small individual contributions. Overall, the total of $1 billion raised was far more than the two presidential candidates in the 2004 US election put together were able to acquire.

The success of the Obama campaign was in part due to his campaign's use of the internet, which not only succeeded in attracting many contributions, but was used to communicate with voters as target markets. This allowed Obama to reach a broad range of Americans through a different mix of messages, emails, blogs and Twitter posts that were targeted at specific segments of the population. It proved to be a very cost-effective and profitable way of reaching the most voters possible and targeting them with the sort of messages that would appeal to voters' specific interests (Wilcox, 2008).

In the Dean and Obama examples, we can perhaps see a glimpse of how all three of Chadwick's suggestions for the potential impact of the internet on politics may pan out. Both campaigns demonstrate how grassroots campaigning and funding was mobilised through clever use of online culture; the Dean campaign certainly demonstrates how outsider candidates can achieve more publicity. Chadwick's third premise, that the democratic potential of the internet could be 'tamed' by mainstream politics, seems reasonable considering that both these candidates, although not frontrunners or incumbents, were from one of two dominating mainstream parties in American politics and the large amounts of funding generated was used to purchase mainstream media coverage.

Overall, the research concerning the effects of the internet on traditional politics has been mixed. After all, mainstream candidates with more financial backing also have the ability to create web pages and internet-based campaigns. For example, Dányi and Galácz (2005), in their analysis of European parliament elections in Hungary, suggest that the internet seemed to reinforce existing power relations in the media, essentially enhancing the incumbency effect.

It will take some time before mainstream politics fully embraces the potential of the internet. Given their privileged place in mainstream mass media, traditional parties in many respects have no real impetus to create a more substantial online political culture. It is clear, however, that the internet has become an increasingly important source for political information for voters, but while the successes of the Obama and Dean campaign to a certain extent demonstrate that outsider's chances and grassroots involvement can be enhanced, it is important to remember that that these successes still involved candidates from mainstream parties.

CYBER POLITICS BY ANOTHER MEANS: CYBER WARFARE

> Nations make war the same way they make wealth. (Cebrowski and Garstka, 1998)

The concept of 'cyber war' or 'information warfare' became part of academic, military, and then popular media discourse in the late 1990s. The rationale behind cyber war is that, as the economies, infrastructures, cultural transmissions and even military capabilities of advanced industrial nations become more and more integrated into, and dependent upon, the internet and other ICTs, the more likely it is that ICT infrastructures could become targets for attack (or themselves used in attacks) by foreign nations or enemy organisations. In that sense, cyber war was deemed as a reasonable – but theoretical – risk to advanced, information age nations.

It must be noted that the discussions revolving around cyber warfare are hampered in two ways. First, the concept itself is often ill-defined, or conflated with other actions (such as internet embezzlement or commercial espionage) that really could be considered 'cybercrime'. Second, the degree of potential risk, number and seriousness of actual incidents, and the scale of activities are largely unknown or classified and are thus open to exaggeration by government security agencies looking for funding, cyber-security firms looking to drum up business, and the media looking for a sensational story.

After a wave of interest that peaked just after the millennium, cyber warfare has returned to the agenda in more recent years, as this potential risk has begun to manifest itself in actual incidents. While many of these incidents are still clouded in secrecy and rumour, some have gained notoriety and have been acknowledged by public officials. A selection of noteworthy incidents include:

- 'Moonlight maze': that in 1999 hackers, suspected to be from the Russian Academy of Sciences, hacked into American Naval networks and obtained large amounts of data, including important naval codes and passwords.

- 'Eligible receiver': a 'no notice' security exercise conducted by the US Pentagon in 1997, in which 35 hackers were given the task of infiltrating defence networks, concentrating on the US Pacific theatre of military operations. Instructed to only use hacking tools readily available on the internet, these hackers were able to (virtually) cripple the US Military's command and control capability for the Pacific, as well as unexpectedly access both public and private critical infrastructure (Verton, 2003).

- In 2006, intruders hacked into the US State Department's networks and downloaded 'terabytes' of classified information. The intruders' identity and location remain unknown, but it is considered a major security breach.

- In May, 2007 and August, 2008, Estonian and Georgian government networks were hacked and disrupted. The assailants were suspected to be Russian hackers, as both nations were having conflicts with Russia at the time.

- In November 2008, the US military 'Centcom' network was breached, giving unknown individuals almost complete access to US military communications and operations in Iraq and Afghanistan for several days. It is suspected that access was gained through the placing of corrupted USB memory sticks in the complex by spies, which were then picked up and used by military staff and infected military computers with malware.

- In March 2009, Canadian researchers uncovered a large cyberspy network of malware-infected host computers called 'ghostnet', which included Embassies and other locations in 103 different countries. Researchers conclude that the malware originated in China, although the Chinese government denied this.

Cyber warfare is often defined as an assault on electronic communication networks. However, this definition is simultaneously both too broad and too narrow. It is too broad in the sense that it is generic in terms of the word 'assault', and thus there is no consideration of motive, intent, or origin. Cyber war actions are politically motivated and originate from rival states, terrorist groups, or state enemies. Without this consideration, cyber war and cybercrime[1] become indistinguishable, and yet it would seem clear that 'cybercrime' as a set of behaviours is distinguished by the motives of financial gain, mischief, deviance, or a non-politically motivated desire to inflict harm on others.

The definition is also too narrow in that it is focussed exclusively on 'offensive' operations and assaults, not on the use of ICTs in organisational capacities, or in attempts to corrupt or obtain information. Cyber warfare refers to a wide range of activities (offensive, defensive and organisational) and, therefore, in the rest of this section, I will discuss the different situations that can be considered, 'cyber warfare'.

Cyber warfare as network-centric warfare

Network-centric warfare can be considered the organisation and conduct of military operations on network-related principles (Cebrowski and Garstka, 1998). It is sometimes also referred to as 'netwar' (Arquilla and Ronfeldt, 1993, 2001). In many respects, it can be seen as the application of many principles of Castells' 'network enterprise' to the conduct of war. Traditional 'modern' warfare, inspired by and enabled through mass production or industrial configurations, possessed a number of features, including:

- Dependence on a very strict hierarchical organisation with top-down chains of command and communication moving from well-informed command units to much less well-informed front-line troops.

- Large massing of opposing forces engaging in 'set piece' battles and direct confrontation.

- A nature of conflict dependent on the incremental acquisition and control over territory or space through the advancements or retreats of 'front lines' or zones of conflict.

Such a style of warfare is perhaps best epitomised in World War I trench warfare, where large masses of infantry resolutely defended their front-line territorial positions through the digging of vast trenches, which ran parallel to the opposing army. These were broken only by the occasional large scale push forward by troops and tanks to overrun the enemy, to advance the front line.

By contrast, network-centric warfare derives its power from the strong networking of well-informed but geographically dispersed forces (Cebrowski and Garstka, 1998). Much like the networked enterprise, network-centric warfare relies on the heavy use of communication technology to create decentralised networks of units or troops. Advanced communications allows individual units more information and overall awareness and, therefore, autonomy. According to Cebrowski and Garstka, network-centric warfare has the features of *speed of command* and *self-synchronisation*. Speed of command refers to the advantage gained over the enemy by the superior use of communication and information. Self-synchronisation is the ability of a well-informed force to organise and synchronise complex warfare activities through bottom-up, as opposed to top-down, processes. This is reminiscent of Rheingold's 'smart mob' and swarming behaviour.

Similarly to the networked enterprise, a network orientation in military tactics creates a different orientation to space. Like Castells' space of flows, the arena of operations becomes much less based on territory and place, and more on nodes or flashpoints of attack. In other words, battle is less tied to a 'front line' in space, but instead can occur almost anywhere. Take, for example, the a-spatial nature of Al Qaeda (or sympathetic) operations, occurring in Kenya, New York, London, Madrid, Bali and other places, which demonstrates that there is no 'front line' in such a conflict.

As Delanda (1991) and Arquilla and Ronfeldt (1993) suggest, such a-spatial, geographically dispersed attacks are more akin to the military tactics of nomadic peoples such as the Mongol armies of Genghis Kahn, which depended on highly mobile, autonomous units and their ability to simultaneously strike from all directions at designated points. This contrasts the military strategies of sedentary agricultural (and later industrial) powers that became nation-states, who relied more on defensive fortifications of territory.

Cyber warfare as information warfare

Information warfare has been defined as 'actions intended to protect, exploit, corrupt, deny or destroy information or information resources to achieve a significant advantage, objective, or victory over and adversary' (Alger, 1996: 12). It is essentially the attempt to gain an informational advantage over one's rival. Cronin and Crawford (1999) suggest that information war revolves around three targets:

- The targeting of *physical assets*, in which the goal is to physically destroy an enemy's communication systems using conventional weapons, so that an adversary's command structure cannot communicate with its own troops, or to the general public, thereby hampering their ability to organise effectively.

- The targeting of the information itself, as opposed to the physical communications infrastructure, also known as *soft assets*. Here the goal is to surreptitiously block, manipulate, or destroy information that is useful to one's adversary. This can be done, for example, through hacking into communication networks and implanting malicious software, or false information.

- The targeting of *psychic assets* (i.e., the morale of troops and citizens) through the shaping of perceptions and the sowing of uncertainty. This can be done through different forms of propaganda, the takeover of mass communications, the hacking and defacement of enemy web sites and the spreading of rumours.

Cyber warfare as espionage

One of the more interesting and increasingly popular forms of cyber war involves the ability to use a dependence on digital ICT systems within advanced military and commercial organisations not to destroy capabilities, but as an inroad to espionage. Of the recent major cyber war incidents listed above, those in 2006, 2008 and 2009 were of this nature. Such attacks have two goals. First, attacks directed at military and commercial organisations are often attempts to steal advanced technology designs that can then be used to advance one's own military capabilities. Second, some attacks are not designed to have an immediate result, but have as their purpose to create a latent capability for information warfare in the future, through the embedding of malicious software such as trojans and other forms of spyware, which allow the capability for an adversary to spy on or disable an advarsary's communication in the future, should conflict arise. Many Western nations feel as though this has been a tactic used in particular by the Chinese military, and has been a source of some protest, although such accusations are hard to prove and are flatly denied by the Chinese government.

Cyber warfare as economic sabotage

One of the main reasons that the World Trade Center in New York City was targeted by Al Qaeda was because of the important role that it played in the economy of the United States. Al Qaeda operatives surmised that its destruction would send shockwaves through the economy of the United States and the rest of the capitalist world.[2] Whether successful or not, such an event is demonstrative of the belief that attacking key economic sites, such as stock exchanges and banks, is one way to cause damage to an enemy. As such, many see a latent potential for internet-based attacks intended to disable stock markets and flows of money.

Cyber warfare as critical infrastructure attack

For many writers such as Lewis (2006), Verton (2003) and others in the popular press, the primary concern in cyber warfare is the risk of a *critical infrastructure attack*. This is an offensive operation that targets and attempts to disable key areas of a nation's infrastructure: power grids, water supplies, air traffic control systems, emergency service communications, nuclear facilities and the like.

One of the main concerns is that many key infrastructures, such as power and water, are run via SCADA (Supervisory Control and Data Acquisition) systems. SCADA systems provide automated control and remote human monitoring of real world processes and are traditionally used by utility companies and industries in the areas of oil and natural gas, electric power, rail transportation, water and waste. While providing massive efficiencies, SCADA systems are seen by some as particularly vulnerable to attack because they allow for the remote manipulation of processes through secured internet linkages. If such systems were compromised, some fear that, for example, power grids could be disabled, drinking water could be poisoned and even nuclear facilities could be encouraged to meltdown, leading to severe loss of life, as well as the disruption of other infrastructures such as air traffic control or emergency services. Many refer to such an incident as a looming 'electronic Pearl Harbour'. This, of course, hasn't happened yet, and many argue that it is unlikely to ever happen. In that respect, critical infrastructure attack is more of a *potential* risk than an *actual* one, but proponents point towards two incidents that are seen as illustrative of the potential risk:

- In March 1997, a teenager managed to hack his way into a telephone company computer in Worcester, Massachusetts. Unbeknownst to him, this computer serviced the local Worcester airport. Telephone service to the airport control tower, security, emergency services and other departments were disabled for over six hours, ultimately causing a ripple effect in air traffic across the entire country.

- In 1992, a former employee for the Chevron petroleum company hacked into company computers and disabled a plant alert system. The system was thus unable to notify Chevron staff of a release of noxious chemicals into the air out of their Richmond, California facility. (Taylor et al., 2006)

The fear is that if such damage can be caused by teenagers inadvertently, or disgruntled employees, then a concerted effort by a team of experts, with all the resources of a foreign power, could produce potentially catastrophic effects.

Adjunct attacks

A last component of cyber warfare is the use of the above methods in combination with conventional terrorist or enemy attacks in order to magnify damage or loss of life (Taylor et al., 2006). For example, if one were to combine a conventional bomb detonated in an urban area, with a concerted virtual attack that disabled emergency communication infrastructures, a scenario could be created in which fire fighting services and medical teams would be severely hampered in completing their tasks, creating confusion and amplifying damage, loss of life and the psychological effect of the incident.

CONCLUSION: NETWORKS AND POWER

One of the fundamental premises of the liberating potential of networked ICTs rests on the assertion that a decentralised communication system invariably distributes power, by decentralising power to the nodes (or individuals) in that network. However, the relationship between power and networks is more complicated than this simple formula would suggest. Indeed, as the internet has become a major part of everyday work, leisure, social and political life, it has typically become enmeshed within these enduring structures of our society. This in itself is significant, as some suggest that in fact, it is within the sphere of everyday life in which the most meaningful struggles between authority, domination and freedom are played out (Lefebvre, 2000). Others have suggested that the push towards the use of different forms of information technology are, like the rise of bureaucracy in the early twentieth century, part of a revolution (of sorts) aiming towards an overall and pervasive increase in economic and social control (Beninger, 1986).

Van Dijk (2000, 2006) has argued that ICTs both spread and concentrate politics in the network society. On the one hand, institutional political forces (particularly governments of nation-states) have to give up power to corporations, supra-national bodies and transnational organisations to operate within the context of globalisation. As the infrastructural backbone of globalisation, networks have no frontiers (i.e., they are a-spatial) and can usually bypass the jurisdictions of state governments. This implies less power for governments. At the same time, as we saw in the previous chapter, networks embody the potential for increased registration, information gathering and surveillance of citizens (and workers), and can strengthen the power of bureaucracies and civil service institutions. Thus, power can be *further* concentrated through the increased collection of information, or it can be *diffused* by being distributed and decentralised to ever more autonomous nodes (or individuals) in a given network.

This power dialectic of the information age is also present in the highly influential (and controversial) work of Hardt and Negri's *Empire* (2000) and *Multitude* (2005). 'Empire' reflects the hegemonic forces of globalisation as a new form of decentralised, supra-national domination through global capitalism, which is built upon the foundation of the globally-networked informational economy. The 'multitude' is the resistance to this global domination through the re-appropriation of the productive capacities of labour in the information age into a weapon of liberation from these oppressive forces. Hardt and Negri suggest that within the form of global informational domination (one could say, its infrastructure) are the very seeds of its own destruction: six billion increasingly networked people that, through their technological connectedness, can be turned into a force of global democracy:

> The hybridization of human and machine is no longer a pro-
> cess that takes place only at the margins of society; rather, it is
> a fundamental episode at the center of the constitution of the
> multitude and its power. (Hardt and Negri, 2000: 405)

Both Van Dijk and Hardt and Negri (and the examples discussed in this chapter) demonstrate that information technology, just like any technological advance, has many potentials, utopian and dystopian. Its Janus-faced nature is not necessarily just about 'which path' a new technology will lead us down, but also about the possibility of several paths being followed at the same time.

One can see this Janus-faced nature in an event such as the 2003 anti-war protests. On 13 February, 2003, in a demonstration of global proportions, millions of people in hundreds of cities around the world gathered to protest the impending invasion of Iraq by the United States and its allies. Not only was this the largest coordinated demonstration that the world has ever seen, but several individual cities, including Rome, London and Madrid, had over one million people take to the streets, the largest protests ever seen in those cities (Bennett et al., 2008: 69). This event became what it was through the use of the internet, and in that sense is an excellent example of the actions of *the multitude* in Hardt and Negri terms. However, an American-led coalition still invaded Iraq in 2003 and, at the time of writing this book (2009), the war is still ongoing.

The examples in this chapter, of anti-globalisation protests, anti-sweatshop campaigns, text-message revolutions, cyber sit-ins, smart mobs and hacktivism also demonstrate how the networked, informational multitude can succeed against Hardt and Negri's 'empire' using the same technology that underpins the success of global capitalism. However, as the problem of selective exposure suggests, *networked* publics are often also *fragmented* publics. Fragmented publics in many respects are easier to ignore, and it is more difficult to get the attention of everyone (either through disturbance or through a message) in a public sphere that is fragmented (see Lessig, 1999). In that respect, digital political action is still not as effective as strikes, protests or riots in the real space of cities.

FURTHER READING

A very good, knowledgeable and detailed account of both the context of political change, and the use of ICTs in politics is Chadwick (2006). Norris (2001) is useful for a discussion of the use of ICTs to enable citizenship and political participation, and Castells (1996) provides a decent overall contextual discussion, and in particular is useful for relating trends in politics to the network society concept. Barney (2004) also does this well. More specifically, Rheingold (2002) is a popular account of new forms of networked organisation resulting from mobile technologies (smart mobs). Dakroury and Birdsall

(2008) provide a good discussion of the political nature of blogging, and Stroud (2008) is a good introduction to the notion of 'selective exposure'. Last, Arquilla and Ronfeldt (2001) provides probably the most interesting set of discussions relating to cyber war.

NOTES

1 One may note here that there is no prolonged discussion of 'cybercrime' in this book. This is because many of the techniques of cybercrime are already dealt with in discussions of political action, or cyber warfare. There are a number of excellent books on the issue of cybercrime, including Yar (2006), Jewkes and Yar (2009), and Taylor et al. (2005).
2 Indeed, there was a short-term impact, stock prices fell, the US dollar declined in value, oil prices rose, but this is now seen to have been a temporary shock, with the attack creating little long term financial impact outside the airline industry (Makinen, 2002).

7

DIGITAL IDENTITY

> I am therefore, precisely speaking, only a thing which thinks, that is to say, a mind, understanding, or a reason, terms whose significance was hitherto unknown to me. I am, however, a real thing and really existing; but what thing? I have already said it: a thing which thinks. (Descartes, 1968 [1637]: 105)

> The hypermediated self is a network of affiliations which are constantly shifting. It is the self of newsgroups and email. (Bolter and Grusin, 2000: 232)

The two quotes above occupy two completely different worlds when it comes to discussions of 'identity' or 'the self'. The first passage by Descartes, begins from what would seem to be the most certain of philosophical positions: that the one thing that can be relied upon and that is beyond doubt, is the disembodied self as a thinking entity:

> But now I come back imperceptibly to the point I sought; for, since it is now known to me that, properly speaking, we perceive bodies only by the understanding which is in us, and not by the imagination, or the senses, and that we do not perceive them through seeing them or touching them but only because we conceive them in thought … (Descartes, 1968[1637]: 112)

Descartes' proposition of radical scepticism, that all things are in doubt apart from the existence of one's own thinking mind and that all else emanates from this one certainty, was the cornerstone in a Western cultural tradition that still emphasises the notion of 'mind/body dualism', where the 'mind' or 'self' is seen as inherently separated from the material world around it, including the body. Since the existence of the mind is the one thing that can be counted upon in an otherwise contingent material world, implicit within this view is the further assumption that this disembodied self must be a consistent, stable, (hopefully) rational, entity.

The tradition of what Gergen (1996) and many others refer to as psychological essentialism in Western culture can be traced back even further to the ancient Greek philosophers such as Aristotle – who argued the superiority of 'mental life' – and Plato, who suggested that it was essences or 'pure forms', not the substances of the material world, which possessed the highest level of reality and that things in nature, including humans, were imperfect versions of such ideal concepts. An example of a 'pure form' would be a perfect circle. No one has ever seen one, but it exists as an ideal form, of which all circles in the material world are pale imitations.

The essentialist tradition solidifies further within the heritage of Judeo-Christianity, which emphasises the notion of the disembodied soul as the location of personness, the centre of healing and the recipient of everlasting life. Within Enlightenment philosophy, and as typified by Descartes above, the notion of the 'soul' is replaced by the notion of the non-material 'mind' as a rational and consistent entity within an irrational and variable material world open to suspicion. The Romantic period challenged the notion of rationality by exploring the significance of passions, drives and urges within the human experience, but still maintained the tradition that assumed an inner life that was, in many respects, more important or substantial than the outer material world (Gergen, 1996).

As Turkel (1999) suggests, the normal requirements of everyday life exert strong pressure on people to see themselves as consistent, unitary actors who must take responsibility for their actions. Indeed, a good portion of people, within Western culture at least, would still firmly identify with statements such as 'I am who I am', 'I was born the way I am', or that there is a 'real me' and 'this "me" inside me doesn't change'. So ingrained in us are these fundamental assumptions of personhood that to challenge them often seems threatening or insulting. After all, the ideal principles of Western society of democracy and freedom are based on the presumption of a civil society built of rational persons with the capacity and responsibility to exercise their individual will and power of choice.

However, by the 1980s and the 1990s, these essentialist modes of thinking were being challenged on the academic front by poststructural and postmodern theories that had emanated from France in the late 1960s and early 1970s through such authors as Barthes, Derrida, Lacan, Foucault, and Deleuze and Guattari. These theorists focussed on the primacy of language in the understanding of the world and of ourselves. Derrida, for example, deconstructed the notion of the self and made the point that identity is something that is always a temporary and unstable effect of relations constructed through marking differences. That is, identity is constructed, and always based on, excluding something, thereby establishing a kind of violent hierarchy between two resultant polls, such as man/woman, or black/white. In order to have an identity of 'man', for example, a negative/opposite identity of 'woman' needs to be created (Hall, 1990).

Lacan, influenced by Derrida, decentred the notion of the self by and arguing that there is no 'ego' at the centre of the self. He portrayed the self as based completely in language. Children, for example, have no sense of self before they acquire language but, as they acquire language, they acquire self-consciousness. In that respect, the self can be said to be seated within a realm of discourses, emerging externally not internally. Foucault follows a similar line, suggesting that identities as categories are constructed within discourses that are produced in specific historical contexts and by institutions with particular practices. So identities emerge from the exercise of power, in which some groups are created and then marked our as 'different' and can therefore be treated in specific ways. These categories of identity emerge and change over time, they are continually in construction, not fixed or essential categories of 'being'. For example, Foucault famously investigated such discursive practices in the historical formation of identities as 'criminal', 'homosexual' and 'insane'.

Identities are thus seen to be contingent upon time and place, and as much about exclusion and domination as they are about unity. People, for their part, embrace identities they see as positive and both embrace and contest identities seen as negative that are ascribed to them.

To sum up, the influential work of Barthes, Lacan, Derrida, Foucault, and Deleuze and Guattari challenged (and still challenges) more essentialist notions of identity by suggesting that:

- Identity is constructed, originating and being maintained in relational processes and through the application of power and the labelling of difference or otherness.

- Identity originates (externally) in language (not internally) and is maintained internally and externally through discourses and discursive practices.

- Identities are historically and geographically contingent, and thus change within different contexts and circumstances.

- As a result, identities are not unified, solid and stable, but maintained, changeable and often contradictory.

This leads Hall (1990) to suggest that the term 'identity' itself is problematic, and the more accurate way of describing processes of self awareness is through the term 'identification', which is more useful for characterising the processes, multiplicities, contradictions and the general 'work' involved in constructing and maintaining identities (see also Bell, 2001). This seems to be a reasonable view, especially within the context of digital culture.

I have set out this rather long introduction in this way because what I intend to do in the rest of this chapter is examine digital identity though a narrative. With the groundwork of the essentialist vs the poststructuralist (or social constructionist) view of identity laid, I would like to tell a story that relates various theories of identity with different forms of self-representation available in digital media as they have risen into prominence within digital culture of the last quarter century. I am following this strategy because different forms of self-presentation and identity construction made available online over time lend themselves to certain theories of identity, which have then been espoused in literature on digital culture. This follows a similar sentiment provided by Zygmunt Bauman:

> I suggest that the spectacular ride of 'identity discourse' can tell us more about the present-day state of human society than its conceptual or analytical results have told us thus far.
> (Bauman, 2001a: 121)

Thus, this chapter will start with a discussion of the poststructuralist turn in early work on the decentred nature of online identity and conclude with the suggestion that identity is now becoming 're-centred' as the internet has moved into a popular mass medium. It will also engage with 'cybersex' as a case of an online identity practice.

'OBJECTS TO THINK WITH': EARLY INTERNET STUDIES AND POSTSTRUCTURALISM

In 1996, Sherry Turkel published *Life on the Screen: Identity in the Age of the Internet.* This was an ambitious text, which dealt with subjects such as artificial intelligence, the relationship between humans and computer interfaces and the 'reality' of online life. However, it made most of its impact in the ethnographic research Turkel conducted in 'Multi-User Domains' (MUDs), which were essentially online text-based chat rooms that often had a fantasy-oriented theme, frequently inspired by the face-to-face role-playing game Dungeons and Dragons.

Within the MUDs, Turkel found that MUDders, herself included, engaged in a significant amount of identity play (for example, the popular MUD *LambdaMoo* had ten genders from which to choose for one's persona) and invested a lot into the particular online personas they had created:

> 'You can be whoever you want to be. You can completely redefine yourself if you want. You can be the opposite sex. You can be more talkative. You can be less talkative. Whatever. You can just be whoever you want, really, whoever you have the capacity to be. You don't have to worry about the slots other people put you in as much. It's easier to change the way people perceive you, because all they've got is what you show them. They don't look at your body and make assumptions. They don't hear your accent and make assumptions. All they see is your words.' (Interview quote from Turkel, 1996: 184)

Not only were MUDders able to 'be whatever they want' by reinventing themselves through an online identity, but they would often reinvent themselves through several online identities. Turkel used the metaphor of 'windows' to describe this practice of switching between contexts and identities in everyday life, where each window on the computer screen represents a different context, set of relations and potential identity, to be called up or minimised at different points. Some of these windows will pertain to the online world of MUDs and some to the offline world. This was a view expressed by many writers at the time, including Bolter and Grusin (2000: 232): 'When we run a multimedia program on our desktop computer, each windowed space ... offers us a different mediation of the subject'.

Indeed, Turkel's work was representative of a larger body of work investigating online culture at the time. Key theorists and texts such as Rheingold (1993), Stone (1995), and Poster (1995) all pointed to MUDs and other types of online interactions to demonstrate the large amount of identity play that was occurring within what was at the time, the new, exciting and mysterious phenomenon that was the internet. This was generally seen as resulting from four aspects of online environments:

1   The degree of anonymity that is possible in online environments creates a freedom not attainable in the offline world.

2   That a person can perform whatever identity one chooses, because online identities are based primarily on self-descriptive text that can be crafted in any manner desired by the user.

3   That multiple selves can be explored in parallel, creating an environment of identity shifting, hybridity and fluidity.

4   That identities can be created that are impossible in offline worlds.

The rising notoriety of the internet in the popular imagination as well as in academic discourse throughout the 1990s corresponded with the explosion of academic debate around identity. The humanities and the social sciences were firmly ensconced in a 'postmodern turn', brought about by the growing popularity of poststructuralist authors such as those mentioned above. Within this context, sentiments such as 'MUDs make possible the creation of an identity so fluid and multiple that it strains the limits of the notion' (Turkel, 1996: 241) were very consistent with the prevailing grain of academic thinking at the time.

Indeed, Turkel thoughtfully suggested that the advent of the online world had the potential to illustrate poststructuralism to a wider public audience. Across several writings, Turkel (1996, 1999) described MUDs and other online arenas as 'objects to think with'. Using her own experience as a postgraduate student in the late 1960s and 1970s, she suggested that her 'French lessons' in poststructuralist concepts of identity remained largely lost on her because these concepts were too abstract to speak to her own (or most other people's) experience in a society that emphasises stable, unified identities. In her encounter of MUDs, these theories that emphasised fluid, decentred identities finally came alive for her and, as result, Turkel suggested that MUDs and other online arenas were the 'objects' that would be able to demonstrate within common sense terms the validity of poststructuralist conceptions of identity: MUDs thus become 'objects to think with' for thinking about postmodern selves (Turkel, 1996: 185).

Gergen (1996) went further to suggest that the profusion of technologies such as the internet have an impact on how selves are constructed and maintained. Technology exposes us to more people, more cultures and increasingly varied understandings of the world. It offers us the opportunities of varied contexts which, when combined with anonymity, freedom of self expression, the ability to lead parallel lives (and introduce a quality of imagination into those lives), creates conditions that are increasingly untenable for the notion of a stable, centred self.

What happened in the early internet studies of the 1990s was a convergence between the prevailing academic discourse at the time, and an emerging technology interpreted within this context as supporting a particular point of view. In this case, authors of the day were emphasising the 'liberation from meat' (Bell, 2001) that cyberspace promised, by having identity constructions that were *disembodied* and, therefore, free from the typical bodily/discursive markers of gender, race, disability and class that tends to mark out 'others' in society.

This 'libertarianism' (Slater, 2002) was probably best articulated in the works of techno or cyber-feminism, which drew heavily on poststructuralism and the work of Judith Butler (1990, 1993). Butler used the work of both Foucault and Derrida to suggest that gender is performative in the sense that the qualities which we associate with a particular gender (and generally see as 'natural' qualities) are indeed not fixed or natural, but collectively created and constructed through social interaction and regulative discourses. People are obliged and expected to demonstrate or perform their gender identity on a daily basis.

In this respect, more attention has been focussed on gender in digital culture or cyberspace discussions than on race. This problem was addressed directly by Kolko et al. (2000) and Fernandez (2002), and a number of studies that have looked at online ethnic and racial identities (for example Parker and Song, 2006) but, nonetheless, the social constructionist platform within online culture has in its majority been built upon cyberfeminism.

Cyberfeminist and technofeminist authors such as Haraway (1991), Stone (1995), Wajcman (1991, 2004) and Plant (1997) saw in the use of the internet and other emerging communication technologies, the practical realisation of the deconstruction of the notion of 'natural', 'real', or 'authentic' (gender) identities based in the body, in favour of the notion of *performance* (Slater, 2002). Decentered, fragmented identities were seen as a liberation from a body-based subjugation of women, as well as ethnic and racial groups. Without a body-based 'identity', the online self could be seen as inherently transgendered (Stone, 1995) and therefore held the potential for the demise of patriarchal (as well as other) forms of oppression.

PERSONAL HOME PAGES AND THE 'RE-CENTRING' OF THE INDIVIDUAL

By the late 1990s, as the novelty of the internet started to wane somewhat, more academic work began to surface that moved away from seeing 'cyberspace' and online identities as separate realms of existence from the material world. There was a move towards exploring how internet use and notions of identity were constructed, which incorporated both online and offline life. Barry Wellman (1997), for example, argued that, at the time, too many academics ignored the fact that:

> People bring into their online interactions such baggage as their gender, stage in the life cycle, cultural milieu, socioeconomic status, and offline connections with others. (Wellman, 1997, cited in Baym, 2002: 67)

The general tone amongst many writing about digital culture in the later part of the 1990s was that there was little evidence to suggest that gender swapping, deception and vast amounts of identity play was the purview of more than a minority of internet users, and thus not typical of mainstream internet activity (Baym, 2002; Slater, 2002).[1] Some even went so far as to suggest that the claims made in the writings of Stone, Turkel and others were sensationalist in nature, and

> runs the risk of marginalising the social study of computing by making it appear fantastic and unrelated to practical projects that could in fact benefit from a social perspective. (Wynn and Katz, 1997: 299)

Often, these studies and writings were a purposeful response to the poststructuralist and postmodern arguments implicitly and explicitly promoted in studies of MUDs and other online text-based environments that emphasised decentred, disembodied and fragmented identities. Sometimes these attacks could be considered openly hostile in nature (for example, Stanley, 2001) and were a manifestation of a larger attack in sociology more generally on certain aspects of postmodernism and poststructuralism.

To counter the examples of fragmented and fluid identity performance in MUDs, many of these studies looked at another web phenomenon that by the late 1990s, was becoming more popular: the personal home page (for examples see Chan, 2000; Schau and Gilly, 2003; Walker, 2000; Wynn and Katz, 1997). Unlike MUDs and chat rooms, which were almost completely text-based, personal home pages incorporated text and image (usually photographs), as well as links to other web pages. They were also much less interactive in nature, in that they were not just conversations (as MUDs basically were), but fashioned web documents with a certain amount of longevity and consistency imposed by a creator.

In contrast to the poststructural leanings of Turkel, Stone and similar authors, most of these studies started from a different theoretical perspective. Although avowedly social constructionist as well, these authors tended to follow the theoretical traditions of symbolic interactionism, phenomenology and ethnomethodology, influenced by authors such as Goffman, Simmel, Mead, Schutz, and Berger and Luckmann.

Perhaps the most complete account, and the most ambitious critique of online poststructuralism in this context, was Wynn and Katz (1997). They openly attacked the MUD-based work of Turkel, Stone and other poststructural and cyberfeminist authors on a number of grounds. On the theoretical front, they took issue with what they called 'deconstructive psychology' models of internet identity for not being based in social theory, but in psychoanalytic and literary theory. Wynn and Katz suggested that this made the deconstructivist argument overly individualistic and not able to properly take into account how identity and self is a group phenomenon and a product and process of social forces. For them, the legacy of symbolic interactionism already effectively demonstrated the notion of a fluid and changing self (and thus an anti-essentialist argument) by situating the self within interactional social contexts.

The difference for Wynn and Katz (informed also by Dreyfus (1972) and his influential Heidegger-based discussion of the impossibility of meaningful artificial intelligence) was that identity, instead of being something inherently and *intrinsically* multiple and fragmented – which is in turn coalesced under the force of discourses and discursive regulation (as the deconstructionists argued) – is *extrinsically* based. That is, they suggested that everyday life is fragmented and multiple in terms of the demands that it makes upon people in different contexts, and that subjects actually work from within to create some sense of a coherent self and identity among a number of different roles, interests and preferences. They argue that personal web pages perform just this function.

Through the empirical example of personal web pages, Wynn and Katz suggested that 'identity' was still indeed grounded in embodied, offline life and that web users generally had a desire to maintain a coherent sense of identity in the online sphere. Rather than portraying a decentred, fragmented, disembodied self, personal home pages are actually attempts at identity integration by demonstrating to others what is important to the individual: 'an attempt to pull together a cohesive presentation of self across eclectic social contexts in which individuals participate' (Wynn and Katz, 1997: 324).

This notion of 'self presentation' is prevalent in much of the work on personal home pages in this period (see Chan, 2000; Schau and Gilly, 2003; Walker, 2000; Wynn and Katz, 1997). This belies a large influence of the work of Erving Goffman (1959, 1975). For Goffman, identity is a contextually related personal and social front that is negotiated in face-to-face encounters, with the goal of presenting oneself as an acceptable person. Goffman's approach is seen as *dramaturgical* in the sense that self-presentation involves a performance of self in front of a particular set of observers, in which there are 'fronts', or public faces where fashioned selves are presented, and 'back' regions or more private contexts where the performance is able to be dropped to a certain extent. This performance will vary among different sets of observers and in that sense, everyday life is made up of different types of role playing within different contexts or 'frames'.

With a Goffman-informed perspective, studies of personal web pages and other internet phenomena such as online dating (Ellison et al., 2006), can easily demonstrate how such sites are ways of integrating the self and both online and offline concerns using new communication resources at hand. Whether these personal web pages happen to be oriented to relationships outside the internet (what Walker, (2000) calls *extrinsic* pages) or ones that are primarily concentrated on cultivating online relationships and personas (what Walker calls *intrinsic* pages), personal web sites are not examples of the free floating fragmented identities depicted in MUDs, but instead are situated in networks of online interaction at least, and usually within offline relationships, identities and affiliations as well.

From this point of view, Wynn and Katz also attack the assumption of (and indeed the preference for) anonymity on the internet as the basis for a liberating environment of identity play. They argue that:

- Anonymous identity play in MUD studies has demonstrated, at best, that such efforts are a way of working out real 'offline' issues, and is ultimately unsatisfactory as a mode of social interaction or social change.

- Anonymity is not the desire of mainstream internet users, who usually integrate aspects of offline life into online identities.

- Anonymity is not really possible to any great degree in online environments. People tend to use cues such as style and grammar to make assumptions about others in terms of education, class, gender. Furthermore, the internet itself is a panoptic technology where anonymity is more under threat than in regular, offline daily life (see Chapter 5).

Overall, Wynn and Katz suggest that the poststructuralist/deconstructivist online research represented by Turkel and Stone depends upon the imposition of a number of false distinctions, between the social and the technical, between the real and the virtual, between the public and the private. All of these are inconsistent with the technology and how it is actively used by the majority of people in everyday life contexts, which tend to blur these distinctions.

The critique of online deconstructionism and the study of MUDs, as represented here by symbolic interactionist studies of personal web pages, certainly provides much food for thought. As we will see, their suggestion that selves were 're-centred' in personal web pages was somewhat prophetic with the later advent and popularity of blogging and social networking. However, it may be fair to say that these studies of web pages repeat the same mistakes levelled at Turkel and Stone. It is entirely reasonable to suggest that excessive identity play within MUDs was a minority activity. However, it is equally fair to point out that the proportion of net users who had their own personal web page in, say, 1998, was also rather small and could not be considered a mainstream internet activity. Indeed, if we take a historical perspective, two points can be made.

First, in terms of the technology, the research conducted by Turkel, Stone and others on MUDs took place at a point in time when the internet was very basic in terms of the environment it could create for its users. Because of bandwidth and memory limitations, it was almost completely made up of text. In that sense, it is not really comparable with the digital environment of the late 1990s, when convergence was starting to take place and when it became possible to include pictures of one's offline life, family and interests. It seems only natural that as the internet became more image-based that offline and 'meat' issues became more prominent, incorporating more of offline life into online identities. This becomes a more important point later on in this chapter.

Second, the explosion of popularity of the internet in the latter part of the 1990s and the demographic effect it had on who were using it, and for what purpose, has to be considered. Reliable demographic information about internet use is difficult to obtain, especially for the 1990s, but to take two examples, the *Computer Industry Almanac* (2006), which has been creating reports since 1990, report that in 1990 the United States had 7.2 internet users per 1000 population (not even one per cent). This number rose to 105 per thousand (or 10.5 per cent) in 1995, and to 476 (or 47.7 per cent) in the year 2000, a massive increase to say the least.

Moreover, if we look at more detailed demographic data from the Graphic Visualisation and Usability Centre's early surveys of internet users (1998), particularly comparing their third survey in 1995, to their tenth survey in 1998, massive demographic changes in internet users is evident. In 1995, the survey showed a four-to-one ratio of men to women, an average age of 35.1 years, a high average income of $69,000, and 55.1 per cent of respondents occupationally involved with the higher education sector (as either students or staff), or from computer related fields. The tenth survey in 1998, just three years later, showed 36 per cent of respondents as women, an increased average age of 37.6 years, a decreased average income of $57,300, and only 34.8 per cent of respondents involved in either higher education or in computer related employment. It is clear that there is already, by 1998, a massive widening of participation and increasing diversity in the types of people using the web. It would be reasonable to assume that as the population of internet users gets older and less concentrated on the education sector, that there will be a smaller proportion of users who are likely to engage in large amounts of identity play and experimentation.

In conclusion, while it might be reasonable to suggest that early MUD-based work on internet identity was perhaps a bit sensational and even a tad technologically fetishist, it should be noted that such studies were, at least in part, a product of their time and technological circumstances as much as they were the products of a particular deconstructionist outlook and political project. The phenomena fit the theory, in the same way that personal web pages later on provided a persuasive counter-example to the decentred identity claims of MUD research. This trend in the saga of digital identity continues as we move on to discuss the phenomena of blogging and then social networking, which emerged as a popular form after the millennium.

PERSONAL BLOGGING, INDIVIDUALISATION AND THE REFLEXIVE PROJECT OF THE SELF

> It is made clear that self-identity, as a coherent phenomenon, presumes a narrative: the narrative of the self is made explicit. Keeping a journal, and working through an autobiography, are central recommendations for sustaining an integrated sense of self …
>
> Yet autobiography – particularly in the broad sense of an interpretative self-history produced by the individual concerned, whether written down or not is actually at the core of self-identity in modern social life. Like any other formalised narrative, it is something that has to be worked at, and calls for creative input as a matter of course. (Giddens, 1991: 76)

The word 'blog' itself (as a contraction of 'web-log') was coined in 1997 and the phenomenon of blogging had its origins among the technologically minded in the late 1990s, who started to compile frequently updated lists and thematic links to interesting or noteworthy web sites. Blogs were popularised by the development of easy-to-use net-based software in 1999 (Pitas and Blogger). The popularity of blogs increased further because of two major political events (9/11 and the invasion of Iraq), which resulted in both a demand for accounts of these events outside mainstream media and a forum to voice opposition to government policies (Carl, 2003). Blogging as a popular phenomenon peaked around 2004/2005, when personal journal blogging was adopted wholeheartedly by youth culture in the developed world. Blogs in particular have been lauded for greatly the expanding the accessibility for the 'average' person to publish on the internet, resulting in an explosion of online content. Many internet observers and academics pointed positively to the revolution in journalism, the democratic potential, and the potential for self expression, communication and communitarianism that blogs embodied.

There are, of course, many types of blogs, but the personal journal blog, a form of often intimate diary writing on the internet, emerged as the next wave of online identity research (see Hevern, 2004; Huffaker and Calvert, 2005; MacDougal, 2005; McCullagh, 2008; Rak, 2005; Schmidt, 2007). While some of this research continued in the deconstructionist tradition (Rak, 2005, for example) and some continued in the symbolic interactionist perspective (MacDougal, 2005), many chose to examine the blogging phenomena from the point of view of the individualisation thesis popularised by Bauman, Beck, and Giddens (Hodkinson, 2007; Hodkinson and Lincoln, 2008; McCulloch, 2008; Miller, 2008; Schmidt, 2007).

In general, individualisation refers to a process in which communities and personal relationships, social forms and commitments are less bound by history, place and tradition. That is, individuals, freed from the contexts of tradition, history, and under globalisation, space, are free to, and perhaps forced to, actively construct their own biographies and social bonds. Due to the increasingly disembedded nature of late modern life, a major task of the individual is to continually rebuild and maintain social bonds, making individualisation by its nature non-linear, open ended and highly ambivalent (Beck and Beck-Gernsheim, 2002). Within this context of disembeddedness, consumer society offers up to the subject a range of choices from which to create biographies and narratives of the self, in addition to a set of relationships that can be seen as somewhat ephemeral or tenuous (Bauman, 2001b): 'I see the praxis of digital culture as an expression of individualization, postnationalism, and globalization' (Deuze, 2006: 64).

According to Giddens (1991), in an environment of disembedding and de-traditionalisation, the subject is 'unshackled' from predetermined life narratives such as class, religion, location and gender, which used to be more determinate in terms of life choices than they are today. This is a kind of double-edged freedom that enables individuals to have a relatively enhanced capacity to reshape and restyle their identities (though still limited by external discursive practices) through a panopoly of lifestyle and consumer choices. Thus, identity becomes a 'reflexive project', a job that is undertaken that must be continually worked on and thought about. The self, for Giddens, is a person's understanding of their own narrative, which they attempt to shape in desirable ways. The struggle to build an identity and create a sense of belonging then gets acted upon through the engagement with consumer culture, an association with brands, types of music and material possessions in order to achieve affinity with others.

In The *Transformation of Intimacy* (1992), Giddens moves on to discuss individualisation within the context of human relationships. He argued that in a context of disembeddedness, trust and security becomes of paramount importance. For Giddens trust, like the 'reflexive project of the self', is something that must be continually worked at. As a result,

Giddens argued that the late modern social milieu has led to a rise of 'pure' relationships: a social relationship entered into for what can be derived from the other. Such relationships are seen as voluntary – and therefore contingent – and have an intimacy based on the trust of mutual reflexivity and self-disclosure (see the case study on p. 176).

One aspect that is particularly relevant to blogging is the assertion that self-disclosure becomes increasingly important as a means to gain trust and achieve authentic (but contingent) relationships with others. Giddens argues that late modern subjects gravitate towards relationships that engender trust through constant communication and reflexive practice. In other words, we crave relationships that allow us to open up to others, and not just in the romantic sense, because in late modernity, the demand for intimacy becomes part of an overall project of self realisation.

In sum, the sociological context of blogging as far as the individualisation thesis is concerned rests on three premises:

1   A general context of social disembeddedness.

2   A need to create and sustain a self-narrative and to present that to others.

3   A need to establish trust, intimacy and understanding in an uncertain world through communication and acts of self-disclosure.

In this regard the internet in general and blogging in particular is seen as the ideal environment – largely because of its potential anonymity and lack of accountability – for pervasive self-disclosure and relationship building. The desire to tell one's life narrative to the world, to write about one's personal experiences of, for example, emotional pain, or one's opinions on world events through a kind of chronological public diary sits quite easily in a contemporary society in which compulsive intimacy has become a major way to overcome disembeddedness and work towards self-realisation. Furthermore, the creation of identity narratives through *bricolage*, the assembling of a number of different artefacts representing a range of interests (such as pictures, texts, sounds, consumer brands) that together are used to create an overall identity impression on blogging sites, leads some to suggest that online journals can be seen as 'virtual bedrooms' for youth who use blogs to carve out a personal space and exhibit their identities on the web (Hodkinson and Lincoln, 2008).

SOCIAL NETWORKS, PROFILES AND NETWORKED IDENTITY

> Our societies are increasingly structured around a bipolar opposition between the net and the self. (Castells, 1996: 3)

Networks cannot be discussed without returning to the work of Manuel Castells in *The Rise of the Network Society* (1996) and *The Power of Identity* (1997). Castells, as intimated by the passage above, sees an antagonistic relationship between 'identity' and the network society. Indeed, Castells views contemporary identity construction as a reaction to the faceless, placeless, anonymous aspects of the network society such as globalisation, timeless time and the space of flows (see Chapter 2). Identity becomes a response to the threat of the homogeneity of globalisation and the concurrent reduction of peculiarity and uniqueness in the world, and thus Castells argues that in the network society, identity becomes a tool of political mobilisation and resistance. This characterisation of the relationship between networks and identity by Castells is somewhat surprising, given the overall thesis in *The Rise of the Network Society*. It could be expected that an argument suggesting how identities in an age of ICTs would become increasingly embedded in networks would be more consistent and plausible.

In the discussion above on personal journal blogs, the point was made that the phenomenon of blogging could be seen as an overt attempt to construct and display a coherent identity narrative as part of the reflexive project of the self. However, constructing a narrative is not particularly meaningful when done in isolation. There is a difference between, for example, the classic (analog) personal diary that is not intended to have an audience outside the writer, and an online personal journal or blog, which has a potential audience and an interactive relationship with that audience. As Somers (1994) suggests:

> The chief characteristic of [identity] narrative is that it renders understanding only by *connecting* (however unstably) parts to a constructed *configuration* or a *social network* of relationships … composed of symbolic, institutional and material practices. (Somers, 1994: 616)

For Somers, the narrative construction of identity is both relational and networked and has to be located within spatial and temporal configurations and cultural practices (Somers, 1994: 625). In its own way, the blog demonstrated this through links to other bloggers and membership in blogging circles, even though it was the text of the personal narrative that was generally emphasised. By 2004, the popularity of the blog within online culture started to be supplanted by Social Networking Web sites (SNWs) such as Friendster, Myspace, Facebook, Orkut and many others. These sites pushed the networking element of 'friends' or contacts into the forefront at the expense of textual content (Miller, 2008). The social networking profile has its roots in a combination of business networking sites (such as LinkedIn and Ryse), dating web sites and blogs. Today, sites such as Myspace, Facebook, Orkut and Flickr are among the most visited destinations on the web.

Within the narrative of this chapter, the rise of social networking profiles continues the move towards the re-centring of online identity within embodied, online life. As many articles have demonstrated, social networking profiles, much like online dating profiles, narrow the gap between multiple (or ideal) selves sometimes depicted in anonymous contexts, and selves that are grounded within corporeal daily life. In dating sites, the representation of self is usually grounded by the possibility of meeting online contacts in an offline setting, with the ambition of a romantic relationship (Ellison et al., 2006; Hardey, 2002). In social networking sites, the self representing profile is grounded within the context of offline friends and contacts (Boyd, 2006; Boyd and Heer, 2006; Zhao et al., 2008), as well as in photographs, in what has developed into a highly image oriented medium (Strano, 2008).

An interesting point made by Zhao et al. (2008), in their analysis of identity construction on Facebook, is the move towards more implicit identity statements in social networking profiles. They suggest that there are three modes of identity construction apparent on Facebook:

1 The visual self or 'self as social actor', which is demonstrated through peer photographs and aimed at implicit identity claims. The aim is to generate desired impressions of self by 'showing without telling' the extent and depth of social ties.

2 The cultural self, which displays consumption and lifestyle tastes and preferences through photographs and lists in an act of self-definition by consumerist proxy.

3 Explicit descriptions of self, for instance, in 'about me' sections. For Zhao et al., this was the least elaborated of the three identity strategies on Facebook profiles.

The interesting thing here is that the defining characteristic of the blog – the explicit description of the self – is the least elaborated strategy on social networking profiles. These profiles instead infer identity statements by relationally situating the self among a network of social contacts and a set of relations to consumer culture, what Liu (2007) calls 'taste performances'. In effect, the identity statement emerges from the constellation of friendship networks and consumerist associations (see also Boyd and Heer, 2006).

In this regard, it may be useful to bring into consideration the concept of the 'situated self' as elaborated by Ismael (2007). For Ismael, the self is a reflexive representation in a continual cycle of self-location and relocation. In other words, the self continually maps itself egocentrically through representation and the creation of locational context. The social networking profile can be seen as one obvious attempt at an egocentric mapping of the self through the relational context of friends, images and consumer tastes.

Situatedness and the metaphor of 'mapping' allows us to consider the social networking profile (and the microblog) within the under-theorised context of mobile technologies. Van den Berg (2009) thoughtfully attempts to consider the notion of *situatedness* and how this has changed in an environment of almost ubiquitous mobile communication, suggesting that the self is becoming centred in a 'distributed presence', maintained by the variety of fixed and mobile communication technologies available. She argues, from a Goffmanesque perspective, that networked information technologies complicate the notion of 'framing' or 'definition' of a particular situation, since a distributed presence means that a person could potentially be involved in several frames or performances at the same time, thus having to continually switch back and forth between frames (this, in a way, brings us back to Turkel's 'windows' metaphor discussed above).

However, one could argue that the effect is the opposite. Instead of continually mixing frames the combination of social networking, especially when involving mobile technologies and pervasive communication (such as microblogging), actually centres the subject even further by mixing frames and blending the diversity of contacts of one's life from a variety of roles and contexts (friends from varied parts and times of life, family members, business associates). There are plenty of examples in the popular press where people have lost their jobs or been suspended from school or university as a result of what they have said (or the kinds of photos displayed) on their social networking profile. It would seem that in these cases, the mixing of performance or identity 'frames' has served to demonstrate how subjects are becoming increasingly policed into more consistent identities by way of a kind of social networking panopticon that demands more consistency in represented identities across many different, sometimes incompatible, contexts.

AVATAR AND IDENTITY

> Every time someone makes an avatar they create a portrait, though it may be little to do with who one is in the real world. But this is nothing new for portraits – portraits have always been combinations of realism and the techniques artists use to communicate the subject's personality. (Meadows, 2008: 106)

The trend thus far discussed in this chapter is towards a centring of identity (both in terms of online identity, but also in the centring of offline and online identities) as the internet has become more image-based, and more oriented towards online/offline social networking. However, the increasing importance of the image in online identity construction and representation is not just confined to the more pragmatic world of social networking. The characteristics of identity have also changed within later generations of online fantasy worlds, more akin to the MUDs discussed at the beginning of this chapter. On the one hand, online worlds such as *World of Warcraft, Everquest, Second Life, Star Wars Galaxies* and *Second Life* are like MUDs in that they are predominantly anonymous online environments, as well as being fantasy-oriented worlds where there is great potential for identity and gender play. On the other hand, instead of text-based self description, characters in contemporary online worlds achieve an identity through the construction of avatars: their visual appearance, their skills and aptitude in the given environment and their social interaction (Lister et al., 2009). An avatar can be defined as 'an interactive social representation of a user' (Meadows, 2008: 13).

In this discussion of 'avatar and identity', there is the potential to return full circle to the phenomenon of MUDs, in terms of the fragmented, decentred postmodern subject as epitomised in the work of Turkel or Stone. Some, such as Jones (2006) see avatar identity in Massively Multiplayer Online Role Playing Games (MMORPG's) and other online worlds very much in these terms. However, there is a larger body of work which argues that the task-oriented nature of these games determines a certain consistency of character that largely works against such fragmentation (Blinka, 2008; Boellstorff, 2008; Chee et al., 2006; Duchenaut and Moore, 2004; Wolfendale, 2007, for examples).

Ambitions such as 'levelling up' (i.e., creating a more powerful character with gameplay experience), acquisition of wealth and power, building a house, acquiring consumer items, becoming more socially popular, are all explicit and implicit goals for players within all types of these worlds, and such ambitions encourage character longevity and identity consistency.

This drive towards consistency is also a function of both intentional and unintentional game design. It is very difficult to engage in, for example, the combat and purposeful exploration involved in fantasy-themed MMORPGs such as *World of Warcraft*, or the less purposeful exploration, chatting and socialising of *Second Life*, successfully, while operating two or more characters at the same time. In addition, game designers often actively prevent players from using multiple avatars at the same time by restricting one login per computer. This prevention of multi-character play is based on the assumption from game designers that too much identity fragmentation in terms of multiple use of avatars harms the building of trust, relationships and community, a necessary part to successful game play (Ducheneaut and Moore, 2004). In this respect, Turkel's (1996) 'windows' metaphor is not applicable to the sorts of identity performances that occur in graphical online worlds.

The preference for consistent identities is seen by players as important for establishing reputations and social contacts, which are a major part of the enjoyment of game play. For example, Krzywinska's (2007: 109) ethnography of *World of Warcraft* notes:

> Many players with greater experience are often more likely to group with people with whom they have played regularly … Most players will add people to the player-generated friends list when they have grouped with another player with whom they feel some sort of affinity.

Similarly, Boellstroff (2008) in his ethnographic study of *Second life*, finds this to be the case even in less task oriented social worlds:

> When I first started, I alternated between two main avatars, and was planning on making more, but since I started actually meeting and hanging out with some people, I haven't really changed my basic look … I started having static relationships and wanted to remain a single entity. (Interview quote from Boellstroff, 2008: 129–130)

Thus, similarly to social networking web sites, the network of friendships on MMORPGs performs the function of situating the avatar identity within a relational network of others. Contacts with others, membership in groups (especially elite groups or 'guilds') creates a context in which the identity of the avatar emerges from a situation.

It must be pointed out that this does not necessarily mean that players have only one online identity. In fact the use of 'alts' or alternative identities is very common. However, given the logistics of game play, these 'alts' are not used simultaneously, but are alternated with the use of the primary character identity or avatar. Research suggests that the use of 'alts' does not conform with free form identity play, but are instead normally used in pragmatic ways to accomplish certain tasks:

- Within fantasy oriented role playing games, 'alts' are used to explore different aspects of the game through different characterisations (for example, to experience the online world as a 'cleric' as opposed to a 'warrior' or a female as opposed to a male) (Duchenaut and Moore, 2004).

- Also typically within fantasy-oriented games, 'alts' are often used in conjunction with other characters to assist in game play success. So for example, if one's 'warrior' becomes wounded, a player will often bring in another character, such as a cleric, who can heal the primary character (Bucheneaut and Moore, 2004).

- In *Second Life*, Boellstroff (2008) notes how many players have 'alts' on reserve for times when they want to accomplish certain tasks, like building, without interruption or social obligations. The anonymous 'alts' allows someone to log on and get things done within a site, without other friends knowing that the person associated with the primary avatar is online.

It seems clear that in the majority, excessive decentred avatar identity play is not compatible with the ambitions or appeal of online worlds. Avatars establish reputations, relationships, and complete short and long term tasks. That is their reason for being. For Chee et al. (2006), this kind of pragmatic outlook is characteristic of the relationship between players and their avatars. They see the avatar/player relationship not so much as representations of self or identification with self. Their interview-based research suggests that *Everquest* players see avatars as tools for accomplishing tasks and the ambitions of the player: social and game-oriented. Wolfendale (2007) similarly suggests that the attachment that people feel towards their avatars is based on what the avatar provides for the player. So while the attachment is real, and even emotional, it is not seen as a reflection of the self but more like a character that one has grown fond of, which might have some aspects of oneself in it. This could be compared with the attachment that people feel towards characters in books or films, or the attachment an author has towards a character he/she has created, or an actor's attachment and engagement with a particular role being performed.

This also seems to be the case, among adult players at least, in research conducted by Blinka (2008), who suggested three types of identity relationships among players and avatars:

1. *Identification* with avatars, where there is a unity expressed between players and avatars. This is rare but more common in adolescent gamers.

2. An *independent status* between player and avatar, where the avatar is seen in terms of its capacity as a game tool, most common among adult players.

3. Avatars as *compensation*, in the sense that the avatar is seen as a kind of idealistic projection of some of the qualities of the player.

This third factor, that avatars can be considered idealised or 'truer' reflections of the player, seems fairly supported in much of the quantitative-based literature (see Bessière et al., 2007; Taylor, 2002; Vasalou et al., 2008). In this sense, there is an expressed link between avatars and offline identity: avatar characters include aspects of offline identity, but realise them in a more idealised form online:

> I am not suggesting that identity is always fixed or indeed 'hard wired', but rather that one of the pleasures of playing games such as *World of Warcraft* might be located in the 'shoring up' of a player's existing identity rather than changing it in any profound sense... (Krzywinska, 2007: 114)

Case Study: Cybersex, Online Intimacy and the Self

Sex appeal is fifty per cent what you've got and fifty per cent what people think you've got. (*Sophia Loren*)

Cybersex has been defined as '...a social interaction between at least two persons who are exchanging real-time digital messages in order to become sexually aroused and satisfied' (Döring, 2000: 863). Basically, cybersex is a sexually-charged computer-mediated personal interaction in which the parties in question are seeking arousal and satisfaction. Thus, it is not merely a conversation about sex, but a form of sexual encounter (Döring, 2000: 864) that has several novel qualities:

- The participants may be completely anonymous to each other.

- The participants will not be co-present in physical space, but are telepresent with each other through the use of real-time digital communication (chat, text, email).

- The sexual encounter, and the relationship more generally, takes place entirely within the virtual space or the imaginations of the participants.

However, far from being a unique phenomenon to the internet, sexually-related activities and eroticism associated with cybersex have typically gone hand-in-hand with technological advances in communication. As Hearn (2006) suggests, ICTs are part of a broader set of trends involving the increasing publicisation of sexualities and technologies of the senses. The inventions of the telephone (and even the telegraph) brought about the idea of remote, real-time erotic chat with others epitomised in 'call girls', and telephone sex services (Hearn, 2006), and currently manifest in controversies over mobile phone 'sexting' in which people exchange erotic text and photos through mobile phone SMS services (for example, see CBS, 2009). In that respect, there has always been a clear link between new communication technologies and eroticism.

The notion of online intimacy or cybersex raises a number of interesting questions about identity and the relationship of online or virtual behaviour to the offline world. As suggested in Chapter 1, the virtual can be considered 'real but not actual' (Shields, 2003). When cybersex is limited to online interaction, it remains in the virtual, and takes on a degree of simulation as the sex act revolves around idealisations and imaginative scenarios that will never be actual.

More recent developments further enhance the simulative nature of online sexual behaviour. In virtual worlds such as *Second Life*, the exchange of text-based sexual chat is supplemented by graphic sexual imagery using avatars that simulate sex. Indeed, *Second Life* has a thriving sexual culture and a wide diversity of sexual subcultures, with two of the largest being 'Furries' and 'Goreans'. The former follow a theme of animal-human hybrids and the latter a theme of hyper-masculine male domination (Boellstorff, 2008; Meadows, 2008). Virtual prostitution has also made a notable presence (Boellstorff, 2008; Wagner, 2007).

In a slightly more wholesome context, the Chinese phenomenon of 'Web Marriage' sites expands the simulation to encompass relationships, marriage, home building and children (McLaren, 2007). Less sexually-oriented, but definitely romantic, web marriage provides an online forum for young Chinese adults to participate in the adult practices of courting, relationship building, marriage and family building with anonymous virtual partners. Many of these virtual relationships last over a year or even several years (McLaren, 2007).

This study will demonstrate how cybersex emerges from a set of late-modern cultural attitudes towards identity, sex and relationships, and how these attitudes have combined with technology to create a new kind of sexual interaction, which may in the long run challenge current cultural norms.

The late-modern context of love and intimacy

In *The Transformation of Intimacy* (1992), Anthony Giddens suggests that romantic relationships have undergone a series of transformations within Western culture from pre-modern, to romantic, to pure or confluent love. Beginning at the mid-twentieth century, Giddens suggests that a cultural shift away from romantic love and towards 'pure' or 'confluent' love, has been taking place. Where romantic love is generally seen as a fated, lifetime commitment towards a 'true love' or a 'soul-mate', pure or confluent relationships – as we will see – are described by Giddens as based on the idea of 'choice' instead of 'fate'. They are seen as more contingent, rather than permanent, lifetime, 'til death do us part' relationships.

Giddens attributes this shift to two general processes, the first being the general framework of *detraditionalisation*. By detraditionalisation, Giddens is referring to the dis-embedding, increased life choices and greater potential number of life narratives offered up to individuals in the context of globalisation and late modern consumer culture (see Chapter 7). This freedom from traditional life narratives and plethora of lifestyles places the burden of identity construction on the individual in the form of the *reflexive project of the self*. These changes are perhaps even more profound for women, as improvements in contraceptive technology (separating sex from reproduction), greater legal and social acceptance of divorce and cohabitation, and feminist campaigns that pushed for equal rights for women in general, have all served to provide women with greater equality and more autonomy in romantic relationships as compared with the past.

In these contexts, Giddens suggests that the 'pure' relationship or confluent love is becoming the archetypal relationship of contemporary times. The pure relationship is:

- *Voluntary* in that commitment is contingent and open to change. Pure relationships are sought as part of a means of self-development. When relationships cease to be seen as useful or are seen as preventative to self-actualisation within the reflexive project of the self, they can be ended. This contrasts the lifelong commitment and 'for better or worse' expectation embodied in romantic love.

- Based on *equality* between parties, who are both expected – and expect – to benefit from the relationship.

- *Reflexive*, in that the relationship is not taken for granted but continually open to scrutiny and evaluation.

- Based on *intimacy*, which is achieved through constant communication (particularly expression of self and needs), and the gaining of knowledge of the other's intimate self. This in turn creates *mutual* trust.

The end result is that pure relationships are based on communication, equality and understanding, and in that sense can be seen as superior to previous forms of romantic relationship. However, the instrumental and contingent nature of confluent love does have its drawbacks, notably the 'until further notice' nature that creates insecurity in the individual as, essentially, the pure relationship is really about one's self and one's own self fulfilment. Giddens suggests this insecurity is manifested in rising rates of compulsive behaviour and addictions within contemporary society, such as additions to drugs, work, sex, as well as eating disorders.

Giddens suggests that sex becomes another tool or property to bring to the reflexive project of the self, becoming simultaneously a means of self-expression and a means towards achieving intimacy and self-disclosure with another. In this sense, sex becomes another way to evaluate a pure relationship and sexual fulfilment, as part of the overall attempt to construct a desirable self-narrative. Moving to the online sphere, Ross (2005) suggests that online sexual behaviour epitomises both Giddens' pure relationship and the reflexive project of the self. It demonstrates the ultimate removal of sex from reproduction, and thus leaves room for sex to be reflexively investigated as a property of the individual in the construction of a sexual identity.

Cybersex: a novel form of intimacy

Ben Ze'ev (2004) suggests that there are four main features that enable online intimacy and make it a novel form of relationship. First, there is *imagination*, in that since the situations are virtual, there are no practical limitations in how settings, scenarios, partners or even selves can be constructed. Thus it becomes extremely easy to idealise situations and people. Second, *interactivity* fosters reciprocity in communications, which both increases self disclosure and places fewer burdens on the actors involved. Third, *availability* suggests that online there is easy access to many available options, meaning that it is easy to find partners (among a large pool of prospects) and that they are continually available through ubiquity of internet and mobile communications. Last, *anonymity* reduces the risk of online activities when compared to offline risks. It decreases vulnerability and the weight of social norms upon behaviour. This makes it easier for people to act according to their desires, increasing self-disclosure and therefore intimacy and seductiveness.

For Ben Ze'ev, these features and contexts create a fundamentally new form of relationship whose feature is *detached attachment*: intimate closeness at a distance. Detached attachment consists of several seemingly contradictory elements that, in Ben Ze'ev's view, make it both appealing and problematic:

- *Distance* and *immediacy*: Temporal immediacy created through real-time and ubiquitous communication technologies can be achieved despite people being separated by physical distance. This creates an emotional immediacy and continued (tele)presence despite a lack of physical contact.

- *Lean and rich communication*: The mostly text-based interaction in online social environments is, on the one hand, a 'lean' form of communication in that it is one-dimensional, but this leanness also paradoxically encourages greater efforts of expression and perception, allowing a communicative richness that promotes intimacy.

- *Anonymity and self-disclosure*: The anonymity available online creates reduced feelings of vulnerability, often encouraging more open and honest communication. Where complete honesty, especially in terms of sexual matters, can sometimes be seen as threatening in real-life relationships, an environment of anonymity can encourage more honesty, and therefore intimacy. This is sometimes also called the 'online disinhibition effect' (Suler, 2004).

- *Continuity and discontinuity*: Online relationships are ultimately very tenuous. People can simply disappear and in that sense such relationships are discontinuous. At the same time, ubiquitous connection through ICTs can create an environment of continual presence in one another's lives.

- *Physical and mental investment*: Online relationships demand relatively little in terms of physical resources, but can demand a lot in terms of mental and emotional investment.

- *Distant relationships*: Online relationships often involve a yearning for circumstances that cannot be bought to bear or cannot exist. They instil a desire for ideal circumstances that are impossible. This gives them a quality of intensity involved with yearning, yet a distance related to the consumption of fantasy.

As a result of these factors, Ben Ze'ev suggests that online intimacy provides an easy and desirable alternative to the difficult circumstances of real life relationships. One can achieve maximum amounts of intimacy with a minimum amount of investment. The distance and potential anonymity allows for a forum in which experimentation and the taking on of different sexual persona allow a continual investigation of the sexual aspects of self, which is only encouraged by the lack of much social control and sexual regulation experienced in offline society. Perhaps most importantly, online intimacy and cybersex, because they normally rely on the exchange of descriptive texts signifying preferences, wants and desires, provides a milieu of reflexivity and self-disclosure intensely compatible with the late-modern need to achieve intimacy through constant communication with valued others.

Similarly, several feminist-inspired studies have also suggested that engaging in cybersex can enhance self-esteem and sexual satisfaction for women in particular by allowing them to engage in consequence-free exploration and expression in a way not possible generally for women offline (Allbright, 2008; Döring, 2000). Ben Ze'ev suggests that online sexual behaviour can be described as 'intrinsically valuable' (meaning sex simply for the pleasure of the act) as opposed to 'goal-oriented' (sex as a means of advancement, as part of a duty or relationship obligation, or as a means of reproduction). Thus, in online sex, people are more likely to treat each other as equal/willing partners engaging in a pleasurable experience, such that the experience can be more intimate and satisfying than in many instances of offline sex. Such sentiments lead some feminist scholars such as Döring (2000) to present cybersex behaviour as largely empowering, for women in particular, as a means of exploring their sexual identities free from the vulnerabilities associated with a patriarchal offline world.[2]

In terms of drawbacks, as some psychological studies will attest, one main concern is addiction or the supporting of obsessive behaviour patterns, especially in individuals who have had previous problems with addictions to sex or pornography. In these cases, cybersex can be a new form of compulsive behaviour, or cause a relapse of prior conditions. Relatedly, there is concern over the increased likelihood of risky sexual behaviour that can occur if behaviour transfers from the online to the offline world. In one study, Schneider (2000) (cited in Allbright, 2008) suggested that 80 per cent of women who engaged in online erotic chat migrated to real-life sex with an online partner (perhaps surprisingly, this contrasted with only 30 per cent of men). This suggests that there is perhaps an increased chance of putting oneself at risk through casual encounters. In addition, moral criticism may be focussed on how the availability of partners for online sexual encounters can be seen as a sexual 'marketplace', in which people are treated as 'off the shelf' consumable objects for gratification or identity experimentation, rendering such relationships as shallow, instrumental and inconsequential (Ross, 2005).

The morally ambiguous nature of online sexual behaviour can also be seen as problematic when it comes to issues of offline relationships. For participants involved in an offline relationship, cybersex is often not considered 'adultery', as it is not 'actual' cheating on a spouse. However, this is often not the opinion of the partners themselves. Indeed, the notion of 'infidelity' (i.e., a betrayal of trust) is often viewed even more seriously than the physical act of adultery or cheating because of the emotional intimacy involved (Ben Ze'ev, 2004; Mileham, 2004). In addition, because it falls into a moral grey area between the virtual and the actual, online sexual activity can easily lead to a 'slippery slope': from online flirting, to explicit sexual discussion, to virtual online sex, to 'actual' sexual encounters. Furthermore, the act of online infidelity can be destructive to the offline relationship both through the amount of emotional work and time involved in the online relationship, and the sexual energy and intimacy that is transferred from the offline relationship to the online one. In this respect, the mundane nature of everyday life in offline relationships can face tough competition from the hassle-free idealisation of online sexual encounters (Ben Ze'ev, 2004). As a result (although firm evidence is difficult), a number of sources suggest that roughly one-third of divorce litigation in the United States, for example, is linked to online infidelity (Infidelitycheck, 2002; Mileham, 2004).

This brings us full circle. If cybersex and online infidelity are contributing to the breakup of marriages and relationships, then such technologies would seem to be reinforcing the move towards more confluent or pure relationships and away from the permanence of romantic love. Indeed, the internet (both in terms of cybersex and in more traditional dating web sites) presents us with a whole world of choice of potential partners, and the ability to continually evaluate these virtual relationships against those in which we are currently involved.

CONCLUSION

This chapter has been as much a story about how different internet phenomena have lent themselves to different theoretical stances in terms of identity construction. Within this narrative, I have attempted to chart a wider move within digital culture from a point in the early 1990s when:

- Self representation was almost exclusively text-based.

- Online social environments were largely anonymous, or characterised as being such.

- There was seen to be little integration between 'online' and 'offline' spheres, which included the view that online identities were 'disembodied' and therefore free from embodied identity discourses.

Such an environment, as epitomised in MUDs, tended to support the poststructuralist view of identity as decentred, fragmented and multiple. Such environments were seen as illustrative of how identity is *performed* and not an *essential* quality. Two decades later, as we move into contemporary uses of the internet and other forms of digital communication technologies, we find:

- An online environment increasingly dominated by images and, in particular, self-representations (for example on social networking sites) based on images, particularly photographs, at the expense of textual self-description.

- Mainstream online social environments have become more 'nonymous' in that social networking profiles in particular have become tools to represent and aid 'offline' selves.

- As a result, there has been an integration of 'offline' and 'online' frames or lifeworlds in a way that leaves little room for identity play or decentred identities. Instead, there has been a centring of the online self within the embodied, offline self.

These factors point to the suggestion that within digital culture, the self has arguably become more centred and situated, as the demands of 'distributed presence' (Van den Berg, 2009) and ubiquitous communication afforded by mobile networking technologies have led to a mixing of different social contexts and the roles associated with them (what Goffman would call 'frames'), in a way that was generally not as prevalent before the advent of these technologies. This can be seen especially well in the diversity of friendship networks on social networking and microblogging profiles, where all manner of contacts, friends and family members from different contexts and stages of life are kept up to date through the use of static and mobile technologies.

Interestingly, the author Ben Elton (2007), in his satirical novel *Blind Faith*, describes a future in which a dictatorial theocratic government demands that the population continually update everything about themselves using 'Face Space', 'podcasts' and 'WorldTube' sites. Attempts at describing selves, things and events using words (as opposed to photographs and video) seem utterly pointless and indeed sinful acts of hubris:

> The Lord has blessed us with digital recording equipment with which we can capture, celebrate and worship in diamond detail the exactitude of every nuance of his creation and yet you, you in your vanity, think that your description, the world of your lowly, humble, inadequate imagination, can somehow do the job better! You believe your description, your fiction, to be a better medium for representing God's work than digitised reality! (Elton, 2007: 28)

Predictably, this is a world where privacy has become offensive, but more implicitly, this is also a world where the idea of identity performance becomes bound, through constant self-reporting and display to others of all aspects of life, to the consistent performance of one single, panoptically policed, centred identity acceptable to all.

FURTHER READING

For a deeper investigation into poststructuralist and (techno)feminist views of identity the work of Butler (1993), Haraway (1991) and Turkel's classic *Life on the Screen* (1996) are important texts. Wynn and Katz (1997) provide a very thorough and important critique of poststructuralist identity theory as related to internet use, as well as a good example of the symbolic interactionist perspective. Anthony Giddens' work on identity (1991) and intimacy (1992) is very influential in later studies of Web 2.0 and user-generated content. Ross (2005) adapts Giddens' theories well to the context of cybersex. Meadows' *I, Avatar* (2008) and Boellstorff's *Coming of Age in Second Life* (2008) are very interesting discussions of identity issues related to virtual worlds. Both also have interesting ethnographic accounts of cybersex in these arenas. Ben Ze'ev (2004) provides a very useful overall discussion of romantic relationships online.

NOTES

1   This claim, like the reverse claim, can be contested. Valkenberg et al. (2005), for example, conducted a quantitative study in which 50 per cent of their sample of adolescents had engaged in identity experimentation on the web.
2   Although some feminist scholars argue the opposite, that cybersex merely reinforces gender stereotypes and the idea of females as primarily sexual objects for men.

8

SOCIAL MEDIA AND THE PROBLEM OF COMMUNITY: SPACE, RELATIONSHIPS, NETWORKS

> In great cities men are brought together by the desire of gain. They are not in a state of cooperation, but of isolation, as to the making of fortunes; and for all the rest they are careless of neighbours. Christianity teaches us to love our neighbour as ourself; modern society acknowledges no neighbour. (Disraeli, 1845: 148)

As many sociological writers will attest, the term 'community' is one of the most fundamental concepts in sociological research, and at the same time perhaps the most ill-defined. The *Penguin Dictionary of Sociology* itself suggests that the terms is so elusive and vague that it is 'now largely without specific meaning' (Abercrombie et al., 2000: 64). By contrast, George Hillery (1955) famously came up with 94 specific definitions of the term. Thus, on the one hand, the term 'community' can be defined so specifically as to have little general value, at the same time wider definitions are often too broad to be meaningful. It is no wonder that sociologists have often poured scorn on the value of 'community' as a concept being able to say anything constructive or useful about the nature of society (Day, 2006: 1).

At the same time, community remains an important term. People want to be part of communities. Politicians, sociologists and journalists constantly tell us that our communities are 'breaking down' (and that something needs to be done about it) and, as we will see, techno-optimists see in online culture the rediscovery of community. In this respect, community is usually used to refer to some sort of ideal state of belonging that we have lost and need to recapture. It is often used as an ideal with which to contrast the present as somehow unsatisfactory.

It is therefore difficult to say exactly what constitutes a community. For some, the term applies to very specific forms of social groupings tied to a common place and mutual interdependence, while for others it can be applied to almost any form of social grouping. This chapter will examine the idea of 'community' as it relates to digital culture, but will set the advent of digital or virtual communities within the longstanding processes of change in the spatial scale of human relationships brought about by the use of technology under capitalist processes and the rise of individualism. It will then consider the pro's and con's of digital communities and consider the concept of the network as a more accurate depiction of relationships within late-modern society.

SEARCHING FOR LOST COMMUNITY: URBANISATION, SPACE AND SCALES OF EXPERIENCE

Classical sociology used 'community' as a way of describing 'group-ness' in contrast to conditions or feelings of isolation or *individualism* (Day, 2006). Indeed, early sociological thinkers often used the concept of community as part of a critique of the industrial revolution and the transformation from a traditional, rural agrarian society to a modern, urban, industrial one. This process was in full swing in northern European countries in the latter half of the nineteenth century, the time that sociology as a discipline arose.

Ferdinand Tönnies' (1955) concepts of *Gemeinschaft* and *Gesellschaft* were particularly foundational in forming the early sociological critique of industrial urban ways of living, as well as concepts of community (Day, 2006; Kumar, 1978). Gemeinschaft (commonly translated from German as 'community') was an abstract ideal 'way of being', which Tönnies suggested was most closely approached in the pre-modern rural village (Day, 2006). Gemeinschaft occurred in small-scale face-to-face contexts of spatial proximity where people were tied together on a number of levels:

- Through kinship and blood relation.

- Through mutual interdependence and multi-dimensional ties or associations where people have a number of different relationships with each other. So your next door neighbour might also be your butcher, friend and cousin, thus possessing family, business, social and locational ties.

- Through historical ties to the place and the land.

Gemeinschaft was characterised as 'organic' or 'natural' in that such interdependence, and the reality of frequent face-to-face contacts, meant that all of the people in a locality broadly shared a common fate and were therefore disposed to each other practically and emotionally.

Gesellschaft (translated as 'association') is the conceptual opposite of gemeinschaft. Gesellschaft refers to a context of individualised social action in which ties between people are rational and calculated, as opposed to natural and emotional. Gesellschaft relationships are based on things like choice, formal contracts and convenience, rather than kinship or mutual interdependence. Tönnies suggested that the large and growing industrial cities of his time (the late nineteenth century) encouraged these kinds of relationships because of the mobility of their populations, the larger spatial scales and the larger spheres of social interaction involved in living in modern industrial cities. The great numbers of people in cities means that face-to-face encounters with the same people in different contexts are relatively rare and, thus, relationships become more one-dimensional or specialised and less interdependent: your butcher is only your butcher.

Other early sociologists such as Engels, Durkheim, Weber, Simmel and Wirth similarly felt that the move to urban life had profound effects on people's sense of belonging and their interactions with each other. For example, Engels (1958) referred to the 'disintegration of society into individuals' in London, Weber (1978) suggested that short-term, immediate, ends-based relationships typical of interactions within city life were not as conducive to the generation of communal sentiments or belonging (Day, 2006; Domingues, 2000). Simmel in *The Metropolis and Mental Life* (1950) saw the over-stimulation of the senses in urban environments resulting in a common blasé attitude, a kind of mental distance used as an insulating layer that contributed towards individuality and at the same time creates a sense of isolation in the urban subject (Kumar, 1978: 71).

In an American context, Louis Wirth (1938) built upon Simmel's arguments to suggest that urban dwellers adopted a kind of relativism in their social relationships. Instead of having deep allegiances to one particular group or set of people, urban dwellers 'acquired membership in widely divergent groups each of which functions only with reference to a single segment of his personality' (Wirth, 1938, cited in Kumar, 1978: 72–73). To put it another way, urban life allows people to specialise or compartmentalise their relationships by establishing them on the basis of one aspect or interest in life (work relationships, family relationships, leisure interests) as opposed to having relationships that intersect or are interdependent on many levels, as they would be in gemeinschaft relationships.

In their own ways, all of these writers propagated a view that 'community', in its more natural or organic form, was something that belonged to the social order of the past (Day, 2006) (most often, a past of living memory) and was set critically against what were seen as the negative trends of the present of the time. It is crucial to emphasise here the importance that transformations in the relationship to space and place from village to city is seen to have had in the transformation of community to gesellschaft relations. The essence of their (and subsequently, our later) conceptions of community came from a caricature of village life and were based on *a particular spatial order* based on the limitations of bodily travel, the rootedness in place and history, the social limitations set by the interweaving, interdependency and obligation of personal relationships tied to an extremely local scale. Changes in this spatial scale and mobility are seen to have a dramatic effect on social scale and mobility.

By the early twentieth century, the shift from village to urban life meant that great industrial cities coordinated the movement of peoples, resources and goods across long distances, which sustained national economies and international trading empires. This altered relationship to space transformed the sense of the local away from a scale that originated in the body and personal relationships with other people, to the scope of mechanised travel (streetcars, trains), which could be imagined on a national scale (Luke, 1996). The space of the 'local' or 'community' expanded to include a sense of belonging that involved entire nations. This was a dramatic shift from the spatial order of agrarian village life and the result was that *nations* became the most important community to which one belonged. But as Anderson (1983) argues, nations are *imagined communities:*

> It is *imagined* because the members of even the smallest nation will never know most of their fellow-members, meet them, or even hear of them, yet in the minds of each lives the image of their communion. (Anderson, 1983: 6)

In such a situation, community is not centred around interaction or face-to-face meeting in everyday life, but is coalesced around symbolic resources (symbols, flags, anthems, sports teams, heroes) and nationally-based media (newspapers, television, literature, history), which encourages a belief among its citizens in a common ground, history and experience. Nonetheless, by the beginning of the twentieth century, whether imagined or not, nations became the predominant focus for feelings of belonging and community within the industrialised world, and this solidified a spatial order which revolved around the scale of the political and economic unit of the nation state.

People had been freed, to a certain extent, from the tyranny of place and were able to gain more physical and social mobility, as well as expanded social circles and increased choice over relationships both commercially and personally. The negative consequences (for many sociologists, at least) of this was a loss of interdependency and a rooted face-to-face social world. In its place rose a more calculated and instrumental individualism. *Community* had started to break down in the face of the *individual.*

COMMUNITY, GLOBALISATION, TECHNOLOGY AND INDIVIDUALISM

The last section described the notion of community as it developed under the spatial order of the urbanised, capitalist nation-state. However, by the early 1970s, the spatial order of the capitalist nation-state (or what Harvey (1989) calls a 'spatial fix') was beginning to disintegrate in the face of increasing pressure to expand the scale of the production and consumption of goods within capitalist economies through globalisation (see Chapter 2). For Harvey (1989), changing the nature of spatial relations is at the heart of capitalism's need for growth, the seeking out of new markets, and the speeding up of capital turnover for profit. In this respect, economic growth under capitalism demands continual re-spatialisation through the overcoming of geographic limits to human exchanges in what he calls 'time-space compression'. Since the early 1970s this has been brought about by improvements in the speed and availability of physical transportation (particularly air travel), as well as the development of digital electronic communications.

Once again, a change in the structure of the economy is responsible for a change in the spatial order by lessening the constraints (or tyranny) of place on the flows of goods, information, money and people. Luke (1996) refers to this as 'third nature' or 'cybernetic spatial orderings', where mechanised forms of organisation and travel begin to give way to forms of organisation and association based on flows of electronic information associated with real-time digital communication. This yet again transforms the spatial order and moves social life even further away from the traditions that preceded.

Indeed, it is the focus on the changing constitution of space – and our relationship to others in space – that pervades much of the globalisation literature as it relates to community, belonging and association. Illustrative of this is Giddens (1991), who suggested that late-modern social life is characterised by three aspects:

- The separation of time and space.

- The disembedding of social relationships and organisations.

- The reflexive ordering of social relations.

First, Giddens argued that in pre-modern social settings, time and space were connected through the situation of place in the sense that activities between people were coordinated by living present in the same time and the same place. In modernity, larger scale coordination of activities meant that people's actions had to still be coordinated according to time, but often the people being coordinated were not in the same place (for example, in the coordination of a national railway system). The 'when' of social action was coordinated but the 'where' was dispersed in space. In late modernity, this coordination is accelerated to a global scale by real-time communication networks. *Time has become effectively separated from space* in terms of social action with others. We no longer have to 'be' together to act together.

The separation of space and time means that social institutions and relationships have become *disembedded*. Giddens suggests that one result is that human interaction is increasingly governed by *abstract systems*. Abstract systems are in place so that people who perhaps don't know each other, or who will never meet in person, can have trustworthy dealings even though they are separated by long distances (for example, using money or contracts). Such systems rationalise human relationships outside face-to-face contexts of known persons. This is similar to Tönnies' characterisation of contractual relationships in gesellschaft societies. Last, the *reflexive ordering* of social relations leaves most forms of relationships open to constant revision in light of increased amounts of information, self-awareness and choice available to the person.

These features of late modern life can be applied to digital culture using the example of the online auction site, eBay. The *separation of time from space* is demonstrated by the ability for several people from all over the world to simultaneously bid on the same good at the same time. Their actions are coordinated, down to winning or losing the auction in the dying seconds, despite the separation of the individuals themselves by huge distances. eBay itself is an *abstract system*, in the sense that the company acts as an intermediary to ensure legal and fair commercial exchanges between complete strangers across long distances. *Reflexive ordering* is present in the awareness of the feedback system. Negative feedback may make one wary of bidding on goods sold by a certain seller, and choose another instead. Conversely, one is always concerned to maintain good feedback because one is reflexively aware of the importance of feedback status in future exchanges.

Giddens' characterisation of reflexivity has many similarities to what is referred to by other academics as *detraditionalisation*, which can be defined as a decline in the belief of a pre-given order of things, or a shift from 'fate' to 'choice, 'virtue' to 'preference' and 'embedded' to 'disembedded' human relations (Heelas, 1996). As many aspects of social life become increasingly disembedded (for example, media), people are exposed to a number of models for living outside the limitations of tradition, and individuals find it possible, to a certain extent, to choose from a number of options to construct their own biographies in a way that revolves less around the limits of tradition and fate and more around choice (Beck, 1992; Beck et al., 1994; Giddens, 1991). Thus, social relations, affiliation and identity become increasingly open to globalising influences.

In this respect it is no surprise that questions of community and belonging have resurfaced in the last two decades alongside discussions of globalisation. A world characterised by global communications, globally interdependent economies, long-distance movements of goods, money and people is one with the potential to radically alter the nature of social life and therefore community by changing, or even destroying, a sense of the local (which now is seen in terms of the imagined community of the nation-state).

Once again, the importance of face-to-face contact is set against a more disembedded social context. Many writers, such as Bellah et al. (1985), Bauman (2001c), Putnam (2000) and Urry (2000) have been explicit in their assertion that community is in 'crisis' in the late-modern world, partly as a result of a further increase in individualism associated with expanded choices, less obligation and more social and physical and imaginative mobility. As Bauman (2001b) comments:

> To sum up: gone are most of the steady and solidly dug-in orientation points which suggested a social setting that was more durable, more secure and more reliable than the times-pan of an individual life. Gone is the certainty that 'we will meet again', and that we will be meeting repeatedly for a very long time to come …
>
> … no aggregate of human beings is experienced as 'community' unless it is 'closely knit' out of biographies shared through a long history and an even longer life expectation of frequent and intense interaction. It is such an experience which is nowadays missing… (Bauman, 2001b: 47–48).

'VIRTUAL' COMMUNITIES: THE NEXT STEP?

From the preceding section, we can suggest that there are several factors that point to online or virtual communities being an inherently reasonable next step in the transformation of community.

- *Detraditionalisation* allows us to imagine new forms of biography and community as older forms, traditions and obligations erode or transform.

- *Disembedding* allows us more choice in our relationships and group affiliations outside spatial limitations.

- *Globalisation* exposes us to a variety of cultural resources and experiences.

- *Reflexivity* allows us to think more freely about who we are and who we want to be as individuals.

- A tradition of *imagined communities* encourages us to find communion with others beyond our locality through media and symbolic resources, and with people who we perhaps may never meet face-to-face.

In this respect, it is not surprising that as the internet has become integral to daily life for many, it also has become a new site for the articulation of all types of groupings and communities. Barney (2004) suggests that as people occupy localised common physical spaces less frequently, communication technologies have begun to take over as the space of community. This certainly seems to be the case when one considers the myriad of ways in which group relationships are manifested online: chat rooms, forums and bulletin board systems, MMORPGs and online worlds, networking facilities, blogging circles, and many more.

Overall, Armstrong and Hegel (2000) coalesce these options into four types of online communities:

- *Communities of transaction* facilitate the exchange or buying and selling of goods and information.

- *Communities of interest* bring together participants who wish to interact about specific topics of interest to them.

- *Communities of fantasy* allow participants to create new environments, identities or imagined worlds.

- *Communities of relationship* centre on intense personal experiences and create networks of support.

As we will see below, opinion is somewhat divided in the social sciences regarding virtual communities. Many writers see a great potential in online or virtual communities to help revitalise community in the late-modern age. Others feel that community in any meaningful way cannot exist purely in offline form and that perhaps these may even be destructive for the 'real world' communities still existing.

The virtues of virtual communities

Proponents of digital/electronic/internet/virtual communities argue that the proliferation of internet-based 'communities' are individually and socially beneficial on a number of levels. First, there is what could be called the nostalgic argument that internet-based communities can help to reverse or compensate for the lack of community in the 'real world'. Rheingold's (1993, 2000), study of his experiences with the close-knit and successful online community called the *Whole Earth 'Lectronic Link, or WELL*, is seen as an exemplar of internet enthusiasm in this regard. He suggests that people in contemporary society have turned to the internet out of a hunger for community spirit, which is no longer provided in the contemporary offline world. Influenced by Putnam's *Bowling Alone* (2000), Rheingold suggests that community spirit has all but disappeared in an auto-centric, suburban, fast-food, shopping-mall culture. He notes, using the work of Oldenburg (1999), a decline in 'third spaces', or informal public spaces such as pubs, café's, squares, which he argues act like a social glue, binding communities together in idle chit chat and informal face-to-face conversation[1] and that it has had a detrimental effect on feelings of community within contemporary urban areas. Rheingold argues that internet spaces such as forums, chat rooms (and presumably now, online worlds, MMORPGs and microblogging) can and do fulfil the function of these informal social spaces. From this perspective, online communities are seen as a compensation for the supposed failings of the offline world in fostering a sense of community (Day, 2006; Fernback, 1999) and combating the isolation of contemporary life (Willson, 1997).

Online community also provides the benefit of increased choice in one's social relationships. The internet and other digital communication technologies liberate individuals from the social, geographical and biological constraints of place and proximity (Willson, 1997). The compressed space of digital communication networks means that (theoretically at least), anyone can establish contact with anyone, despite their 'real world' location. This frees up individuals to associate with like-minded others, those with common interests, values, beliefs or passions (Baym, 2002). No one needs to feel socially isolated because we will always be able to search online and find others with whom to share some sort of interest or communion:

> Life will be happier for the on-line individual because the people
> with whom one interacts most strongly will be selected more
> by commonality of interests and goals *rather than by accidents
> of proximity*. (Licklider et al., 1968, cited in Rheingold, 2000: 9;
> my emphasis)

In this way, internet communities could be considered more meaningful, relevant or 'authentic' because people freely choose to be in them, as opposed to being obliged to membership because of the happenstance of birth or residential location. Instead, online interaction takes place within an environment shaped by the actors themselves (Bruckman, 1998; Willson, 1997).

This element of choice relates to the *freedom of engagement* within online communities. Members of online communities choose when and how to engage with other community members. They may, for example as many *WELL* members do, choose to meet face-to-face as well as online. But ultimately, this is a decision made by individuals on their own terms. Similarly, community members can choose their level of involvement in the community itself. One could be an intensive member, a frequent poster, or even a moderator, and contribute a lot of time and resources to the greater good of the community, or one could be a casual member, infrequent poster, or even a 'lurker'. All have their place and are accorded varying degrees of prestige within the community itself on the basis of their involvement. No one is obliged to contribute more than they want to contribute.

Fourth, by overcoming space and distance, online communities also overcome the problem of mobility, in that belonging or membership to a community is not necessarily interrupted by the physical movement of people (Day, 2006). People can move, but can still be a member and keep in contact with others online. The presence of the person (or person's profile) is within the space of the internet, so the actual physical location of the body becomes much less important when it comes to maintaining communal ties. The importance of this is particularly salient when it comes to diasporic communities such as migrants from India (Adams and Ghose, 2003; Mitra, 1997) or the Caribbean (Miller and Slater, 2000) who wish to maintain contact and a connectedness to their home countries and the people in them.

Fifth, virtual communities have a purpose in which membership provides perceived tangible benefits to their members. Rheingold, for example, suggests that virtual communities can be used to expand social and knowledge capital (i.e., to create useful social links or obtain knowledge) as well as provide feelings of communion. 'Real world' communities that are based on accidents of geography often foster a sense of *obligation*, but often seem to do little to demonstrate a sense of *benefit* from being in them or, at least, the benefits always seem to be outweighed by the burdens. In this respect, the demands of the larger community, and membership in it, are often seen by many as not providing much reward in return: 'I pay my taxes, and still I can't find a police officer when I need one …'.

By contrast, online communities are created and sought out specifically to provide people with something that they want or do not have. There is a point/benefit to them that is evident for the members and if these benefits have been obtained or are no longer needed, a member can leave the group. There is a reason for the existence of the community, and a reason to be in it.

Last, there is the suggestion that online communities do not have material limits. There are a potentially limitless number of online communities and these communities can have, in theory, a limitless number of members. Thus, there is the potential for creating forms of solidarity in all sorts of new ways and through new channels (Day, 2006). Further, there are no constraints on the ways in which people could be affiliated or attached to others. This makes online notions of community more open-ended and potentially less exclusionary than offline, place-based forms.

The vices of virtual community

As with any new form of communication or socialisation, proponents are balanced by critics and sceptics. One of the earliest worries was that internet use in general, and engagement with online communities in particular (especially when addiction is involved), is a distraction from real-world relationships and communities. This is based on the logic that time spent online would potentially cut time spent offline with families or other members of the community (Barlow, 1996; Lockhard, 1997; Nie, 2001).

These concerns have largely been discounted in research that has since demonstrated the integrated nature of online and offline activities, as we will see in the next section (Anderson and Tracey, 2001; Wellman et al., 2002).

However, a more convincing rebuttal to the suggestion that online communities can help to compensate for the failings of offline community in contemporary society is the suggestion that abstracted a-spatial communities do not combat, but continue, the general trend of compressing time and space under capitalism and the disembedding human relationships further from locality, local contexts and mutual interdependence. Here the emphasis on the benefit of choice to be gained by a liberation from place in online environments can be seen also as part of the current trend towards individualism that is said to have started in the period of urbanisation. The fact that individuals can pick and choose what communities they belong to can be seen as antithetical to the notion of obligation and interdependence, which is characteristic of the concept of community in a meaningful sense (Sunstein, 2001).

Interdependency in physical space encourages a sense of obligation, and responsibility and conflict avoidance, for better or for worse. This emerges from being stuck together in the same place. In online environments, there is very little 'stickiness', because all membership is based on choice, no one is 'stuck'. Members choose not only to join a community, but when and how to engage (if at all) with that community. Thus, there is no 'burden' of mutual responsibility. So, for example, Willson (1997) has pointed out that 50 per cent of postings on the *WELL* (that most utopian of internet communities) were actually made by only one per cent of its members. The 'community' was actually sustained by a very small minority of members.

It is important to demonstrate how community sometimes does not work on the basis of common interests and choice. To use a personal example, I have been a member of an online forum called 'The Big Chill'. This forum was dedicated to people who have the unenviable pastime of surfing in Kent, a south-eastern county in the UK. The forum had a couple of hundred members, and was a place for people to exchange tips, discuss surfing forecasts, buy and sell surfing equipment and, in general, acted as a resource and online locus for the 'community' of people who surf at the one (or perhaps two) surfable beaches in Kent. When I moved to the area I joined the site and became a reasonably active member of the boards, checking them several times a day and contributing to the conversation. I used the forum to get advice, buy equipment, and find others to surf with (which resulted in a few face-to-face meetings and surf sessions). This forum had all the elements of an online community: a thematic purpose; a common interest among members; the longevity of several years of operation; regular members; the added dimension of a geographical basis (the Kent area and the beaches involved); and an obvious pretext for face-to-face meetings.

However, closer inspection of my behaviour may suggest some problems with this ideal. When I was interested in surfing, I was interested in the site and the people on it. When I became busy with work or other interests in life, my activity on the site disappeared along with my surfing activity. My involvement in the community was *instrumental*, purely linked to my interest in surfing. Indeed, at the time of writing this book (August 2009),

The Big Chill forum no longer exists, as the commercial enterprise that was running the site decided not to maintain it anymore. So, was The Big Chill a community? Or was it a *resource* that people used, not a 'community' in any meaningful way?

The other option is to suggest that The Big Chill was a 'failed' community: one that just didn't capture a communal sentiment and thus eventually died out. This may be the case, but it is reasonable to suggest that there are several more cases like The Big Chill (and my use of it) than there are like the *WELL*. The web is littered with non-active forums, abandoned blogs and moribund profiles that people have abandoned when their interests have changed, or when they have got what they want from them. In this context, places like the *WELL* would seem to be the exception, not the rule.

This can be seen as a logical and fair consequence of communities that are based primarily around choice and interest. Very similarly to urban contexts, online contexts can be said to contribute to increasingly instrumental and one-dimensional interactions with others, leading to yet more individualisation, as Willson (1997) notes:

> I would suggest that the dissolution or fragmentation of the subject and the instantaneous, transient nature of all communication disconnect or abstract the individual from physical action and a sense of social and personal responsibility to others. (Willson, 1997: 153)

In this respect, Willson's view has much in common with Dreyfus' (2001) suggestion that the internet disembeds the subject from local physical contexts and encourages a 'God's eye' point of view. People in such a position become increasingly nihilistic in their attitudes towards events and others, resulting in a disinterested curiosity or reflection towards the world around them. For Dreyfus, such a blasé pursuit of 'interesting things' leads people away from investing a personal stake in their local circumstances and the people around them.

Dreyfus' point leads us to a further suggestion. Many internet enthusiasts would suggest that it benefits those who feel odd or socially isolated in offline contexts by allowing such people to establish reassuring connections with others who share the same interests or passions. In that way, people can find intimacy, encouragement, understanding and 'community' among each other in a-spatial online communities. But what if these interests are the sorts of things that society sees as pathological or destructive? For example, there are suicide forums on the web that cater to depressed people (mostly teenagers) who are feeling suicidal (see Scheeres, 2003). Such forums exist to provide mutual understanding, share thoughts and exchange advice about pain-free or effective means of commiting suicide in an environment where such thoughts are not considered taboo. Similarly, there is also a large 'pro-ana' community promoting the view of anorexia as a (desirable) lifestyle choice, rather than telling their members (as the rest of society does) that they suffer from a medical condition or a mental health problem.

In both of these cases, it is clear that some people are finding a solace or reassurance in an online community of like-minded individuals. But such an engagement is easily considered destructive, both for larger society, and for the individuals involved, in that in cases such as these (as well as other 'communities' which revolve around illegal practices), there is a trend to normalise and even encourage pathological behaviour. By contrast, in the normal course of events, an offline community would usually seek to help the individual or, more cynically, to pressure the individual to modify their behaviour to the norms of the community. There is generally an interest in discouraging the destructive behaviour because those living in the same place are confronted both by the pathology and the results of it, such as death, grieving parents, suffering, and funerals. Those in an a-spatial online community have no such consequences to deal with. They will not be 'confronted' by anything and therefore have less incentive to intervene, and are perhaps more likely to encourage the behaviour.

The gist of the argument against online community is that, instead of combating what observers see as the decline of communal relations by creating new forms of solidarity, online communication is actually furthering the process of individualisation. This is seen as damaging under the assumption that place – and the lack of choice imposed by the physical reality of place – itself plays an important part in creating the interdependence (and therefore sense of social responsibility and obligation) seen by many as important to the creation and sustenance of communities. As a result, many writers would agree with Barney's statement that 'if one is interested in the relationship between network technologies and the prospects of community, perhaps "virtual community" is not the place to look' (Barney 2004: 162).

The reality of the situation

The reality of online or virtual communities seems to lie somewhere between the two above viewpoints. In this respect, Wellman and Gulia (1996) have characterised the debate (at the time) over online community as:

- *Manichean*: a sort of 'either/or' scenario in which online sociality is seen as either the saviour of community, or the destroyer of it, with little room to recognise that the actual situation may be a combination of the two.

- *Presentist*: in the sense that there was very little effort to see the 'online' as anything but 'new' and thus there was no attempt to place fears of community, or the potential of online relations, into any historical context.

- *Unscholarly*: in that much of the work was speculative, anecdotal, and not grounded in either historical literature or empirical study.

- *Parochial*: in that the internet was often portrayed as an isolated social phenomena. Thus, it was not really taken into account how much the boundary between online and offline life might be blurred, or how online interactions might fit in with aspects of offline life.

Around the millennium, several large-scale empirical studies and ethnographic work (Anderson and Tracey, 2001; Howard et al., 2002; Nip, 2004; Tutt, 2005) has demonstrated that, far from being separate spheres, the offline and the online are well integrated into everyday life. Thus, in terms of the debate about whether or not internet and participation in online communities 'harms' real life community or social interactions (on an individual level at least), the empirical results are quite mixed.

For example, Wellman et al. (2001) found that online interactions tended to supplement face-to-face contact without increasing or decreasing such contact. They also found that, in general, socially active people online tend to be socially active offline and, as a result, heavy internet users tend also to be more involved in offline volunteerism and politics.[2] Similarly, Katz and Rice (2002) found that internet users were no more no less involved or socially active than non-users as a whole, suggesting that internet use has no real impact on measurable aspects of community participation. Instead, they found that people used the internet to find individuals with common interests or concerns, or to engage in forms of exchange.

Overall, large scale empirical studies do not tell us very much. The broad consensus seems to be that internet use does not have much effect on offline relationships, apart from that the internet becomes integrated into the maintenance of offline relationships. But it is important to note here that these kinds of empirical studies do not really measure 'cause and effect', they measure relationships between variables. What is really being found in studies like Wellman et al. (2001), or Katz and Rice (2002), is a relationship between high internet use and high participation in offline social life. Community-oriented or sociable people are sociable online as well as offline, and the internet is yet another tool with which to be sociable. In some ways, this is not much of a conclusion when discussing the merit, worth or significance of online communities.

Thus, it is reasonable to agree with Wellman's (2002) tacit suggestion that 'community' is not really a workable concept for online sociability, or even for contemporary social life:

> Rather than increasing or destroying community, perhaps the Internet can best be seen as integrated into rhythms of daily life, with life online viewed as an extension of offline activities. Thus, the Internet provides an additional means of communication to telephone and face-to-face contact, one that can be more convenient and affordable. This suggests that the Internet's effects on society will be evolutionary, like the telephone has been, continuing and intensifying the interpersonal transformation from 'door-to-door' to individualized 'place-to-place' and 'person-to-person' networks. (Wellman, 2001: 46)

It is perhaps more appropriate in contemporary times to talk about 'my community', as in an ego-centric network of relationships centred around oneself and one's interests (as visually articulated in a social networking profile), than to talk about 'the community', as a set of people who all have things in common, a mutual interdependence and who share a common fate. In this respect, Wellman is right to suggest that the internet is one part of a larger shift away from place-based 'groups' or 'communities' to person-centred social 'networks' (Wellman 2002; Wellman and Gulia, 1996), a move that was actually well underway a number of decades before the advent of the web (Wellman, 1979). It is to this idea of networks to which we now turn.

NETWORK SOCIETIES, NETWORK SOCIALITIES AND NETWORKED INDIVIDUALISM

The Internet is a perfect instrument for a world in which community is understood as a network. (Barney, 2004: 164)

The final part of this chapter will build on from the conclusions of the last section: that 'community' is not an accurate term to describe the current state of social relations in contemporary post-industrial societies. Instead, the concept of 'networks' will be proposed and investigated form two points of view. First, it will reconsider Manuel Castells' analysis of the network society, which emphasises the economic, technological and spatial basis for the move away from 'groups' to networks as the fundamental form of social organisation. Then we will examine Barry Wellman's notion of 'networked individualism' (2002), which originates from the tradition of social network analysis.

Both of these approaches emphasise the role of information and communication technology in accelerating larger scale changes that have been ongoing for decades, notably increased physical mobility and the rise of individualism. In the final section, these two perspectives will be brought together to suggest some key elements for the conceptualisation of technology-enhanced social networks.

The network society revisited

Chapter 2 introduced Manuel Castells' notion of the network society. In Castells' (1996, 1997, 2001) formulation, the network has replaced the group as the basic socio-economic unit of contemporary society. This shift was based on a number of changes in the economic structure of later modern societies, the most important (for our current purposes) being:

- A transition from an economic model based on standardised mass production (Fordism) to one based on flexible customisation (post-Fordism), which envisiones the production of goods as a coordination of a series of decentralised, semi-autonomous nodes.

- The economic pressure to change the spatial order of industrial production and consumption (i.e., to globalise and deregulate), in order to allow firms to benefit

197

from locational advantages (normally access to cheaper labour and raw materials) on a worldwide scale.

- The development of a worldwide communication infrastructure and digital networks which, in turn, allowed for the decentralisation of firms and the coordination of their production, distribution and consumption on a global scale.

These changes meant, in effect, that the restrictions of place became less of an issue for businesses who could now pursue their activities on a global scale. Thus, Castells suggested the development of a 'space of flows', essentially, the space-transcending interactions of a global economy, which contrasted the more fixed and vulnerable 'space of places'.

This resulted in the 'networked enterprise' (see also Chapters 2 and 6), an 'agency of economic activity actively based around specific business projects' (Castells, 2001: 67). The purpose of the networked enterprise is to be flexible enough to expand production when demand is high and contract when demand is low, by having a flexible system of production and workforce. The networked enterprise needs flexible labour, and labour has responded to the networked enterprise by becoming more flexible, nomadic and networked itself as work has become less reliable, more ad-hoc, and more project oriented (see Chapter 2).

Andreas Wittel (2001) places the uncertain condition of work in the network society alongside observations of the erosion of enduring social relationships posited by writers such as Giddens, Bauman and Sennett. He provides an excellent account of how these macro-scale economic shifts trickle their way down to the individual level in the form of 'networked sociality': a disembedded intersubjectivity that contrasts the 'belonging' of 'community' with the concept of 'integration' and 'disintegration' in a network.

Wittel argues that the key to success in the network society on both social and economic levels revolves around the skill of 'networking' and the creation of an extensive network of 'weak ties', in the sense of Granovetter's (1973) concept of strong and weak ties – weak ties referring to loose, one-dimensional connections to people outside one's close social circle. Granovetter's argument was that weak ties are beneficial instrumentally in that they provide access to non-redundant information, practically manifested in things like increased employment opportunities. Wittel suggests that insecure, project-related employment leads to a proliferation of weak ties in the employment and social sphere that must continually be maintained. In this context the creation of instrumentally useful contacts is prioritised over loyalties to employers or fellow workers.

Thus, the foundations of the network society, specifically its working conditions of flexibility and uncertainty, and its relation to space (in the form of the a-spatial space of flows), creates social conditions that undermine the basis for community by emphasising the instrumental value of diverse, wide ranging and individual network connections to others over strong, long-lasting relationships and communities. This has an obvious link to social networking web sites (see the case study in this chapter).

Networked individualism

Van Dijk (2006) agrees with the general conclusion above when he suggests that:

> At the individual level, we are witnessing the rise of networking as an explicit and increasingly systematic method of making contacts and improving social relations. (Van Dijk, 2006: 29)

Indeed, Van Dijk, Barney (2004) and Wellman (2002) specifically make the link between the practice of networking and the rise of individualism. Van Dijk even describes networks as the 'social counterparts' to individualism. There are strong links between the two concepts. As we suggested earlier in this chapter, the rise of individualism during the period of industrial urbanisation involved increased mobility, choice, and specialised relationships.

Similarly, Wellman (2002) has argued that networked individualism has been furthered by the liberation of community (as networks) by further physical mobility, as well as advances in communication technologies, leading to further choice and specialisation in social relationships. For Wellman, this move from communities to networks is not new, and was well underway by the 1970s (Wellman, 1979). However, increased mobility and advances in communication technology have intensified this process to the point where social relations are in the process of moving from being completely place-centred, to being completely person-centred and a-spatial. He charts this move as one from 'little boxes' to glocalisation, to networked individualism (Figure 8.1a).

By 'little boxes', Wellman (2002) is referring to pre-industrial social relations, which were intensely centred around (isolated) places. Wellman suggests that this gave way to *glocalisation* and involved a shift away from isolated settlements to more modern urban contexts of social and physical mobility. In glocalisation, place is still important, but places (typically households) are now connected over longer distances outside the locality (Figure 8.1b). In *networked individualism*, place to place connection deteriorates in favour of person to person connection via the advent of mobile phones and other wireless technologies (or indeed virtual networking profiles that can be accessed from anywhere) (Figure 8.1c).

The result is a decoupling of social relationships and linkages from place as social relationships become centred increasingly around the person. But Wellman argues that (just as Simmel and Wirth suggested with regard to urbanisation), the shift to networked individualism means that relationships become increasingly specialised. That is, the people to which one is connected perform a specific instrumental role of function in one's life, as does membership in a specific network. This is an important point about networks, which needs to be elaborated further. Networks (social networks, economic networks or otherwise) have a goal, point, project or purpose for their existence. They exist for a specific purpose and therefore can be seen as the products of instrumental reasoning. This puts them in contrast with place-centred communities, which exist merely by the fact of location.

The truth about networks

While the work emanating from Castells and Wellman come from two different traditions, they both portray the foundations of social organisation in a similar way by suggesting

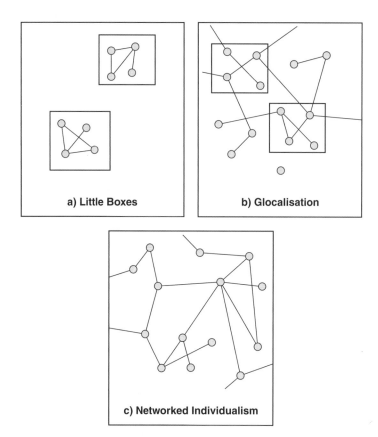

a) Little Boxes

b) Glocalisation

c) Networked Individualism

Figure 8.1 Little boxes, glocalisation, networked individualism (from Wellman, 2002)

that networks – and not groups or communities – are increasingly the heart of social life. Ultimately, both approaches outline very similar understandings of what networks as a form of social organisation entail, and this can be boiled down to five interrelated features of social networks in the information age (Figure 8.2).

First they are *a-spatial* in the sense that membership in networks enhanced by ICT technology is based on connectivity versus geographical proximity. Castells describes this in terms of connectivity in the space of flows. Wellman refers to the person-centred (as opposed to place-centred) networks created through mobile technology.

Second, ICT-enhanced networks are based on *choice*, in the sense that without restrictions of geography, people are much freer to choose who to establish and maintain contacts with. One can establish links on the internet with unmet others on the basis of common interest, no matter their location. Furthermore, one can also choose to maintain links with others through facilities like social networking profiles, with people who might once have been face-to-face contacts.

Third, social relationships in networked sociality are a product of *instrumentalism*, in the sense that all kinds of networks exist because of some purpose, project, or goal. This contrasts them with traditional communities that exist through the fact of location.

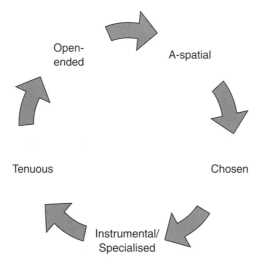

Figure 8.2   Elements of ICT-enhanced social networks

For Castells and Wittel, the basis of the networked enterprise revolves around 'projects' related to the production of certain goods in a globalised economic milieu. Certain nodes (people or contacts) in the network attain relevance by being potentially useful in uncertain economic conditions and a dynamic labour market. For Wellman, networked individualism is made up of a network of ties with others based on specialisation and the fulfilment of certain roles or functions within one's life. Online, this is demonstrated by online forums and other networks, which usually focus on specific themes, for example technical advice, celebrities or soap operas, surfing, politics or music, to name a few.

At the same time, such technologically enhanced ties are tenuous in that one has to demonstrate a worth or relevance to be included in a network. Being an instrumental and not obligatory form of organisation, one cannot simply be born into a network and remain in it in perpetuity, one has to prove one's relevance or usefulness to be included.

Last, ICT enhanced social networks have no limits in terms of size and are thus *open-ended*. There are no limits to how many networks one can be a part of or how many relationships one can establish, as networks (unlike placed-based affiliations) are not mutually exclusive. It is very easy to belong to several different networks. Indeed, if one was to follow the logic of networked sociality, the more the better.

Case Study: Social Networking, Microblogging, Language and Phatic Culture

I hate paying bills ... Son, don't say 'me too.' I didn't say that looking to relate to you. I said it instead of 'go away.' (http://twitter.com/Shitmydadsays)

Earlier in the chapter, we reviewed the concept of 'network sociality' as formulated by Andreas Wittel (2001). To briefly recap, his argument was that the foundations of the network society, specifically its working conditions of flexibility and uncertainty and its relation to space in the form of the a-spatial space of flows (specifically flows of people or 'labour'), created social conditions that undermine the basis for community by emphasising the instrumental value of diverse, wide ranging network connections to others. In such a scenario, communication becomes essential because social connections in networks have to be maintained, and thus consistently be renewed, reconstructed, refreshed and revalued in the disembedded and a-spatial context of late-modern society. Therefore, one could suggest that a key problem in a network society is the maintenance of presence within networks. After all, without a continued presence, social connections would be lost, networks would shrink and insecurity would increase. Thus, in a mobile network society where people increasingly move and travel long distances, social presence in physical absence presents a challenge that needs to be overcome.

Technology, presence and the post-social

At the time of Wittel's writing, he argued that operations that are designed to maintain connections were typified in the compressed social acts of 'catching up'. He gave relatively little attention to the role of new communications technologies in this process. However, he did note that a fundamental aspect of network sociality is its dependency on technological objects to spread networks and to maintain 'live' social contacts to others.

Karin Knorr-Cetina (1997) suggests that in contemporary times, processes of individualisation and disembedding has resulted in social relations that are increasingly mediated by, dependent on, and even displaced by, objects. She argues that the use of objects and technologies needs to be taken more into account in human relationships and that the concept of 'the social' needs to move from a focus solely on human groups to something that includes the variety of objects, tools and technologies which increasingly help us engage with others.

In an age where, first, almost ubiquitous communication (through phones, mobile phones, email, blogs, text messaging, microblogging and wireless technologies) means that many people are continually 'in touch' with others, and second, where a network sociality encourages an ever-growing network of contacts that would not be personally maintainable without the use of technologies to store and retrieve these contacts, this assertion makes sense. Technologies often 'stand in' for people by making them almost continually contactable no matter their physical location. This has contributed to a situation where we increasingly use social objects as communicative bodies in constant conversation with others, in what Knorr-Cetina refers to as a *post-social* context.

Licoppe (2004) suggests that in this context relationships – and the interactions that sustain them – are altered. He notes that one way in which these transformations take place is through a change in the notions of 'presence' and 'absence', which he suggests are being blurred into what he calls 'connected presence'. Licoppe argues that a new sociability pattern of the constantly contactable has resulted in relationships becoming webs of quasi-continuous exchanges.

In this context, social networking web sites such as Facebook, MySpace and Orkut are particularly useful. According to Facebook (2010), the average user on their site has 130 friends on their profile, which in itself is a lot of social connections to keep track of and maintain. Social networking profiles make this easy by providing the means for many types of communication: messages, comments, photographs, gifts and status updates. All of these ways of 'catching up' are combined into one easy to use technology that can be accessed virtually anywhere and through a large array of digital communication devices, including mobile ones. The overriding point of the networking profile is to reach out and sustain network linkages through the maintenance of a continuous communicative social presence with others.

Language, technology and phatic communion

Culture and community are maintained through conversation and communication. Not only are dialogues, conversation and communication in general the way in which beliefs, ideas, perspectives, opinions, ideologies and information in general are transmitted between persons, but the use of language is also a thing that binds people together by making them interact. Malinowski (1923) refers to these two simultaneous functions of language as 'the mode of reflection', in which language is used to exchange information from one to another, and 'the mode of action', in which the act of communicating itself creates sociability through the acknowledgement of another's presence. In that sense, one of the main functions of communications is to cultivate and sustain relationships through acknowledgement (Menely, 2007).

At the extreme end of the mode of action is what linguists (and anthropologists such as Malinowski) refer to as 'phatic' communication. Phatic exchange is a term used to describe a communicative gesture that does not inform or exchange any meaningful information or facts about the world. Its purpose is a social one, to express sociability and maintain connections or bonds:

> They fulfil a social function, and that is their principal aim, but they are neither the result of intellectual reflection, nor do they necessarily arouse reflection in the listener. Once again we may say that language does not function here as a means of transmission of thought. (Malinowski, 1923: 315)

As a result, our daily lives are filled with interactions and gestures that basically convey no information, but serve to enhance a general sense of sociability and community by acknowledging the presence of other people and establishing a connection with them. Gestures such as nods, winks and waves; small talk such as 'how are you?' and 'hi';

idle chit chat about banal or uncontroversial topics such as the weather ('nice day'), the annoyances of modern life ('these trains are always late'), or the fate of local sports teams are all more about making a connection with others around us than they are about saying anything in particular (Menely, 2007). They basically say 'I am here, and so are you. We're here together'.

Thus, phatic communications are not intended to carry information for the receiver, but are essentially more about connection than content. They act as a kind of social adhesive, which helps to maintain relationships with others (Menely, 2007) and reinforce a sense of communion by acknowledging the presence of others.

While overcoming the challenge of social presence would seem to be fundamental to success in the mobile network society, facilitating social presence in mobile contexts is a problem. This has also been a concern in the discipline of Human–Computer Interaction (HCI), where many have investigated how social presence can be facilitated through communication technologies in spite of physical absence. For example, a growing amount of HCI research has concentrated on the development of 'phatic technologies', which build relationships and sustain social interaction through pervasive, non-informational contact and intimacy (see for example Howard et al., 2006; Vetere et al., 2005).

Such research suggests that *social* presence across distances is enhanced by technologies that facilitate easy connection to others but are relatively lean in the amount of information they provide, whereas *physical* presence or *telepresence* is enhanced by technologies that put more emphasis on information depth and breadth (see also Chapter 1). In short, *contact* more so than content encourages a 'here and now' social union among people who are physically dispersed (Howard et al., 2006) and, as a result, phatic communications have become central to digital culture (Miller, 2008).

Such findings confirm popular new media trends, in particular the phenomenal popularity of social networking sites and microblogging. Social network sites such as Facebook encourage and support networking practices by placing more prominence on friends and links to others than on any content being produced by the author. In contrast to a *content*-laden practice such as blogging, which relies on information provision and dialogue, social network profiles provide a means to *connection* by prioritising phatic communion through gestures such as 'pokes', 'likes', brief status updates, comments on status updates and gifts. These communications essentially provide a means of maintaining presence, and on having that presence acknowledged by others in one's network.

Perhaps the most striking current example of the rise of digital phatic communion currently is the increasing popularity of microblogging. In essence, microblogging is a kind of cross between social networking, text and instant messaging. It allows people to keep in touch with friends through the internet, as well as mobile devices, through messages that are normally restricted to no more than 200 characters. These communications are designed to be read as soon as they are sent. Essentially they are 'up to date' updates and status reports sent to one's network.

For example, we can examine the most popular microblogging service, Twitter, a microblogging service started in 2006. The central theme of Twitter is 'what are you doing?' One is expected to answer this in a maximum of 140 characters. In comparison to both blogs and social networking profiles, Twitter profiles are stripped down to the minimum and contain almost no information about the user. The 140 character limitation and the nature of the medium also severely curtail the amount of potential content in any given posting. All updates are visible to everyone in one's network.

This is because the point of Twitter is the maintenance of connected presence and a sense of communion among a network of friends. To efficiently sustain this presence, Twitter is necessarily almost completely devoid of content and relies in the main on phatic communications: plans for the evening, what one has had for lunch, general comments on daily routine. Java et al. (2007), in their study of Twitter usage and postings, found that over half of posts were of this nature. One eighth of communications were attempts at conversation with specific people, 13 per cent shared information in the form of a URL link, and a small proportion of posts reported on news or current events.

Social networking and especially microblogging are good examples of how the problem of presence is being overcome in an increasingly global mobile network society. The result, at least in these cases, is the creation of a digital culture which is increasingly reliant on the production of a phatic intimacy that prioritises connection and acknowledgement over content and dialogue. While some criticisms can be made of such a phatic media culture (see Miller, 2008; or Baron, 2008), such technologies are a novel attempt at solving an unprecedented problem: producing a sense of presence and belonging in an uncertain world of constant movement and change.

CONCLUSION

This chapter has navigated a long journey to investigate the relationship between community, space and communications technologies. First, the origins of the community problem were presented as emerging from the context of industrialisation in the latter half of the nineteenth and early twentieth century in the latter stages of the industrial revolution. At this time, the emerging discipline of sociology linked the decline of communal bonds and a rise in individualism with the process of urbanisation and the spatial contexts of cities. It then demonstrated how similar claims for a crisis of community were made with regard to the period associated with globalisation (the last two decades of the twentieth century until the present).

It was argued that ultimately, the concept of community is related to a specific spatial context in which face-to-face interaction dominates. In an age where physical mobility and interactions through communication technology have dramatically lessened the influence of place as a determining factor in social relationship building, it was suggested that community is no longer the right word to describe social organisation and affiliation in the late modern era. In this respect, when one considers the impact of the internet and other digital technologies, it is not particularly constructive to talk about the enhancement or the destruction of community, but a further precipitant to the transformations that were already taking place under the process of capitalism. As a result, the concept of the network was put forward as a reasonable way to view attachments and social organisation in the late-modern world of mobility and digital communications.

FURTHER READING

Perhaps one of the more useful general overviews of the community debate within online contexts can be found (albeit briefly) in chapter five of Barney (2004). More general discussion about community, and the decline of it in contemporary times can be seen in Bauman (2001), for a European discussion, and Putnam (2000), for an American context. Both are wildly popular accounts, and Putnam in particular has been very influential. Luke (1996) provides a nice discussion of the changing nature of space and its relationship to community, tradition and belonging. Wittel (2001) is an excellent discussion of the social consequences of network sociality and the conditions of informational labour in contemporary capitalism, and Wellman et al. (2002) links the discussion of online community with the notion of networked individualism.

For more cyber culture-oriented discussions, Rheingold (2000) is the classic cyber-optimist text about online community, and Mitra (1997) provides a (perhaps now dated, but still interesting) look at the use of the internet in the Indian global diaspora. Last, Lockhard (1997) is a very good theoretical critique of online community.

With regard to social networking and microblogging, Wittel (2001) on network sociality, and Knorr-Cetina (1997) on post sociality are relevant theoretical discussions. In terms of a more detailed critique of the types of communication endemic to ICT use, Baron (2008) and Miller (2008) on phatic media culture may be useful. Menely (2007) provides an interesting and thoughtful discussion on the ideological dimensions of dialogue (associated with the exchange of content) versus expression (associated with phatic content).

NOTES

1 Although Rheingold generalises to all of America, and even the world, this observation would seem to be very particular to the San Francisco bay area in which he lived. Most urban centres these days, I would argue, are ripe with cafés and pubs, as anyone who complains about seeing a Starbuck's on every corner will attest. Certainly this is the case in Europe and in many large North American cities as well. There is no shortage of establishments that will exchange ones money for drinks, food, and an opportunity to shoot the breeze with others. The 'third places' are certainly there, but whether or not people who choose to live in large houses in suburban areas actually prioritise these spaces in their housing decisions is perhaps the more important issue

2 Interestingly, this study also found that heavy internet users were also the least committed to online community. Wellman et al. speculated that bad experiences or disappointments in online interactions has left heavy internet users somewhat jaded.

9

THE BODY AND INFORMATION TECHNOLOGY

'Commerce is our goal here at Tyrell. "More human than human" is our motto.'

'If only you could see what I have seen, with your eyes.'

(Both from *Bladerunner*, 1982)

Both of these opening quotes are taken from the 1982 Ridley Scott film, *Bladerunner*. Based on the Philip K. Dick novel, *Do Androids Dream of Electric Sheep?*, the film has been a popular topic of discussion among academics with an interest in technological matters. The plot revolves around protagonist Rick Dekard (played by Harrison Ford), who is assigned the task of terminating a set of rogue 'Replicants' (androids). The difficulty of this task lies in the fact that Replicants are almost perfect likenesses of humans on physical and intellectual levels (for example, they have been implanted with real human memories), to the point where Replicants are usually not even aware that they are not human (there is even an intimation in some versions of *Bladerunner* that Dekard *himself* is a Replicant but is not aware). Only through the administration of a subtle verbal cognitive test is one able to separate humans from Replicants.

This dystopian version of a future world is not uncommon in science fiction literature, and this sense of boundary blurring between machines and humans is particularly fundamental to the genre known as cyberpunk, epitomised in the work of authors such as Phillip K. Dick, William Gibson, Bruce Bethke and Bruce Sterling. These writers describe a future in which the application of technology to forms of life – and especially the human body – proceeds in unexpected ways and results in (often ramshackle) human-machine or biological hybrids.

In one sense, such fictional characterisations of the future serve as a warning that if technological advances and their application to the human body continue uncontrolled, unimpeded and dominated by the forces of the market, we might end up with a situation where 'humans' become unrecognisable from what we consider to be human today. In another sense, the chimeric bio-tec future of humans depicted within cyberpunk can be seen as the inevitable next step in the evolution of human beings, not to be feared, but to be embraced.

Setting aside the tendencies towards speculative futurism described in cyberpunk fiction, it seems clear that within contemporary culture there is an ongoing ambivalence between, on the one hand, a desire to use technological advances to prolong and improve the quality of human life and, on the other, concern about how the use of such technologies might move humanity away from its 'humanness' or create further inequalities and conflict in society. This has been seen in controversies surrounding research into stem cells, anti-ageing, reproductive technologies and plastic surgery. Our increasing manipulation of bodies through technology leads us to question what 'the body' (and 'the human') is, what they could or should be, and how we should control these processes.

This chapter examines the relationship between the body (human bodies) and technology, with a specific focus on the body and its relationship to information technology. It begins with a brief examination of the relationship between the body, technology and society, then engages with a set of ideas known collectively as posthumanism and, finally, looks at more phenomenologically-inspired approaches to the relationship between the body, with a focus on mobile technologies.

THE BODY, TECHNOLOGY AND SOCIETY

In Chapter 7 it was argued that identity is not essential, that is, it is not something predetermined but something that is created within social contexts and through societal discourses. Much the same can be said about the body. The body is not something given, it is something *made* (Shilling, 1993). Contemporary societies have seen a rise in the degree of control over bodies not only from external forces (see Chapter 5 on cybercrime and surveillance), but also in the degree of control we exercise over our own bodies. The decline of religious authority in the West has meant that the behaviour and appearance of bodies, and what is done with them, has become more of an individual judgement. Increased leisure time in post industrial economies has given us more time to work 'on ourselves' and the milieu of consumer culture has encouraged outward expressions of identity through body appearance and lifestyle pursuits, leading the body to increasingly become a bearer of symbolic value. Overall, more affluent material circumstances have allowed many within later modern society the luxury of diets, exercise and even surgery, creating a historically unparalleled degree of control over our bodies (Shilling, 1993; Turner, 1984; Williams and Bendelow, 1998).

Indeed, it is not difficult to suggest that contemporary Western society (at least) has taken a massive interest (if not obsession) with bodily matters. Growing numbers of people (as well as governments) are increasingly concerned with the health, shape and appearance of their bodies and see their bodies – at least in part – as expressions of themselves. This is manifested in popular cultural by diet fads, fitness regimes, aesthetic body modification practices such as tattooing, as well as by the rise of more extreme body oriented psychopathologies such as anorexia, body dysmorphia and addictions to plastic surgery, as well as plain old gym memberships.

Within sociology and cultural studies there has also been a shift in focus to bodily matters and an increasing recognition of the relevance of embodiment to social life. Shilling (1993) suggests that the rise of academic interest in the body is a result of several factors: second-wave feminism, which views gender as a social construction and the female body as a site of oppression, (see also Chapter 7 on identity), the increasing influence of Michel Foucault and his concentration on the body as a target of power relations, and the control and disciplining of bodies. Increasingly, the body is seen as the principal site for the exercise of power and surveillance through their policing, restrictions on their movement, the monitoring of them by health authorities, and incarceration of them for transgression. At the same time, technological and medical advances have encouraged a greater uncertainty about the 'reality' of the body and, together with the ageing populations of post-industrial societies, we are creating a vanguard of people keen and financially able to exploit technology to delay the adverse effects of ageing bodies.

Williams and Bendelow (1998) have suggested that contemporary medical science and technology in particular have played an important part in problematising the body in contemporary society in a number of ways:

- Bodies have become more *plastic*, in that they have become more able to be honed, crafted and moulded by cosmetic surgery and other medical procedures.

- They have also become more *bionic*, with the introduction of synthetic machines, such as artificial hips, hearts, pacemakers, and the like.

- Bodies are becoming increasingly *communal* or *interchangeable* in the sense that organ donation, transplantation and stem cell research have become successful enough to develop into a commercial enterprises, both 'legitimate' and 'black market'. Consequently, human bodies are being seen more like machines with interchangeable, standardised, commodified parts that break down and can be replaced as needed.

- Bodies are becoming more *interchangeable across species*, as animals such as pigs are used as sources of replacement organs and other species are used to grow human organs by way of tissue engineering (eg., the mouse with the human ear).

- Last, bodies have become more *virtual* or *hyperreal* (see Chapter 1), wherein representations of bodies have increasingly been the focus of action for medical technology.

It seems clear that we now, individually and collectively, have more control over our bodies than ever before. In no small part is this due to our increasing technological mastery of bodies, especially within the medical sciences. While on the one hand this situation has resulted in longer life spans and improved quality of life, it has also created a certain amount of uncertainty over 'how much is too much?', and even concerns over 'playing God' by manipulating the basic building blocks of life. This can be seen in the continuing controversy over advances in cloning and stem-cell research within popular, scientific and political culture (for example, Clements, 2008; Tierney, 2007). It seems that, as science has facilitated ever greater degrees of intervention into the body, our knowledge of what bodies are and how to change them has leaped ahead of our ability to make moral judgements about how far science should go in the ability to deconstruct and reconstruct the body (Shilling, 1993: 3). The problem of the body and its present and future relationship with technology is addressed in a set of diverse discussions known collectively as 'posthumanism'.

THE POSTHUMAN

Bruce Mazlish (1993) suggests in *The Fourth Discontinuity* that the intellectual history of the West can be seen in having overcome a series of 'discontinuities': foundational beliefs that had set humans apart from the world as special. First was the separation of humans from the cosmos: the belief that humanity was placed in a different cosmological system than the heavens. When Copernicus proved that the solar system was centred around the sun and not the earth, and that the earth was simply one of many planets orbiting the sun, this discontinuity was overcome. The second discontinuity, that humans were apart from other life forms, was overcome by Charles Darwin, who proved that humans were affiliated with other animals through the evolutionary chain of life. The third discontinuity, that humans were governed by a rational, conscious self (as a fundamental characteristic of what it is to be human), was undone by Sigmund Freud, who demonstrated the existence of an unconscious, and the power of irrational drives formed in early childhood experiences. The fourth discontinuity, still yet to be overcome, is the distinction between humans and machines (see Graham, 2002; Gray et al., 1995).

Posthumanism is a term that has many uses within literature on technology and the body. Lister et al. (2009) have attempted to separate this rather vague and messy term into three approaches:

1   A critique of the notion of humanism and the human subject within critical theory – that is – a kind of philosophical posthumanism.

2   A range of debates that examine the potential changes in the human body and its relationship with technology and technoscience.

3   An approach which addresses critically the relationship between technology and the human.

Posthumanism throws open the debate about what makes us human (Bell, 2001) on a number of levels, but especially with regard to our relationships with technology. In its predictive or speculative capacity, it envisages a not too distant world in which humans are mixtures of machine and organism, and speculates on what the consequences of that might be. Posthumanism moves this debate from the philosophical realm and looks directly into the realms of current science and politics.

The first step on the way to the 'fourth discontinuity' or posthumanism can be seen in the modern development of the field of *cybernetics*, the study of regulatory systems and self governing mechanisms (Hayles, 1999). The importance of cybernetics, and particularly of Norbert Wiener's work on cybernetics in this regard, is discussed at length by Hayles (1999) as well as Graham (2002). After World War II, Wiener was researching ways in which the flight paths of enemy aircraft could be predicted, even when trying to avoid hostile fire, so that they could be destroyed. He suggested that the pilot/airplane could be seen as a self-governing mechanism that continually processes and tries to respond to external stimuli under a set of complex, though ultimately predictable rules, in order to maintain homeostasis (that is, stability and control). For Hayles (1999), this becomes a foundational moment in the move towards the posthuman.

Cybernetics was a foundational step towards the posthuman, because this is the point when machines and humans begin to be imagined as self-regulating patterned information processing systems (Hayles, 1999; Naylor, 2004) and the world itself starts to be seen as bits of information that can be processed by humans and machines with varying complexity (Hayles, 1999; Thacker, 2003). Thus, three fundamental themes of posthumanism emerge from Wiener:

1   The aircraft/pilot are viewed as a single entity in which organic and inorganic are merged.

2   The aircraft/pilot entity is seen as an information processor which responds to environmental information in a patterned way (feedback loops) that can be reduced to information. In that sense, there is no conceptual difference between the two.

3   The material environment around the aircraft/pilot, as well as the aircraft/pilot itself, is viewed as ultimately reducible to patterned and unpatterned information. In that sense, 'information' becomes decontextualised, and seen as a universal essence of all material and organic things (Thacker, 2003).

These points mark out the three main streams of posthumanist thought: *cyborg* constructions, and the conversion of the material into the informational in two ways: as the conversion of flesh into data (or *extropianism*) and the conversion of data into flesh (or *technological embodiment*). These will be discussed in turn in the rest of this section.

Cyborgs

The term cyborg is a contraction of 'cybernetic organism' and is generally referred to as an organism that has both organic and inorganic elements to it. It is in effect a 'melding of the organic and the machinic' (Gray et al., 1995: 2) or the biological and the technical. The term was originally coined by Manfred Clynes and Nathan Kline (1960) to describe the need for humans to have their bodies technologically enhanced in order to be able to travel and explore space.

Most people's first introduction to the cyborg is within popular media – and particularly science fiction – where the notion of the cyborg has almost always taken on a threatening quality. Characters such as Darth Vader (*Star Wars*), the Borg (*Star Trek*) and *The Terminator* are popular examples of how the merging of human and machine denigrate what it is to be human, as well as threatening humanity itself. At the same time, more benign cyborgs in popular media, such as *The Six Million Dollar Man* or *Robocop*, portray cyborgs as helpful, as opposed to threatening, but still with a sense of pathos associated with the denigrated human.

In her seminal essay 'A manifesto for cyborgs', Donna Haraway (1985, 1991) suggests that not only are cyborgs powerful images in fiction, but that they are also becoming an increasing fact of life:

> Contemporary science fiction is full of cyborgs – creatures simultaneously animal and machine, who populate worlds ambiguously natural and crafted. Modern medicine is also full of cyborgs, of couplings between organism and machine … Modern production seems like a dream of cyborg colonization work, a dream that makes the nightmare of Taylorism seem idyllic. And modern war is a cyborg orgy … I am making an argument for the cyborg as a fiction mapping our social and bodily reality …
>
> By the late twentieth century, our time, a mythic time, we are all chimeras, theorized and fabricated hybrids of machine and organism; in short, we are cyborgs. The cyborg is our ontology; it gives us our politics. The cyborg is a condensed image of both imagination and material reality … (Haraway, 1991: 149–150)

Here the notion of the cyborg is being used in a more generalised way, and in particular it references the growing number of ways in which technological apparatuses have been used to fix and alter the human body. We can refer to Gray et al.'s (1995) highlighting of the restorative, normalising, enhancing and reconfiguring relationships that contemporary bodies have with machines. In this respect Gray et al. make the point that cyborgs are 'not just Robocop, it is our grandmother with a pacemaker'. Indeed anyone with artificial limbs or organs and anyone who is prescribed mood altering or cognitive behavioural medicines can rightly be considered cyborgs (Gray et al., 1995: 2).

In this respect, human–machine relationships can be characterised in a number of ways which relate to the function that the technology performs (Gray et al., 1995):

- *Restorative* Tools or machines that restore lost functions or limbs. Artificial hearts and prosthetic limbs are examples.

- *Normalising* Technologies that return existing limbs or organs to normality, such as hearing aids, spectacles, pacemakers, or reconstructive surgery.

- *Enhancing* Technologies that improve human performance, such as night vision goggles, forklifts, or communication technologies.

- *Reconfiguring* Technologies that create differences, but do not enhance human bodies, such as cosmetic breast implants, collagen injections, tattooing and body modification. An extreme example of this is 'cat-man' Denis Avner, who has gone through a large amount of body modification to, as much as possible, transform himself into a cat. His modifications include the bifurcation (splitting) of his upper lip, surgical pointing of the ears, silicon cheek and forehead implants, tooth filing, tattoos and facial piercings to which he can attach whiskers.

Still more generally, the notion of the cyborg can be seen as a kind of relationship describing the interface between humans and technology. The example of the aircraft/pilot from above describes this relationship, although the human/computer or car/driver are more popular examples to describe more everyday couplings of humans and machines, which together create an entity that is neither human, nor machine, but an assemblage of both that has unique properties not available to either (Dant, 2004, cited in Lister et al., 2009). Although many, such as Gray et al. and Dant himself would argue with the premise that such interfaces are strictly cyborg, because of their temporary nature and because they are not fully integrated into the body. Hayles (1999) has suggested that human computer interfaces, in particular, create a kind of embodied functionality in which the computers become transformed by being increasingly sophisticated in their ability to sense human movement and intentionality (for example learning to recognise voices), and humans become increasingly adept at learning to move in ways that computers understand (learning to type and use a mouse, for example) (see also Nayar, 2004). As time goes on, this coupling has transformed each to be a little more like the other.[1]

The Nintendo Wii console is a contemporary example that demonstrates how the computer/human interface has resulted in changes on both sides. The point of the Wii console is to make interaction with the computer more 'natural' by using biomechanical movements that simulate embodied 'real world' movement: a transformation on the part of the computer. At the same time, playing with a Wii baton/console is not completely effortless, but necessitates exaggerated or parodic movements by the human user in order for inputs to be detected: a concession on the part of the human player.

Unlike some of the other shades of posthumanism (notably 'extropianism' below), the notion of the cyborg keeps the body firmly in view by emphasising technology as embodied (Bell, 2001). As a result, cyborgs mark out a series of questions about the boundaries of the body. It is in this respect that Haraway sees the cyborg not only as an outcome of technology merging with bodies, but also, from a feminist standpoint, sees the cyborg as a liberating character which embodies the questioning of many boundaries in our society that need questioning. In that sense, the notion of the cyborg is also seen as part of the technofeminist project discussed in Chapter 7 on identity.

Part of the monstrous character of cyborgs as depicted in popular culture is their transgression of binary boundaries that have a powerful weight in Western culture, most notably (as referenced in the *Fourth Discontinuity*), the boundary between human and machine. As Haraway points out, blurring binary boundaries is what cyborgs do on many levels: nature/culture, organic/machine, physical/non-physical, human/animal. As a result, (postgendered) cyborgs are productively troubling figures for feminist thought and Haraway sees their monstrous, hybridised straddling of categories as politically liberating precisely because they cannot be pinned down. For the kind of productive anxieties demonstrated by the blurring of corporeal boundaries, one need look no further than the popular fixation with the appearance of the late Michael Jackson. Through his many facial surgeries and alterations, Jackson's appearance increasingly came to be seen as troubling or disturbing. This was arguably due to his visual transgression of binary categories such as black/white, male/female, natural/artificial (see Davis, 2003). Similarly, cyborgs are seen as tools for the deconstruction of oppressive, essentialist binaries based on the body, such as man/woman, black/white, pure/impure. This leads Haraway to proclaim 'I would rather be a cyborg than a goddess'.

Material as information 1: extropianism and disembodiment, or 'flesh made data'

The second foundational point made by Wiener was that the human pilot and the machine aircraft would be seen as analogous to each other because, in their basic essence, they could both be seen as entities which processed and responded to information in patterned ways that could eventually be understood at the level of information theory (Graham, 2002; Hayles, 1999; Thacker, 2003). Fundamentally, there is seen to be no difference between what a computer or a machine does and what an organism does, they both respond to certain stimuli in a way that attempts to maintain stability:

> The medium of information (to be distinguished from the message and from information) is transparent with respect to information, so that information is taken to be abstracted and self-identical across different media, or across different technological platforms. As the central unit operating within systems that work towards a homeostatic state, information is seen to play a central role in maintaining, restoring, or producing a normative, regulatory operational state for the system ... (Thacker, 2003: 85)[2]

In this respect, information is viewed or defined in a very universal, abstract way. Thacker (2003) suggests that this universalist way of viewing information and the processing of information provides the foundation for a version of posthumanism referred to as 'extropianism'. The premise of extropianism is that if human thought can be seen as merely a set of neural activity patterns (ultimately a set of informational channels) that occur in the brain, then these patterns can be 'mapped' and ultimately duplicated. Furthermore, advances in computing and neural networking will eventually get to a point where they will be able to host the informational channels of the human mind within technology. Essentially, the human 'mind' can (and will) be seen as 'software' that can be located in a 'hardware' of more durable, powerful, manufactured bodies (Kurzweil, 1999; Moravec, 1999; Thacker, 2004).

Extropianism, and its partner, 'transhumanism' (see Bostrom, 2005), are both seen as starting from two principles. First, that 'humanness' is located within the thinking mind and not a particular function of a 'natural' human body. In that sense they very much identify with the tradition of mind/body dualism of Descartes (see Chapter 7) that the essence of what it is to be human is the power of reason and consciousness, and not particularly rooted in the body. In that respect, extropians and transhumanists are both receptive to the 'mind as software' model of disembodied intelligence as not only possible, but even preferable.

> We will enhance our brains gradually through direct contact with machine intelligence until the essence of our thinking has fully migrated to the far more capable and reliable new mechanism.
> (Kurzweil, 1999: 135)

Second, extropians and transhumanists promote the view that human advancement will occur through technological augmentation and even the replacement of the fragile human body by more durable forms:

> We challenge the inevitability of aging and death, and we seek continuing enhancements to our intellectual abilities, our physical capacities, and our emotional development. We see humanity as a transitory stage in the evolutionary development of intelligence. We advocate using science to accelerate our move from human to a transhuman or posthuman condition.
> (More, 1999, paragraph 3; cited in Thacker, 2004: 75)

This kind of posthumanism is demonstrated in the work of the performance artist, Stelarc (http://www.stelarc.va.com.au/), who emphasises the obsolescence of the body and the stagnation of 'natural' human evolution. Through a series of spectacular engagements between his body and technology (such as the grafting of a mechanical, functioning third hand onto one of his forearms), Stelarc makes the point that the next step in human evolution will be dependent on embracing technological bodies.

Extropianism and transhumanism are, of course, highly contentious positions subject to criticism on many fronts. Bioconservatives (those opposed to significant alteration of the body through technology) usually oppose this view on ethical and even quasi-religious grounds. They believe that too much augmentation of humans through technology might not only be dangerous because of the potential for such trends to cause inequalities and conflict between augmented human beings and those not augmented, but also result in a debasement of human character and dignity (Bostrom, 2005).

Others criticise the extropian view by asserting that a disembodied human intelligence, which can be uploaded or downloaded onto machines like software, is an impossibility based on a flawed conception of human intelligence. The most persuasive argument in this regard is Dreyfus' (1972, 1992) attack on the notion of artificial intelligence. In *What Computers Can't Do*, he lampooned the predictions of thinking computers and artificial intelligence by undermining four basic assumptions underpinning the possibility of artificial intelligence:

1   A *biological* assumption that human brains work like binary computers.

2   A *psychological* assumption that thought is a type of calculation.

3   An *epistemological* assumption that intelligent behaviour is formalised, rule-based, and therefore reproducible by a computer.

4   An *ontological* assumption that everything that is essential to intelligent behaviour can be portrayed as understandable, context-free information, i.e., a confusion of *perception* and *conception*.

Dreyfus then went on to demonstrate the importance of the body in terms of human behaviour, particularly in how the environmental and social situation of humans in their bodies, produces shared forms of life and experience by which people are able to understand each other and possess shared meanings necessary for what we deem to be human intelligence. In other words, the way that human bodies fit into the physical and social world makes the world available to them, and thus allows humans to think about themselves and the world.

While the focus of Dreyfus' argument was the notion of building a thinking computer that thinks the way humans think, his criticisms are also relevant for the critique of the kind of disembodied 'software' model of intelligence sought for by the likes of Kurtzwiel, Moravac and other extropian posthumanists. Others, such as Stock (2003), attack transhumanism and extropian posthumanism on the basis of the technical unfeasibility of its vision. He argues that speculation of a near future merging of either biology and machine (on a large scale) in the form of a cyborg future, or the integration of human thought with computers, massively underestimates the complexities of integrating organic and non-organic matter. For Stock, the future of the posthuman is a biological one, where the mapping and manipulation of the codes of biological form will provide the next step in human evolution. This thought leads us to the next section.

Material as information 2: technological embodiment or 'data made flesh'

Hayles (1999) notes the potential danger of disembodiment thinking when thinking of information as a decontextualised universal element common to both humans and machines. She is at pains to suggest that a strategic definition of information does not exclude the body or the material from the domain of consciousness, but rather ties the material world to information *as* information (Hayles, 1999; Thacker, 2003: 80). This relates to the third point that emerged from Wiener's work on cybernetics: all forms of materiality can be seen in terms of bits of information, what Thacker (2003) refers to as 'informatic essentialism'.

In that sense, the materiality of the body becomes reduced to a set of codes (DNA, genomes, stem-cells) that are ultimately programmable when understood. Thus,

Thacker (2005: 89) notes three things about how the body is now viewed in the life sciences:

- Bodies are viewed essentially as information, codes and patterns.

- A body that is viewed as information can be technically manipulated, controlled and maintained.

- A body viewed as information does not exclude it from being a material body.

Far from the speculative futurism of extropian posthumanism, the arguments that Stock (2003), Hayles (1999) and especially Thacker (2003) make are more rooted in current and very real developments taking place within the biological sciences and medicine, where the merging of the biological and computer sciences has been manifested in projects such as The Human Genome Project, an international, multi-billion dollar undertaking to map the entire genetic makeup of the human species. This took 13 years and was completed in 2003. A genome, simply put, is a complete set of coding instructions for the behaviour of cells and organisms, thus it is the 'code' of a particular life form, in this case, humans (http://www.ornl.gov/sci/techresources/Human_Genome/home.shtml).

The Visible Human Project is an ongoing digital archive of the human body, which aims to function as a resource for biomedical research and teaching. The project in its first stages involved the freezing and fine slicing of two corpses, each slice being digitally scanned to produce high resolution images. This resulted in three dimensional sets of virtual bodies that can be explored from any angle or at any depth. In the process, the actual bodies were completely destroyed (Bell, 2001; Waldby, 2007) (http://www.nlm.nih.gov/research/visible/visible_human.html).

Both projects demonstrate the reduction of the body to information. In the case of the Human Genome project, we see the reduction of organic bodies into their foundational building blocks, represented as informational pattern and codes. In the case of the Visible Human Project, we see the exact opposite of the vision of uploaded consciousness and release from the human body put forward by the extropian movement, instead we are left with the uploaded body with no consciousness (Bell, 2001). What it also demonstrates is the increasing virtualisation of the body brought about by bioinformational imperatives. Gaggiolo et al. (2003), Balsamo (1996), Williams and Bendelow (1998) and Frank (1992) all point to the growing virtualisation of the body, represented in the form of computer codes and displayed on screens (which become ever more numerous in hospitals and health centres), scans and, increasingly, through medical avatars. Balsamo (1996) refers to this as one aspect of the *disappearing body*, where the 'meat' of the body is coded into large electronic databases. Gaggiolo et al.'s (2003) discussion of medical avatars is another example on how the body, viewed as information, results in increasing amounts of attention being paid to simulations of bodies in medical science, rather than bodies themselves.

However, as Thacker (2003) points out, the reduction of bodies to information is only one half of the bioinformatic cycle. This cycle proceeds with a view to ultimately manipulate and transform real-life, material bodies:

> biotech research directs its resources toward an investment in generating materiality, in actually producing the body through informatics. If areas such as genomics and bioinformatics are predominantly concerned with programming the (genetic) body, other areas such as tissue engineering and stem cell research are predominantly concerned with being able to grow cells, tissues, and even organs in vitro, in silico, and in vivo. The trajectory of biotech's informatic essentialism completes a loop, from an interest in encoding the body into data to an interest in programming and reprogramming that genetic-informatic body, and finally to an investment in the capabilities of informatics to help synthesize and generate biological materiality. (Thacker, 2003: 92)

For Thacker, Stock, Hayles and many others, the reconfiguring of bodies is much more likely to take place through the manipulation of the organic at the informational level, rather than the merging of the organic and inorganic. The contemporary successes with regard to cloning, gene therapy, organ transplants and stem cell research for the moment seem to support this view as more realistic, although this raises just as many questions in terms of what is seen as a 'natural' or 'human' body; or what is 'nature' and what is 'culture'; whether or not such reconfiguring in some way degrades 'humanness'; or whether one can productively even speak of such a category.

TECHNOLOGY, EMBODIMENT RELATIONS AND 'HOMO FABER'

> Man is not only *homo sapiens* or *homo ludens*, he is also *homo faber*, the maker and user of objects, his self to a large extent a reflection of things with which he interacts. (Csikszentmihalyi and Rochberg-Halton, 1981: 1)

While the overall lesson in sociological discussions of the body may be that bodies are interpreted through the lens of culture and shaped by social forces, many authors, such as Featherstone and Burrows (1995), are of the opinion that this may be the last generation of 'natural' humans due to the increasing influence of technology on the body, as described above. But what is a 'natural human'? Looking more specifically at the relationship between the body, technology and society, Shilling (2005) suggests that there is a tendency to view these spheres as separate and even competing elements, especially when it comes to the relationship between technology and the body. That is, technology is seen as something inherently 'unhuman' or 'artificial' as compared to the 'natural' human body.

As an antidote to this, Shilling looks to Georg Simmel (1971), who characterised the human desire to manipulate inorganic matter and create tools and machines as a way of overcoming bodily boundaries and limitations in the pursuit of physical transcendence. Humans use their capacities of imagination and calculation to create technologies that extend their corporeal limits. Thus, technologies emerge from the functional relationship between bodies and their physical environment, and the imagination to overcome both. In that sense, technologies are not 'inhuman' or apart from humanness, but are things integrated into people's plans, projects and desires. In that sense, the body is a source of technology, not separate from it, nor the subject of it (Shilling, 2005).

The emphasis on humans as tool/technology using creatures contrasts with the mind/body dualism associated with post-Renaissance Western culture and grounded in the philosophy of Rene Descartes (see Chapter 7). In this view, the essence of the human lies in the disembodied rational mind, and is summed up in the term *homo sapiens* ('thinking man'), separated from animals by their ability to think. However, this is by no means the only thing that distinguishes humans from animals. Humans are also referred to as *homo faber*: 'tool-making man'. Seeing humans as tool-makers may be particularly useful when exploring the relationship between the body and technology. After all, many would argue – as Latour (1994) does – that humans live in symbiosis with both tools and society. The tendency to separate the person or body from the tool is a distinction made in theory but not in the doing of the act itself (Latour, 1994, cited in Dwight, 2004). Indeed, the human without tools is a kind of anthropological abstraction (Dwight, 2004), perhaps as much of an abstraction as the notion of the disembodied mind. Ihde (1990) makes a similar point by asking what kind of human exists that is not always and already bound up in a technological relationship with the world, arguing that humanity's existence has been from almost the very beginning, a technological existence (Eason, 2003; Ihde, 1990). Such conceptions lead some, such as Clarke (2002), to see humans (*homo faber*) as ontologically a cyborg species (Selinger and Engström, 2007).

The phenomenologically-inspired approach of Ihde (1990, 2002) is a useful way of examining the relationship between bodies and technology. Inspired by Merleau-Ponty (1962), who attacked Cartesian mind–body dualism as inadequate for explaining human existence in the world, Ihde (1990) argues that humans have three types of relationships with technology: embodiment, hermeneutic and alterity. The first two relations are particularly relevant to this discussion.

The embodiment relation refers to the situation in which tools or technologies are being used. He suggests that when technologies are being used, the tool and the tool user become 'one' in the sense that, in use, the tool 'withdraws' from us as a separate object and becomes part of the body image and overall identity of the person. Tools recede into the body and are no longer seen as separate from the body by the user until they break or cannot perform the function intended (Eason, 2003). So, for example, when wearing a pair of eyeglasses, the eyeglasses cease to be an object of their own and become incorporated into the body of the wearer. This incorporation is illustrated by the fact that the wearer of the glasses ceases to be aware of the glasses as something on his or her head.

Second, Ihde speaks of a hermeneutic relation with technology, in which the tool not only ceases to be a separate *object* of experience, but also becomes part of the *means* of experience. The eyeglasses, therefore, not only are integrated into the body, but also become part of the way in which the wearer perceives the world and thus alters the wearer's relationship with the world. To further illustrate, Ihde (2002) uses Heidegger's famous example of using a hammer, in which the craftsman is able to feel the hardness and position of the nail through the hammer as though the hammer was an extended limb of the body. He also notes Merleau-Ponty's (1962) example of the blind man's cane, which is used as a limb that enables the man to feel the pavement in contact with the cane. This in turn helps to shape the blind man's experience of the world.

To take a more complex example, but one already mentioned, Richardson (2007) describes the relationship between the car and driver. Learning to drive a car involves a great deal of perceptual and bodily reorganisation. We have to judge distances and speed in a different way, learn to perceive the world through mirrors, get used to steering and brakes as ways of moving, as well as adjust our perception of size to accommodate the car that surrounds us. We have to learn an entirely new way of perceiving and being in the world which, at first, we find confusing and intense, but after a surprisingly short time this becomes mundane and habitual. Once more, it is easy for us to instantly shift from the car/driver state of being in the world, back to the 'pedestrian' state of being because our embodiment relation is variable according to whatever technology we happen to be using.

The point that Ihde is making is similar to Simmel's. Technology is not inhuman or artificial, but part of being human. It is through technological embodiment relations that humans exist in and perceive the world around them.

Embodiment relation and mobile technologies

> Mobile media technologies, and tele-technologies more generally, are therefore not simply prosthesis or augmentations of our sensorium, but tools which impact upon our bodily limits, shifting the variable boundaries of embodiment, and altering our sense of having a body: they educe altered 'involvements' of the soma. (Richardson, 2007: 207)

Mobile phones and, to a lesser extent other mobile communication technologies, have become an almost ubiquitous part of life for the vast majority of people living in advanced market economies, and are spreading through the developing world at unprecedented rates. For many people they are now seen as indispensable – the great sense of anxiety which follows the loss of a mobile phone certainly seems to suggest that mobile phones have achieved an intimacy with their users that other communication technologies have yet to match. And yet despite this, there has been little research on the relationship between the body and the mobile phone (or other mobile technologies).

A notable exception to this is Richardson (2007), who attributes the intense relationship that people have with their mobile phones to two things. First, there is the almost ever-presence of the mobile phone on the body or in close proximity of the body. Second, the mobile phone engages several bodily senses, including hearing (involved in ring tones and conversation), vision (involved in using the screen interface) and touch (involving continual proximity to the body, vibrating ring tones, and the interaction with the keypad or interactive screen). As a result, the mobile phone demands much more somatic involvement than other forms of digital information technology (Richardson, 2007). This intimacy with the body is further expressed in the importance of mobile phones as an object of fashion, where they are seen as indicative of the self in the same way as clothing (Campbell and Park, 2008).

However, it is arguable that mobile phones do more to the body than just extend the senses in a McLuhan-esque fashion. True, they can be seen as 'enhancing' technologies (enhancing the power of hearing, memory, and speech) and in that sense can be seen as engaging the body in a cyborg-like relationship or as an assemblage similar to the aircraft/pilot or the car/driver, but Richardson (2007) looks to the phenomenological perspective of Ihde (2002) to make the point that mobile phones alter our sense of being in the world through embodiment and hermeneutic relations. Similarly to cars, our union with mobile communication technologies involves us in a new way of being, in that it shifts the variable boundaries of embodiment and our bodily limits and embeds in us new ways of perceiving and interacting with the world.

Mobile phones, for example, alter the connection between physical and social proximity (Arnold, 2003) by creating a simultaneous presence in the space of places and in the space of flows (Castells, 1996). This gives us an experience of what Licoppe (2004) calls 'connected presence', in which we feel connected and present to others not in bodily proximity. At the same time, we can also experience an absent presence to those that are within our bodily proximity (Gergen, 2002). In addition, Van den Berg (2009) suggests that mobile technologies allow us a 'distributed presence', in that we are able to be present in several contexts (including the immediate physical context) at the same time. Aside from a presence with others, mobile technologies alter our bodily presence and our perception in the world when they are used as navigational devices, allowing us to pay less sensory attention to our surroundings, transcend our ground level pedestrian viewpoint and navigate our way through the world from a (God's eye) view of the digital map.

The increasing use and importance of mobile technologies in everyday life will no doubt create new ways of perceiving and being in the world, leading to ever more varieties of embodiment relation to technology and to our surroundings. In a more speculative example, the mobile embodiment relation may take an even more profound step with the advent of ambient intelligence (Bohn et al., 2004; Gaggioli et al., 2003; Raisinghani et al., 2004). Ambient intelligence is an emerging technology that brings together three contemporary fields of information technology:

1 Ubiquitous computing, in which increasingly small microprocessors are inserted into everyday objects such as clothes, vehicles or furniture to make them more interactive or responsive to user needs.

2 Ubiquitous communication achieved to ever more robust wireless networking technology.

3 Intelligent or adaptive user interfaces, which allow humans and computers to interact in more natural or personalised ways. (Gagglioli et al., 2003)

Current technological research on ambient intelligence imagines a future in which ubiquitous computing and mobile connectivity create environments in which 'smart' everyday objects react to the presence of individual bodies as individuals, in customised ways. Blind people, for example, could be guided through unfamiliar environments by smart signposts that 'talk' to them (Bohn et al., 2004). Domestic settings could be attuned to the bodily state of the occupant (for example, body temperature) and automatically alter the surrounding environment by turning on heat or air conditioning.

Within the medical sciences, mobile technologies are seen increasingly as instruments to be used in the diagnosis, repair and maintenance of bodies through research into ambient intelligence (Gaggioli et al., 2003; Jovanov et al., 2005; Riva, 2003). Ambient intelligence (for example, in the form of clothing with embedded sensors and microprocessors) could be used to retrieve or monitor information about patients' bodily states inside and outside medical facilities, leading to more accurate and efficient diagnosis, as well as treatment. Heart rates or insulin levels could be monitored for patients with chronic conditions, victims of stroke or injury can have physical therapy and rehabilitation improved by monitoring progress at home.

While such pervasive technologies are still in the design stage and come with a host of moral and ethical questions concerning privacy, surveillance and many other issues (Bohn et al., 2004), they do serve as examples of how the increasing mobility and pervasiveness of digital technologies has the potential to further alter our embodied relationships to our surroundings.

CONCLUSION

This chapter started with a dystopian vision of cyberpunk literature, which depicts a future where human bodies are continually altered by technologies to the point where they become unrecognisable as humans. It then went on to discuss the current fixation on the body within contemporary culture and how current technological advances as applied to the body have already problematised the notion of the 'natural' body.

We then looked at a set of academic discourses known as posthumanism, which engage with the problem of the body and technology through three ways of thinking: the notion of human–machine hybrids or cyborgs, the idea that the body can be surpassed altogether by technology (extropianism and transhumanism) and, lastly that bodies can be viewed as information patterns and codes (bioinformationalism), which allows for the transformation of bodies through the manipulation of organic matter (genes and geonomes) as opposed to human–machine hybrids or digital transcendence of the mind from the body.

Finally, we examined the relationship between technology and the body, which was more grounded in phenomenological approaches and the notion of humans as always technologically embedded in the world. The example of mobile technologies was used to demonstrate how technologies alter our being in the world and our perception of the world through embodiment and hermeneutic relations with the tools and environments around us.

One of the main points in the last section was the suggestion that tool making and tool using can be seen as an integral part of what humans do when they are being humans. From this perspective, technologies are not viewed as 'inhuman' or set in opposition to human bodies, but are seen as part of the complex symbiosis between human bodies, tools and the social and physical environment. This view of humans as *homo faber*, or technologically embedded tool-users, opens up a different view on what it means to be human in a technological world, where the motivation for making tools and machines stems from a wish or need to extend the boundaries of the body and to overcome its limitations in response to the surrounding environment. In this respect, one could argue that humans have never really been 'natural humans', because they have always had an intimate relationship with technology. To go even further, one may suggest that part of being human is 'to seek to escape from one's humanity by the creation of machines' (Mazlish, 1993: 229, cited in Graham, 2002: 186).

FURTHER READING

To get a broad yet informative sociological discussion about the body and its relationship to technology, Shilling (2005) is very useful. Feminist and technofeminist discussions of the body and cyborgs are well represented in Graham (2002) and in Haraway's (1991) influential text. For a flavour of extropian posthumanism, Kurzweil (1999) is a popular representative, and the web site of STELARC (http://www.stelarc.va.com.au/) is both intellectually interesting and artistically provocative. As counterpoints to posthumanism and extropian arguments, Thacker (2003) has an excellent analysis of both sides of the debate, and Dreyfus (1992) provides a landmark critique of the idea of artificial intelligence. Lastly, Ihde (2002) provides an excellent discussion of the phenomenological relationship between technology and the body.

NOTES

1   In that respect, we can refer back to the discussion of 'becoming', 'decalcomania', 'the wasp and the orchid' and Deleuze and Guattari in Chapter 1.
2   The parallels with technological and functional convergence, discussed in Chapter 3, are interesting to note here.

CONCLUSION
Base, Superstructure, Infrastructure (Revisited)

This book has attempted to give the reader a sense of the scope and scale to which digital communication technologies have permeated the everyday life of those in modern industrialised nations. In it, I have endeavoured to situate the use of these technologies within a wider framework of the economic, social and cultural processes taking place, and how these processes integrate the influences of technological innovations, economic structures and cultural creativity.

I began with the suggestion that digital communication technologies should not be seen as scientific innovations which then directly effect society and culture, but should instead be seen as *enabling infrastructures*, part of the 'base' in the base-superstructure relationship between economy and culture. What this means is that the infrastructures of digital communication were developed because of a certain set of economic conditions, namely, a crisis of profit in Fordist-based economies by the 1970s. We learned in Chapter 2 how innovations in communications technology are not only pushed by this set of economic circumstances looking for a solution (the 'creative destruction' of globalization), but how these innovations helped to further set these processes in motion in a kind of virtuous circle. Thus, technological innovations that helped to encourage globalisation, which meant that manufacturers and producers of goods could take better advantage of cheap pools of labour around the world, also created the conditions whereby consumers, using services like eBay or a myriad of other consumer web sites, could themselves search for products and information on a global scale. This helps to increase competition among those very producers and even, in the case of media and software companies, allows consumers to easily access their products illegally and for free.

This drive to innovate and globalise is part of a wider tendency within capitalism to overcome the problem of space in order to maximise the speed at which investments in raw materials and labour can be turned into a profit (Harvey, 1989). Technologically, this is manifested in Manuel Castells' notion of the space of flows (in contrast to the geographically-based space of places). Socially, this is manifested not only through the increase in mobility of consumer and labour markets, but also in a reconsideration of the types of groupings formed by society in a move towards networks and away from more static hierarchical structures and 'communities'. This situation produces two consequences.

First, it contributes to adaptations and transformations in societal structures and cultural forms. It is important to stress that in most cases, these are transformations that were already taking place as part of transformations under capitalist processes. Looking at the issues discussed in this book:

- Digital divides follow from a long legacy of the production of inequalities under capitalism. But in this case, information technology reproduces the domestic and global disparities that already exist.

- Privacy, and the right to it, becomes redefined on the basis of state concerns for security and control, as well as the need to understand more about consumer behaviour in a competitive global marketplace.

- Under the restructuring of labour in global post-Fordism, the class-based nature of national politics increasingly moves to more individualised, lifestyle-oriented, international issue-based new social movements. The internet contributes to this trend through providing an architecture what encourages networked organisation, multiple affiliations and easy access to information about issues of concern on a global scale.

- Processes of detraditionalisation, disembedding and globalisation were already ushering in changes in how we think about ourselves and perform our identities. Advances in ICTs merely opened up these processes further by increasing our ability to portray ourselves to others in virtual arenas.

- These same processes suggest that virtual communities are fundamentally nothing new, but are part of the continuing processes of individualism and the overcoming of the limitations of space, which sociologists commented upon in the early years of the industrial revolution as part of the consequence of capitalism.

- Our changing relationship to the body under digital culture can be seen to be the result of the rising value of information under post-Fordism, and the increasing use of mobile communication and information technologies in everyday life.

Second, while digital culture can be seen as one part of an overall societal process based on transformations in the economic base of society, and enabled through innovations in technological infrastructures, the 'superstructure' being created includes not only the continuation of older trends, but also the evolution of novel cultural forms, as demonstrated by the case studies we have examined:

- Digital video games, alternate reality games, ubiquitous games and MMORPGs are innovative forms of play, uniquely created through contemporary digital media technologies and thus defy traditional cultural categorisation.

- New forms of music production and distribution defy the basic of 'ownership' and 'authorship', which have been the bedrock of the cultural industries for centuries.

- The cybersexual relationship, enabled by and lived through digital communication technologies, becomes, especially in virtual worlds and real-time video interactions, a new form of human sexual encounter.

- Ubiquitous communications technologies allow us to decouple co-presence in space from social presence in time, leading to new forms of distributed or ambient presence within which we can maintain a sense of community or belonging with others in spite of physical distances.

While digital culture has become an unremarkable part of everyday life, it also continues to be a source of never-ending creativity. Whether an iPhone application that creates a treadmill for fingers, interactive paint on walls created by research into ambient intelligence, the random and often perverse global interactions enabled though *Chatroulette*, or the disruption of classrooms by using mobile phones to play downloaded high-frequency noises that only teens and children can hear, the continual manifestations of digital culture never ceases to be surprising in its developments.

REFERENCES

Aarseth, E. (1997) *Cybertext: Perspectives on Ergodic Literature*. Baltimore: Johns Hopkins University Press.

Aas, K. (2004) 'From narrative to database: technological change and penal culture', *Punishment & Society*, 6(4): 379–393.

Abercrombie, N., Hill, S. and Turner, B. (2000) *The Penguin Dictionary of Sociology*, 4th edn. London: Penguin.

Abercrombie, N. and Longhurst, B. (1998) *Audiences*. London: Sage.

Adams, P. and Ghose, R. (2003) 'India.com: the construction of a space between', *Progress in Human Geography*, 27(4): 414–437.

Adorno, T. and Horkheimer, M. (1991) *The Culture Industry: Selected Essays on Mass Culture*. London: Routledge.

Agamben, G. (1998) *Homo Sacer: Sovereign Power and Bare Life*. Stanford: Stanford University Press.

Agamben, G. (2005) *State of Exception*. London: University of Chicago Press.

Akyeanpong, E. and Winters, J. (1993) 'Perspectives on labour and income', *Statistics Canada*, 5(2): Summer.

Alderman, J. (2001) *Sonic Boom: Napster, MP3, and the New Pioneers of Music*. London: Fourth Estate.

Alger, J. (1996) 'Introduction', in W. Schwartau (ed.) *Information Warfare. Cyberterrorism: Protecting Your Personal Security in the Electronic Age*, 2nd edn. New York: Thunder's Mouth Press, pp. 8–14.

Allbright, J. (2008) 'Sex in America online: an exploration of sex, marital status, and sexual identity in internet sex-seeking and its impacts', *Journal of Sex Research*, 45(2): 175–186.

Anandarajan, M., Thompson, S., Teo, H. and Simmers, C. (2006) 'The Internet and workplace transformation', in M. Anandarajan, S. Thompson, H. Teo and C. Simmers (eds) *Advancements in Management Information Systems* (Vol. 7). Arnak, N.Y.: M.E. Sharpe Publications, pp. 3–11.

Anderson, B. (1983) *Imagined Communities: Reflections of the Spread of Nationalism*. London: Verso.

Anderson, B. and Tracey, K. (2001) 'Digital living: the impact (or otherwise) of the Internet on everyday life', *American Behavioral Scientist*, 45(3): 456–475.

Ansolabehere, S., Snowberg, E. and Snyder, M. (2005) 'Television and the incumbency advantage in U.S. Elections'. Typescript. Massachusetts Institute of Technology. Located at http://www.hss.caltech.edu/~snowberg/papers/Ansolabehere-Snowberg-Snyder%20TV%20and%20Incumbency%20Advatage.pdf (accessed 26 August 2009).

Armstrong, A. and Hegel, J. (2000) 'The real value of online communities', in E. Lesser, M. Fontaine and J. Slusher (eds) *Knowledge and Communities*. Oxford: Butterworth-Heinemann, pp. 85–97.

Arnold, M. (2003) 'On the phenomenology of technology: the "Janus-faces" of mobile phones', *Information and Organization*, 13(4): 231–256.

Arquilla, J. and Ronfeldt, D. (1993) 'Cyber war is coming', *Comparative Strategy*, 12(2):141–165.

Arquilla, J. and Ronfeldt, D. (eds) (2001) *Networks and Netwars: The Future of Terror, Crime, and Militancy*. Santa Monica: RAND.

Atton, C. (2006) 'Far-right media on the internet: culture, discourse and power', *New Media & Society*, 8(4): 573–587.

Ayres, R. (2006) 'Did the fifth K-wave begin in 1990–92? Has it been aborted by globalization?', in T. Devezas (ed.) *Kondratieff Waves, Warfare and World Security*. Amsterdam: IOS Press, pp. 57–71.

Back, L. (2002) 'Aryans reading Adorno: cyber-culture and twenty-first century racism', *Ethnic and Racial Studies*, 25(4): 628–651.

Badmington, N. (2003) 'Theorizing posthumanism', *Cultural Critique*, 53(4): 10–27.

Bagdikian, B. (2000) *The Media Monopoly*. Boston: Beacon Press.

Balsamo, A. (1996) *Technologies of the Gendered Body: Reading Cyborg Women*. London: Duke University Press.

Bank for International Settlements, Monetary and Economic Department (2007) *Triennia Central Bank Survey of Foreign Exchange and Derivatives Market Activity in April 2007: Preliminary Global Results*, located at http://www.bis.org/publ/rpfx07.pdf (accessed 5 March 2008).

Barlow, J.P. (1996) 'A declaration of the independence of cyberspace', located at http://homes.eff.org/~barlow/Declaration-Final.html (accessed 12 May 2009).

Barney, D. (2004) *The Network Society*. Cambridge: Polity.

Baron, N. (2008) *Always On: Language in an Online and Mobile World*. Oxford: Oxford University Press.

Barthes, R. (1974) *S/Z*, (translated by Richard Miller; preface by Richard Howard). New York: Hill and Wang.

Baudrillard, J. (1994) *Simulacra and Simulation*. Ann Arbour: University of Michigan Press.

Baudrillard, J. (1995) *The Gulf War Did Not Take Place*. Sydney: Power Publications.

Bauman, Z. (2001a) 'Identity in the globalising world', *Social Anthropology*, 9(2): 121–129.

Bauman, Z. (2001b) *The Individualized Society*. Cambridge: Polity.

Bauman, Z. (2001c) *Community: Seeking Safety in an Insecure World*. Cambridge: Polity.

Baym, N. (2002) 'Interpersonal life online', in L. Lievrouw and S. Livingstone (eds) *Handbook of New Media*. London: Sage, pp. 62–76.

BBC (2006) 'How we are being watched', *BBC News*, located at http://news.bbc.co.uk/1/hi/uk/6110866.stm (accessed 28 August 2009).

Beck, U. (1992) *Risk Society: Towards a New Modernity*. London: Sage.

Beck, U. (1997) *The Reinvention of Politics: Rethinking Modernity in the Global Social Order* (trans. Mark Ritter). Cambridge: Polity.

Beck, U. and Beck-Gernsheim, E. (2002) *Individualization: Institutionalized Individualism and its Social and Political Consequences*. London: Sage.

Beck, U., Giddens, A. and Lash, S. (1994) *Reflexive Modernization: Politics, Tradition and Aesthetics in the Modern Social Order*. London: Sage.

Beer, D. (2008) 'Making friends with Jarvis Cocker: music culture in the context of Web 2.0', *Cultural Sociology*, 2(2): 222–241.

Belhocine, N. (2008) 'Treating intangible inputs as investment goods: the impact on Canadian GDP'. Queen's Economics Department Working Papers No. 1215. Located at http://www.econ.queensu.ca/working_papers/papers/qed_wp_1215.pdf (accessed October 19 2009).

Bell, D. (1973) *The Coming of the Post Industrial Society: A Venture in Social Forecasting*. Harmondsworth: Penguin.

Bell, D. (1979) 'The social framework of the information society', in M. Dertouzous and J. Moses (eds) *The Computer Age: A Twenty Year View*. Cambridge: MIT Press, pp. 163–211.

Bell, D. (2001) *An Introduction to Cybercultures*. London: Routledge.

Bellah, R., Robert, N., Masden, R., Sullivan, W., Swindler, A. and Tipton, S. (1985) *Habits of the Heart*. Berkeley: University of California Press.

Ben Ze'ev, A. (2004*) Love Online: Emotions on the Internet*. Cambridge: Cambridge University Press.

Beninger, J. (1986) *The Control Revolution*. London: Harvard University Press.

Benjamin, W. (1936) 'The work of art in the age of mechanical reproduction', in F. Frascina and J. Harris (eds) (1992) *Art in Modern Culture*. London: Phaidon, pp. 297–307.

Bennett, L., Breunig, C. and Givens, T. (2008) 'Communication and political mobilization: digital media and the organization of anti-Iraq war demonstrations in the US', *Political Communication*, 25(3): 269–89.

Bennett, W.L. (2004) 'Branded political communication: lifestyle politics, logo campaigns, and the rise of global citizenship', in M. Micheletti, A. Follesdal and D. Stolle (eds) *Products and Markets: Exploring Political Consumerism Past and Present*. New Brunswick, NJ: Transaction Press, pp. 101–126.

Bessière, K., Seay, F. and Kiesler, S. (2007) 'The ideal elf: identity exploration in *World of Warcraft*', *CyberPsychology & Behavior*, 10(4): 530–535.

Beststuff.com (2001) 'LG internet refrigerator is at the heart of the digital home network', located at http://www.beststuff.com/fromthewire/lg-internet-refrigerator-is-at-the-heart-of-the-digital-home-network.html (accessed 24 June 2009).

Bigami, F. (2007) 'Privacy and law enforcement in the European Union: the data retention directive', *Chicago International Law*, 8 (Summer): 233–255.

Bimber, B. (1990) 'Karl Marx and the three faces of technological determinism', *Social Studies of Science*, 20(2): 333–351.

Bingham, N. (1996) 'Objections: from technological determinism towards geographies of relations', *Environment and Planning D: Society and Space*, 14(6): 635–657.

Blanchette, J-F. and Johnson, D. (2002) 'Data retention and the panoptic society: the social benefits of forgetfulness', *The Information Society*, 18(1): 33–45.

Blinka, L. (2008). 'The relationship of players to their avatars in MMORPGs: differences between adolescents, emerging adults and adults' *Cyberpsychology: Journal of Psychosocial Research on Cyberspace*, 2(1), article 5 located at http://cyberpsychology.eu/view.php?cisl oclanku=2008060901&article=5 (accessed 5 January 2010)

Boellstorff, T. (2008) *Coming of Age in Second Life*. Oxford: Princeton University Press.

Bohn, J., Coroama, V., Langheinrich, M., Mattern, F. and Rohs, M. (2004) 'Social, economic, and ethical implications of ambient intelligence and ubiquitous computing', in W. Weber, J. Rabaey and E. Aarts (eds) *Ambient Intelligence*. Berlin: Springer-Verlag, pp. 5–29.

Bolter, J. and Grusin, R. (2000) *Remediation: Understanding New Media*. Cambridge/London: MIT Press.

Bostrom, N. (2005) 'In defence of posthuman dignity', *Bioethics*, 19(3): 202–214.

Boyd, D. (2006) 'Friends, friendsters, and *MySpace* top 8: writing community into being on social network sites', *First Monday*, 11(12), located at http://www.firstmonday.org/issues/issue11_12/boyd/ (accessed October 15 2007).

Boyd, D. and Heer, J. (2006) 'Profiles as conversation: networked identity performances on Friendster', in Proceedings of the Hawai'i International Conference on System Sciences (HICSS-39), Persistent Conversation Track, Kaui, HI: IEEE Computer Society. January 4–7, 2006, located at http://www.danah.org/papers/HICSS2006.pdf (accessed 15 October 2007).

Bruckman, A. (1998) 'Finding one's own in cyberspace', in R. Holeton (ed.), *Composing Cyberspace: Identity, Community and Knowledge in the Electronic Age*. London: McGraw-Hill, pp. 171–179.

Bruns, A. (2008) *Blogs, Wikipedia, Second Life and Beyond: From Production to Produsage*. New York: Peter Lang.

Buchanan, I. (2007) 'Deleuze and the Internet', *Australian Humanities Review*, 43 (December), located at http://www.australianhumanitiesreview.org/archive/Issue-December-2007/Buchanan.html (accessed 15 June 2009).

Bush, V. (1945) 'As we may think', *The Atlantic Monthly* (July): 101–108, located at http://www.theatlantic.com/doc/194507/bush (accessed June 12 2009).

Butler, J. (1990) *Gender Trouble: Feminism and the Subversion of Identity*. London: Routledge.

Butler, J. (1993) *Bodies that Matter: On the Discursive Limits of 'Sex'*. London and New York: Routledge.

Callois, R. (1961) *Man, Play and Games*. New York: The Free Press.

Cameron, G. (1998) 'Economic growth in the information age: from physical capital to weightless economy', *Journal of International Affairs*, 51(2): 447–471.

Campbell, S. and Park, Y. (2008) 'Social implications of mobile telephony: the rise of personal communication society', *Sociology Compass* 2(2): 371–387.

Carl, C. (2003) *Bloggers and Their Blogs: A Depiction of the Users and Usage of Weblogs on the World Wide Web*. MA dissertation, Georgetown University, Washington DC.

Carr, N. (2008) *The Big Switch: Rewiring the World from Edison to Google*. London: Norton and Co.

Carty, V. (2002) 'Technology and counter-hegemonic movements: the case of Nike Corporation', *Social Movement Studies*, 1(2): 129–146.

Castells, M. (1996/2000) *The Rise of the Network Society*. Oxford: Blackwell.

Castells, M. (1997) *The Power of Identity*. Oxford: Blackwell.

Castells, M. (2001) *The Internet Galaxy: Reflections on the Internet, Business, and Society*. Oxford: Oxford University Press.

Castells, M., Fernández-Ardèvol, M., Qiu, J. and Sey, A. (2007) *Mobile Communication and Society: A Global Perspective*. Cambridge: MIT Press.

Castronova, E. (2006) *Synthetic Worlds: The Business and Culture of Online Games*. Chicago: University of Chicago Press.

CBS (2009) '"Sexting" shockingly common among teens', *CBS News Online*, Jan 15, located at http://www.cbsnews.com/stories/2009/01/15/national/main4723161.shtml (accessed 28 December 2009).

Cebrowski, A. and Garstka, J. J. (1998) 'Network-centric warfare: its origin and future', Naval Institute Proceedings, January, located at http://www.kinection.com/ncoic/ncw_origin_future.pdf (accessed 10 December 2009).

Chadwick, A. (2006) *Internet Politics: States, Citizens, and New Communication Technologies*. Oxford: Oxford University Press.

Chan, S. (2000) 'Wired_selves: from artefact to performance', *CyberPsychology & Behavior*, 3(2): 271–285.

Chancellor, J. (2010) '2009 was a record-breaking year for music sales', *Scene Tulsa World*, located at http://www.tulsaworld.com/scene/article.aspx?subjectid=269&articleid=20100106_371_0_Musics422096 (accessed 6 January 2010).

Chazerand, P. and Geeroms, C. (2008) 'The business of playing games: players as developers and entrepreneurs', *Digital Creativity*. 19(3): 185–193.

Chee, F., Vieta, M. and Smith, R. (2006) 'Online gaming and the interactional self: identity interplay in situated practice', in J.P. Williams, S.Q. Hendricks and W.K. Winkler (eds),

Gaming as Culture: Essays on Reality, Identity, and Experience in Fantasy Games. Jefferson, NC: McFarland Publishing, pp.154–174.

Choemprayong, S. (2006) 'Closing digital divides: the United States' policies', *Libri*, 56: 201–212.

Chon, B., Choi, J., Barnet, G., Dankowski, J. and Joo, S. (2003) 'A structural analysis of media convergence: cross industry mergers and acquisitions in the information industries', *Journal of Media Economics*, 16(3): 141–157.

Clark, A. (2003) *Natural Born Cyborgs: Mind, Technologies, and the Future of Human Intelligence*. Oxford: Oxford University Press.

Clarke, R. (1993). 'Profiling: a hidden challenge to the regulation of data surveillance', *Journal of Law and Information Science*, 4(2), 403–419.

Clements, A. (2008) 'Stem-cell research – playing God?' *The Times Online*, May 10, located at http://business.timesonline.co.uk/tol/business/specials/stemcell_research/article 3903841.ece (accessed on 25 July 2009).

Clinton, B. (1996) 'Remarks made by the President and the Vice President to the people of Knoxville, October 10, 1996', located at http://www.clintonpresidentialcenter.org/legacy/101096-remarks-y-resident-and-vp-in-knoxville-tn.htm. (accessed 28 July 2008).

Clynes, M. and Kline, N. (1960) 'Cyborgs and space', *Astronautics*, September: 29–34.

Coleman, S. (1999) 'Cutting out the middle man: from virtual representation to direct deliberation', in B. Hague and B. Loader (eds) *Digital Democracy: Discourse and Decision Making in the Information Age*. London: Routledge, pp. 195–210.

Computer Industry Almanac (2006) Press release 28 February, located at http://www.c-i-a.com/pr0206.htm (accessed 3 July 2009).

Comscore (2009) 'Americans viewed 12 billion videos online in May 2008, press release, located at http://ir.comscore.com/releasedetail.cfm?releaseid=321908 (accessed on 3 November 2009).

Conklin, J. (1987) 'Hypertext: an introduction and survey', *Computer*, 20(9): 17–41.

Coyle, D. (1997) *Weightless World: Strategies for Managing the Digital Economy*. Cambridge, Mass: MIT Press.

Coyle, D. (2005) 'Overview' in *Africa: The Impact of Mobile Phones: Moving the Debate Forward*. Vodaphone Policy Paper Series #3, pp 03–09, located at http://www.vodaphone.com/ect/medialib/attachments/cr_downloads (accessed on 15 July 2008).

Crawford, C. (2003) 'Interactive storytelling', in M. Wolf and B. Perron (eds) *The Video Game Theory Reader*. New York and London: Routledge, pp. 259–274.

Cronin, B. and Crawford, H. (1999) 'Information warefare: its application in military and civilian contexts', *The Information Society*, 15(4): 257–263.

Csikszentmihalyi, M. and Rochberg-Halton, E. (1981) *The Meaning of Things: Domestic Symbols and the Self*. Cambridge: Cambridge University Press.

CSIS (Canadian Security Intelligence Service) (2000) 'Anti-globalization: a spreading phenomenon. Report No. 2000/08', August 22, located at http://www.csis-scrs.gc.ca/pblctns/prspctvs/200008-eng.asp (accessed 22 May 2009).

Cullen, R. (2001) 'Addressing the digital divide', *Online Information Review*, 25(5): 311–320.

Dahlgren, P. (2004) 'Forward', in van de Wonk, W., Loader, B., Nixon, P. and Rucht, D. (eds) *Cyberprotest: New Media, Citizens and Social Movements*. London: Routledge, pp. xi–xvi.

Dahms, H. (1995) 'From creative action to the social rationalization of the economy: Joseph A. Schumpeter's social theory', *Sociological Theory*, 13(1): 1–13.

Dakroury, A. and Birdsall, W. (2008) 'Blogs and the right to communicate: towards creating a space-less public sphere?', *International Symposium on Technology and Society, ISTAS*

2008. IEEE, 1–8. Located at http://ieeexplore.ieee.org/stamp/stamp.jsp?arnumber=455 9762andisnumber=4559749 (accessed 26 January 2009).

Dant, T. (2004) 'The driver-car', *Theory, Culture & Society*, 21(4/5): 61–79.

Dányi, E. and Galácz, A. (2005) 'Internet and elections: changing political strategies and citizen tactics in Hungary', *Information Polity*, 10(3/4): 219–232.

Davis, K. (2003) 'Surgical passing: or why Michael Jackson's nose makes us uneasy', *Feminist Theory*, 4(1): 73–92.

Dawson, M. and Bellamy-Foster, J. (1998) 'Virtual capitalism: monopoly capital, marketing, and the information highway', in R. McChesney, E. Wood and J. Bellamy-Foster (eds) *Capitalism and the Information Age.* New York: Monthly Review Press, pp. 51–67.

Day, G. (2006) *Community and Everyday Life.* New York: Routledge.

Delanda, M. (1991) *War in the Age of Intelligent Machines.* New York: Zone Books.

Deleuze, G. and Guattari, F. (1988) *A Thousand Plateaus: Capitalism and Schizophrenia.* London: Athlone.

Dena, C. (2008) 'Emerging participatory culture practices: player-created tiers in alternate reality games', *Convergence: The International Journal of Research into New Media Technologies*, 14(5): 41–57.

Department of Trade and Industry & Department of Culture, Media and Sport (DTI & DCMS) (1998, July) *Regulating Communications: Approaching Convergence in the Information Age* (CM4022). London: HMSO.

Descartes, R. (1968 [1637]) *Discourse on Method and The Meditations* (trans by F.E. Sutcliffe). London: Penguin Books.

Deuze, M. (2006) 'Participation, remediation, bricolage: considering principal components of a digital culture', *The Information Society*, 22(2): 63–75.

Devereaux, A. (2007) '"What chew know about down the hill?": Baltimore club music, subgenre crossover, and the new subcultural capital of race and space', *Journal of Popular Music Studies*, 19(4): 311–341.

Dilley, R. (2000) 'The blockade that grew', BBC Online News, 11 September, located at http://news.bbc.co.uk/2/hi/uk_news/919852.stm (accessed 28 August 2009).

Disraeli, B. (1845) *Sybil; or, the Two Nations* (Volume 1, 3rd edn). London: Henry Colborn Pubs.

Domingues, J. (2000) 'The city', *Philosophy & Social Criticism*, 26(4): 107–126.

Donner, J. (2005) 'The mobile behaviors of Kigali's microentrepeneurs: whom they call ... and why', in K. Nyíri (ed.) *A Sense of Place: The Local and the Global in Mobile Communication.* Vienna: Passengen Verlag, pp. 293–301.

Donner, J. (2008) 'Research approaches to mobile use in the developing world: a review of the literature', *The Information Society*, 24: 140–159.

Döring, N. (2000) 'Feminist views of cybersex: victimization, liberation and empowerment', *Cyberpsychology and Behavior*, 3(5): 863–884.

Downes, E. and McMillan, S. (2000) 'Defining interactivity: a qualitative identification of key dimensions', *New Media & Society* 2(2): 157–179.

Drahos, P. and Brathwaite, J. (2002) *Information Feudalism: Who Owns the Knowledge Economy?* London: Earthscan.

Dreyfus, H. (1972) What *Computers Can't Do: A Critique of Artificial Reason.* New York: Harper and Row.

Dreyfus, H. (1992) What *Computers Still Can't Do: A Critique of Artificial Reason.* London: MIT Press.

Dreyfus, H. (2001) *On the Internet.* London: Routledge.

Drucker, P. (1979) *The Age of Discontinuity*. London: Heinemann.

Ducheneaut, N. and Moore, R.J. (2004) 'Let me get my alt: digital identiti(es) in multiplayer games', in *Proceedings of The CSCW2004 Workshop on Representation of Digital Identities*, Chicago, IL. located at http://people.ischool.berkeley.edu/~dmb/cscw2004–identity/papers/Ducheneaut-Moore.pdf (accessed 12 November 2009).

Dwight, J. (2004) 'Review essay: on the internet', *E-learning* 1(1): 146–152.

Dyer, C. (2007) 'Warning to abusive bloggers as judge tells site to reveal names', the *Guardian*, October 22, located at http://www.guardian.co.uk/technology/2007/oct/22/news.blogging (accessed 28 August 2009).

Eagleton-Pierce, M. (2001) 'The internet and the Seattle WTO protests', *Peace Review*, 13(3): 331–337.

Eason, R. (2003) 'Hypertext: Rortean links between Ihde and Haraway', in D. Ihde and E. Selinger (eds) *Chasing Technoscience: Matrix for Materiality*. Bloomington: Indiana University Press, pp. 67–181.

Ellison, N., Heino, R. and Gibbs, J. (2006) 'Managing impressions online: self-presentation processes in the online dating environment', *Journal of Computer-Mediated Communication*, 11(2): 415–441.

Ellul, J. (2001) *The Technological System*. New York: Continuum.

Elmer, G. (2004) *Profiling Machines*. London: MIT Press.

Elton, B. (2007) *Blind Faith*. London: Black Swan.

ELZN (1998) 'Fifth Declaration from the Lacandon Jungle, Mexico, July 1998', located at http://www.struggle.ws/mexico/ezln/ccri_5_dec_lj_july98.html (accessed 25 November 2009)

Engels, F. (1958) *The Condition of the Working Class in England in 1844* (trans. W. Henderson and W. Chaloner). New York: Macmillan. (First Published in German in 1845.)

Facebook (2010) 'Press room: Facebook statistics', located at http://www.facebook.com/press/info.php?statistics (accessed January 5 2010).

Featherstone, M. (2000) 'Archiving cultures', *British Journal of Sociology*, 51(1): 161–184.

Featherstone, M. and Burrows, R. (1995) 'Cultures of technological embodiment: an introduction', *Body & Society*, 1(3/4): 1–20.

Fernandez, M. (2002) 'Cyberfeminism, racism and embodiment', in M. Fernandez, F. Wilding and M.M. Wright (eds) *Domain Errors! Cyberfeminist Practices*. Brooklyn: Autonomedia.

Fernback, J. (1999) 'There is a there there: notes toward a definition of cybercommunity', in S. Jones (ed.) *Doing Internet Research: Critical Issues and Methods for Examining the Net*. Thousand Oaks: Sage, pp. 203–220.

Ferree, M. (2003) 'Women and the web: cybersex activity and its implications', *Sexual and Relationship Therapy*, 18(3): 385–393.

Flew, T. (2005) *New Media: An Introduction*. Oxford: Oxford University Press.

Frank, A. (1992) 'Twin nightmares of the medical simulacrum: Jean Baudrillard and David Cronenberg', in W. Stearns and W. Chaloupkea (eds) *Jean Baudrillard: The Disappearance of Art and Politics*. London: Macmillan, pp. 82–97.

Frasca, G. (2003) 'Simulation versus narrative: an introduction to Ludology', in M. Wolf and B. Perron (eds) *The Video Game Theory Reader*. New York and London: Routledge, pp. 221–236.

Frascina, F. and Harris, J. (1992) *Art in Modern Culture*. London: Phaidon Press.

Froehling, O. (1997) 'The cyberspace "war of ink and internet" in Chiapas, Mexico', *Geographical Review*, 87(2): 291–208.

Fuchs, V. (1980) 'Economic growth and the rise of service sector employment', Working Paper no. 486. Cambridge, MA: National Bureau of Economic Research.

Gaggioli, A., Vettorello, M. and Riva, G. (2003) 'From cyborgs to cyberbodies: the evolution of the concept of techno-body in modern medicine', *PsychNology*, 1(2): 75–86.

Galloway, A. (2004) 'Social realism in gaming', *Game Studies: The International Journal of Computer Game Research*, 4(1) located at http://www.gamestudies.org/0401/galloway/ (accessed 4 January 2010).

Garfinkel, S. (2001) *Database Nation: The Death of Privacy in the 21st Century*. Cambridge: O'Reilly.

Gauntlett, D. (1998) 'Ten things wrong with the "effects model"', in R. Dickinson, R. Harindranath and O. Linné (eds) *Approaches to Audiences – A Reader*. London: Arnold.

Gere, C. (2002) *Digital Culture*. London: Reaktion Books.

Gergen, K. (1996) 'Technology and the self: from the essential to the sublime', in D. Grodin and T. Lindlof (eds) *Constructing the Self in a Mediated World*. London: Sage, pp. 127–140.

Gergen, K. (2002) 'The challenge of absent presence', in J. Katz and M. Aakhus (eds) *Perpetual Contact: Mobile Communication, Private Talk, Public Performance*. Cambridge: Cambridge University Press, pp. 227–241.

Gibb, F. (2009) 'Ruling on *Nightjack* author Richard Horton killer blogger anonymity', *The Times Online*, 17 June, located at http://technology.timesonline.co.uk/tol/news/tech_and_web/the_web/article6509677.ece# (accessed on 28 August 2009).

Giddens, A. (1991) *Modernity and Self Identity: Self and Society in the Late Modern Age*. Cambridge: Polity.

Giddens, A. (1992) *The Transformation of Intimacy: Sexuality, Love and Eroticism in Modern Societies*. Cambridge: Polity.

Gilpin, R. (2001) *Global Political Economy: Understanding the International Economic Order*. Princeton and Oxford: Princeton University Press.

Goffman, E. (1959) *The Presentation of Self in Everyday Life*. Garden City, NJ: Doubleday.

Goffman, E. (1975) *Frame Analysis: An Essay on the Organization of Experience*. Harmondsworth: Penguin.

Graham, E. (2002) *Representations of the Post/Human*. Manchester: Manchester University Press.

Graham, S. and Marvin, S. (1996) *Telecommunications and the City: Electronic Spaces, Urban Places*. London: Routledge.

Graham, S. and Marvin, S. (2001) *Splintering Urbanism*. London: Routledge.

Granovetter, M. (1973) 'The strength of weak ties', *The American Journal of Sociology*, 78(6): 1360–1380.

Graphic Visualisation and Usability Centre (1998) 'GVU Center's WWW Surveys', located at http://www.cc.gatech.edu/gvu/user_surveys/User_Survey_Home.html (accessed 3 June 2009).

Gray, C., Mentor S. and Figueroa-Sarriera, H. (1995) 'Cyborgology: constructing the knowledge of cybernetic organisms', in C. Gray (ed.) *The Cyborg Handbook*, London: Routledge, pp. 1–15.

Gunkel, D. (2008) Rethinking the digital remix: mash-ups and the metaphysics of sound recording', *Popular Music and Society*. 31(4): 489–510.

Gunter, B., Campbell, V., Touri, M. and Gibson, R. (2009) 'Blogs, news and credibility', *Aslib Proceedings: New Information Perspectives*, 61(2): 185–204.

Habermas, J. (1989) *The Structural Transformation of the Public Sphere* (trans. T. Burger). Cambridge: Polity.

Hague, B. and Loader, B. (eds) (1999) *Digital Democracy: Discourse and Decision Making in the Information Age*. London: Routledge.

Hall, S. (1990) 'Who needs "identity"?' in P. du Gay, J. Evans and P. Redman (eds) *Identity: A Reader*. London: Sage, pp. 15–30.

Hamman, R. (1996) 'Rhizome@Internet: using the Internet as an example of Deleuze and Guattari's "Rhizome"', located at http://www.swinburne.infoxchange.net.au/media/halm316/gallery/david/pg11b.htm (accessed 15 June 2009).

Hansen, M. (2006) *New Philosophy for New Media*. Cambridge: MIT Press.

Haraway, D. (1985) 'A manifesto for cyborgs', *Socialist Review*, 80: 65–108.

Haraway, D. (1991) *Simians, Cyborgs and Women: The Reinvention of Nature*. London: Free Association Books.

Hardey, M. (2002) 'Life beyond the screen: embodiment and identity through the Internet', *The Sociological Review*, 50(4): 570–585.

Hardt, M. and Negri, A. (2000) *Empire*. London: Harvard University Press.

Hardt, M. and Negri, A. (2005) *Multitude: War and Democracy in the Age of Empire*. London: Hamish Hamilton.

Harris, A. (2008) 'Young women, late modern politics, and the participatory possibilities of online cultures', *Journal of Youth Studies*, 11(5): 481–95.

Harvey, D. (1989) *The Condition of Postmodernity*. Oxford: Blackwell.

Hayles, K. (1999) *How We Became Posthuman*. London: University of Chicago Press.

Hayward, P. (1990) 'Technology and the (trans) formation of culture' in P. Hayward (ed.) *Culture, Technology and Creativity in the Late Twentieth Century*. London: John Libbey, pp. 1–14.

Hearn, J. (2006) 'The implications of information and communication technologies for sexualities and sexualised violences: contradictions of sexual citizenships', *Political Geography*, 25(8): 944–963.

Hebdige, D. (1979) *Subculture: The Meaning of Style*. London: Methuen.

Heelas, P. (1996) 'Introduction: detraditionalization and its rivals', in Heelas, P., Lash, S. and Morris, P. (eds) *Detraditionalization*. Oxford: Blackwell, pp. 1–20.

Henwood, F., Wyatt, S., Miller, N. and Senker, P. (2000) 'Critical perspectives on technologies, in/equalities and the information society', in S. Wyatt, F. Henwood, N. Miller, and P. Senker (eds) *Technology and in/Equality: Questioning the Information Society*. London: Routledge, pp. 1–18.

Herman, E. and Chomsky, N. (1988) *Manufacturing Consent: The Political Economy of the Mass Media*. New York: Pantheon.

Hermanns, H. (2008) 'Mobile democracy: mobile phones as democratic tools', *Politics*, 28(2): 74–82.

Herz, J. (2005) 'Harnessing the hive', in J. Hartley (ed.) *Creative Industries*. Malden, MA: Blackwell, pp. 327–341.

Hess, A. (2008) 'Reconsidering the rhizome: a textual analysis of web search engines as gatekeepers of the internet', in A. Spink and M. Zimmer (eds) *Web Search, Springer Series in Information Science and Knowledge Management Volume 14*. Berlin: Springer, pp. 35–50.

Hevern, V. (2004) 'Threaded identity in cyberspace: weblogs and positioning in the dialogical self', *Identity*, 4(4): 321–335.

Hill, K. and Hughes, J. (1998) *Cyberpolitics: Citizen Activism in the Age of the Internet*. New York: Rowman & Littlefield.

Hillery, G. (1955) 'Definitions of community: areas of agreement', *Rural Sociology*, 20(2): 111–124.

Hindman, M. (2005) 'The real lessons of Howard Dean', *Perspectives on Politics*, 3(11): 121–128.

Hine, C. (2006) 'Databases as scientific instruments and their role in the ordering of scientific work', *Social Studies of Science* 36(2): 269–298.

Hodkinson, P. (2007) 'Interactive online journals and individualization', *New Media & Society*, 9(4): 625–650.

Hodkinson, P. and Lincoln, S. (2008) 'Online journals as virtual bedrooms? Young people, identity and personal space', *Young*, 16(1): 27–46.

Holmes, D. (1997) 'Introduction: virtual politics – identity and community in cyberspace', in D. Holmes (ed.) *Virtual Politics: Identity & Community in Cyberspace*, London: Sage, pp. 1–24.

Horrigan, J. (2009) *Home Broadband Adoption 2009*. Pew Internet and American Life Project, located at http://www.pewinternet.org/~/media//Files/Reports/2009/Home-Broadband-Adoption-2009.pdf (accessed 10 June 2009).

Howard, P., Rainie, L. and Jones, S. (2002) 'Days and nights on the Internet: the impact of a diffusing technology', *American Behavioral Scientist*, 45(3): 382–404.

Howard, S., Kjeldskov, J., Skov, M., Garnæs, K. and Grünberger, O. (2006) 'Negotiating presence inabsence: contact, content and context', *Proceedings of the SIGCHI Conference on Human Factors in Computing Systems* (Montréal, Québec, Canada, 22–27 April). Located at http://portal.acm.org/citation.cfm?id=1124906 (accessed 4 January 2010).

Howard-Spink, S. (2005) 'Grey Tuesday, online cultural activism and the mash-up of music and politics', First Monday, 9(10), located at http://firstmonday.org/issues/issue9_10/howard/ index.html (accessed 4 January 2010).

Huffaker, D. and Calvert, S. (2005) 'Gender, identity and language in teenage blogs', *Journal of Computer-Mediated Communication*, 10(2), article 1, located at http://jcmc.indiana.edu/vol10/issue2/huffaker.html (accessed 12 July 2009).

Ihde, D. (1990) *Technology and the Lifeworld: From Garden to Earth*. Bloomington: Indiana University Press.

Ihde, D. (2002) *Bodies in Technology*. Minneapolis: Minnesota University Press.

Ilan, J. (2010) 'Decade in review: bass, from ghetto to global', *Bodytonic*, located at http://www.bodytonicmusic.com/words/2009/dec/01/decade-review-bass/page/5/ (accessed 6 January 2010).

Infidelitycheck (2002) 'Cheating spouse statistics', located at www.infidelitycheck.org/statistics/htm (accessed 10 October 2010).

International Federation of the Phonographic Industry (2009) 'Digital music report', located at www.IFPI.org/contact/DMR2009-real.pdf (accessed 11 October 2010).

Internet World Stats: Usage and Population Statistics (2008) located at http://www.internetworldstats.com/ (accessed 1 August 2008).

Iosifidis, P. (2002) 'Digital convergence: challenges for European regulation', *The Public*, 9(3): 27–48.

Irion, K. (2009) 'Privacy and security-international communications surveillance', *Communications of the ACM*, 52(2): 26–28.

Ismael, J.T. (2007) *The Situated Self*. Oxford: Oxford University Press.

ITU (2008) Online Statistics. International Telecommunications Union, located at http://www.itu.int/ITU–D/icteye/Default.aspx (accessed 20 July 2008).

James, J. (2006) 'Information technology and mass poverty', *International Journal of Development Issues*, 5(1): 85–107.

James, J. and Versteeg, M. (2007) 'Mobile phones in Africa: how much do we really know?', *Social Indicators Research* 84(1): 117–126.

Java, A., Finin, T., Song, X. and Tseng, B. (2007) 'Why we Twitter: understanding microblogging usage and communities', *Procedings of the Joint 9th WEBKD*.

Jenkins, H. (2004) 'The cultural logic of media convergence', *International Journal of Cultural Studies*, 7(1): 33–43.

Jenkins, H. (2006) *Convergence Culture: Where Old and New Media Collide*. New York and London: New York University Press.

Jenkins, H. and Deuze, M. (2008) 'Editorial: convergence culture', *Convergence: The International Journal of Research into New Media Technologies*, 14(5): 5–12.

Jensen, J. (1998) 'Interactivity: tracing a new concept in media and communication studies', *Nordicom Review*, 19(1): 185–204.

Jensen, R. (2007) 'The digital provide: information (technology), market performance, and welfare in the south Indian fisheries sector', *Quarterly Journal of Economics*, 122(3): 879–924.

Jewkes, Y. and Yar, M. (eds) (2009) *Handbook of Internet Crime*. Portland: Willan.

Johnson, S. (2009) 'How Twitter will change the way we live', *Time Magazine Online*, 5 June, located at http://www.time.com/time/business/article/0,8599,1902604,00.html (accessed 15 January 2010).

Johnston, H. (1994) 'New social movements and old regional nationalisms', in E. Larana, H. Johnston and J. Gusfield (eds) *New Social Movements*. Philadelphia: Temple University Press, pp. 267–286.

Jones, D.E. (2006) 'I, avatar: constructions of self and place in *Second Life* and the Technological Imagination', *Gnovis*, 6, located at http://gnovisjournal.org/files/Donald-E-ones-I-Avatar.pdf (accessed 1 November 2009).

Jones, J. (2003) *Bridging the Global Digital Divide*. Cheltenham: Edward Elgar.

Jones, S. (2002) 'Music that moves: popular music, distribution and network technologies', *Cultural Studies*, 16(2): 213–232.

Jovanov, E., Milenkovic, A., Otto, C. and de Groen, P. (2005) 'A wireless body area network of intelligent motion sensors for computer assisted physical rehabilitation', *Journal of NeuroEngineering and Rehabilitation*, 2(1): 6–15.

Jupiter Media Metrix (2001) 'Rapid media consolidation dramatically narrows number of companies controlling time spent online, reports Jupiter Media metrix', 4 June, located at http://www.comscore.com/press/displaycontent.asp?press=245&suffix=htm (accessed 28 April 2009).

Juul, J. (2001) 'Games telling stories? A brief note on games and narrative', *Game Studies: The International Journal of Computer Game Research*, 1(1),: located at http://gamestudies.org/0101/juul–gts/ (accessed 12 September 2009).

Kahn, J. (2005) 'Yahoo helped Chinese to prosecute journalist', *The New York Times*, 8 September, located at http://www.nytimes.com/2005/09/07/business/worldbusiness/07iht-yahoo.html (accessed 15 September 2009).

Kahn, R. and Kellner, D. (2004) 'New media and internet activism: from the "Battle of Seattle" to blogging', *New Media and Society*, 6(1): 87–95.

Kalleberg, A. (2000) 'Nonstandard employment relations: part time, temporary and contract work', *Annual Review of Sociology*, 26(1): 341–365.

Katz, J. and Rice, R. (2002) 'Project syntopia: social consequences of internet use', *IT & Society*, 1(1): 166–179.

Kiousis, S. (2002) 'Interactivity: a concept explication', *New Media & Society,* 4(3): 355–383.

Kleinknecht, A. (1986) 'Long waves, depression and innovation', *De Economist*, 134(1): 84–108.

Kleinknecht, A. (1987) *Innovation Patterns in Crisis and Prosperity*. Basingstoke: Macmillan.

Knorr-Cetina, K. (1997) 'Sociality with objects', *Theory, Culture & Society*, 14(4): 1–30.

Kolko, B., Nakamura, L. and Rodman, G. (eds) (2000) *Race in Cyberspace*. London: Routledge.

Kondratieff, N. (1935) 'The long waves in economic life', *Review of Economic Statistics*, 17(6): 105–115.

Krahn, H., Lowe, G. and Hughes, K. (2007) *Work, Industry and Canadian Society*, 5th edn. Toronto: Thompson/Nelson.

Krzywinska, T. (2007) 'Being a determined agent in (the) *World of Warcraft*: text/play/identity', in B. Atkins and T. Krzywinska (eds) *Videogame, Player, Text*. Manchester: Manchester University Press, pp. 101–119.

Kumar, K. (1978) *Prophesy and Progress*. Middlesex: Penguin.

Kumar, K. (2005) *From Post-Industrial to Post-Modern Society*. Oxford: Blackwell.

Kurzweil, R. (1999) *The Age of Spiritual Machines: When Computers Exceed Human Intelligence*. New York: Viking.

Kurzweil, R. (2005) *The Singularity is Near*. New York: Penguin.

Kusek, D. and Leonhard, G. (2005) *The Future of Music: Manifest for the Digital Music Revolution*. Boston: Berkley Press.

Landow, G. (1994) *Hyper/Text/Theory*. Baltimore: Johns Hopkins University Press.

Landow, G. (2006) *Hypertext 3.0. Critical Theory and New Media in an Era of Globalization*. Baltimore: Johns Hopkins University Press.

Lasn, K. (2000) *Culture Jam: How to Reverse America's Suicidal Consumer Binge, and Why We Must*. New York: Quill Press.

Latour, B. (1994) 'On technical mediation – philosophy, sociology, genealogy', *Common Knowledge*, 3(2): 29–64.

Laurel, B. (1991) *Computers as Theatre*. Reading, MA: Addison-Weseley.

Lawson-Borders, G. (2006) *Media Organizations and Convergence Pioneers*. Mahwah, NJ: Lawrence Erlbaum Associates.

Leadbeater, C. (2008) *We-Think*. London: Profile Books.

Lee, J. (2009) 'Contesting the digital economy and culture: digital technologies and the transformation of popular music in Korea', located at http://sonicscape.koreanpop.org/wp-content/uploads/2009/07/jylee090625contesting-the-digital-economy-and-culture.pdf (accessed 6 January 2010).

Lefebvre, H. (2000) *Critique of Everyday Life*. London: Verso.

Lehman, B. (1996) 'Intellectual property: America's competitive advantage in the 21st century', *Columbia Journal of World Business*, 31(1): 6–16.

Lessig, L. (1999) *Code and Other Laws of Cyberspace*. New York: Basic Books.

Lessig, L. (2001) *The Future of Ideas: The Fate of the Commons in a Connected World*. New York: Random House.

Levy, P. (1997) *Collective Intelligence: Mankind's Emerging World in Cyberspace*. Cambridge, MA: Perseus Books.

Lewis, T. (2006) *Critical Infrastructure Protection in Homeland Security: Defending a Networked Nation*. Hoboken, NJ: Wiley.

Licklider, J., Taylor, R. and Herbert, E. (1968) 'The computer as a computational device', *International Science and Technology*, April.

Licoppe, C. (2004) '"Connected" presence: the emergence of a new repertoire for managing social relationships in a changing communication technoscape', *Environment and Planning D: Society and Space*, 22(1): 135–156.

Lister, M., Dovey, J., Giddings, S., Grant, I. and Kelley, K. (2009) *New Media: A Critical Introduction*. London: Routledge.

Liu, H. (2007) 'Social network profiles as taste performances', *Journal of Computer-Mediated Communication*, 13(1), article 13, located at http://jcmc.indiana.edu/vol13/issue1/liu.html (accessed 29 October 2009).

Lockhard, J. (1997) 'Progressive politics, electronic individualism and the myth of the virtual community', in D. Porter (ed.) *Internet Culture*. London: Routledge, pp. 219–232.

Longan, M. (2005) 'Visions of community and mobility: the community networking movement in the USA', *Social & Cultural Geography*. 6(6): 849–864.

Luke, T. (1996) 'Identity, meaning and globalization: detraditionalization in postmodern time–space compression', in P. Heelas, S. Lash and P. Morris, (eds) *Detraditionalization*. Oxford: Blackwell, pp. 109–133.

Lyon, D. (1988) *The Information Society: Issues and Illusions*. Cambridge: Polity.

Lyon, D. (2001) *Surveillance Society: Monitoring Everyday Life*. Buckingham: Open University Press.

Lyon, D. (2003) 'Surveillance as social sorting: computer codes and mobile bodies', in D. Lyon (ed.) *Surveillance as Social Sorting*. New York: Routledge, pp. 13–30.

MacDougal, R. (2005) 'Identity, electronic ethos, and blogs', *American Behavioral Scientist* 49(4): 575–599.

Mackenzie, D. and Wajcman, J. (1999) 'Introductory essay and general issues', in D. Mackenzie and J. Wajcman (eds) *The Social Shaping of Technology*, 2nd edn. Buckingham: Open University Press, pp. 3–27.

Madden, M. and Jones, S. (2008) *Networked Workers*. Pew Internet and American Life Project, 24 September, 2008, located at http://www.pewinternet.org/pdfs/PIP_Networked_Workers_FINAL.pdf (accessed 26 January 2009).

Mager, N. (1987) *The Kondratieff Waves*. New York: Praeger.

Makinen, G. (2002) 'The economic effects of 9/11: a retrospective assessment', Washington, DC: Congressional Research Service – Report for Congress. Located at http://www.fas.org/irp/crs/RL31617.pdf (accessed 13 December 2009).

Malchup, F. (1962) *The Production and Distribution of Knowledge in the United States*. Princeton, NJ: Princeton University Press.

Malinowski, B. (1923) 'Supplement 1: the problem of meaning in primitive languages' in C. Ogden and I. Richards (eds). *The Meaning of Meaning*. London: Routledge & Keegan Paul, pp. 296–336.

Mallon, B. and Webb, B. (2005) 'Stand up and take your place: identifying narrative elements in narrative adventure and role-play games', *ACM Computers in Entertainment*, 3(1): 6–6.

Mandel, E. (1980) *Long Waves of Capitalist Development. The Marxist Explanation*. Cambridge: Cambridge University Press.

Manovich, L. (2001) *The Language of New Media*. Cambridge/London: MIT Press.

Mansch, G. (1979) *Stalemate in Technology. Innovations Overcome Depression*. Cambridge: Ballinger.

Marcuse, P. (2002) 'Depoliticizing globalization: the information age and the network society of Manuel Castells', in J. Ede and C. Mele (eds) *Investigating the City: Contemporary and Future*. Oxford: Blackwell, pp. 131–158.

Marlin-Bennett, R. (2004) *Knowledge Power: Intellectual Property, Information and Privacy*. London: Lynne Rienner Publications.

Marx, K. (1932) *Capital, the Communist Manifesto and Other Writings* (M. Foster, ed.), New York: The Modern Library.

Marx, K. (1977 [1853]) 'The future results of British rule in India', in D. McLellan (ed.) *Karl Marx: Selected Writings*. Oxford: Oxford University Press, pp. 332–337.

Marx, K. (1990 [1867]) *Capital, Volume 1*. London: Penguin.

Masuda, Y. (1981) *The Information Society as a Post-Industrial Society*. Bethesda, MD: World Future Society.

Mazlish, B. (1993) *The Fourth Discontinuity: The Co-Evolution of Humans and Machines*. New Haven: Yale University Press.

McChesney, R. and Shiller, D. (2003) *The Political Economy of International Communications: Foundations for the Emerging Global Debate about Media Ownership and Regulation*. United Nations Research Institute for Social Development; Technology, Business and Society Programme Paper Number 11, October.

McCullagh, K. (2008) 'Blogging: self presentation and privacy', *Information and Communications Technology Law*, 17(1): 3–23.

McGonigal, J. (2008) 'Why I love bees', in K. Salen (ed.) *The Ecology of Games: Connecting Youth, Games, and Learning*. The John D. and Catherine T. MacArthur Foundation Series on Digital Media and Learning. Cambridge, MA: MIT Press, pp. 199–228.

McGrath, J. (2004) *Loving Big Brother: Performance, Privacy and Surveillance Space*. London: Routledge.

McLaren, A. (2007) 'Online intimacy in a Chinese setting', *Asian Studies Review*, 31(4): 409–422.

McLeod, K. (2005) 'Confessions of an intellectual (property): Danger Mouse, Mickey Mouse, Sonny Bono, and my long and winding path as a copyright activist-academic', *Popular Music and Society*, 28(1): 79–93.

McQuail, D. and Suine, K (1998) *Media Policy: Convergence, Concentration and Commerce*. London: Sage.

Meadows, M. (2008) *I, Avatar: The Culture and Consequences of Having a Second Life*. Berkeley CA: New Riders.

MediaPost (2001) 'Media Consolidation Narrows Number Of Companies Controlling Time Spent Online', location at http://www.mediapost.com/publications/index.cfm?fa=Articles.showArticle&art_aid=11794 (accessed 28 April 2009).

Menely, T. (2007) '"Forgive me if I am forthright" – or, conversational freedom', *Campus Conversations*, 1(1): 94–111, located at http://www.willamette.edu/events/conversations/past/conversations/pdf/conversations.pdf (accessed 10 November 2009).

Merlau-Ponty, M. (1962) *Phenomenology of Perception*. London: Routledge & Kegan Paul.

Mileham, B. (2007) 'Online infidelity in Internet chat rooms: an ethnographic exploration', *Computers in Human Behavior*, 23(1): 11–31.

Miller, D. and Slater, D. (2000) *The Internet*. Oxford: Berg.

Miller, V. (2008) 'New media, networking and phatic culture', *Convergence*, 14(4): 387–400.

Mills, J. (2008) *Privacy: The Lost Right*. New York: Oxford University Press.

Mitcham C. (1994) *Thinking Through Technology: The Path Between Engineering and Philosophy*. London: The University of Chicago Press.

Mitra, A. (1997) 'Virtual community: looking for India on the Internet', in S.G. Jones (ed.) *Virtual Culture: Identity and Communication in Cybersociety*, Thousand Oaks, CA: Sage, pp. 55–79.

Mitra, A. (2005) 'Creating immigrant identities in cybernetic space: examples from a non-resident Indian website', *Media, Culture & Society*, 27(3): 371–390.

Mitra, S. (2009) 'Wall street vs. "virtual street"', *Forbes.com*, located at http://www.forbes.com/2009/08/20/virtual-worlds-economy-intelligent-technology-virtual-worlds.html, (accessed 25 October 2009).

Moravec, H. (1999) *Robot: Mere Machine to transcendent Mind*. Oxford: Cambridge University Press.

More, M. (1999) 'The extropian principles: a transhumanist declaration', located at http://www.extropy.org/extprn3.htm (accessed 12 August 2009).

Nakada, M. and Tamura, T. (2005) 'Japanese conceptions of privacy: an intercultural perspective', *Ethics and Information Technology*, 7(1): 27–36.

Nasaw, D. (2009) 'Court orders "Skanks in NYC" blogger to reveal identity', the *Guardian*, 19 August, located at http://www.guardian.co.uk/technology/2009/aug/19/google-model-blogger-liskula-cohen (accessed 28 August 2009).

Nayar, P. (2004) *Virtual Worlds: Culture and Politics in the Age of Cybertechnology*. London: Sage.

Newman, J. (2004) *Videogames*. London: Routledge.

Nie, N. (2001) 'Sociability, interpersonal relations, and the Internet: reconciling conflicting findings', *American Behavioral Scientist*, 45(3): 420–435.

Nietzsche, F. (1968) *Thus Spoke Zarathustra*, (trans. W. Kaufmann). London: Penguin Books.

Nip, J. (2004) 'The relationship between online and offline communities: the case of the Queer Sisters', *Media, Culture & Society*, 26(3): 409–428.

Nora, S. and Minc, A. (1980) *The Computerization of Society: A Report to the President of France*. Cambridge, MA: MIT Press.

Norris, P. (2001) *Digital Divide: Civic Engagement, Information Poverty, and the Internet Worldwide*. Cambridge: Cambridge University Press.

NPD Group (2009) 'Press Release: more Americans play video games than go out to the movies', located at http://www.npd.com/press/releases/press_090520.html (accessed 2 January 2010).

O'Hara, K. and Brown, B. (eds) (2006) *Consuming Music Together: Social and Collaborative Aspects of Music Consumption Technologies*. London: Springer.

Obama, B. (2009) 'Remarks by the President at the National Academy of Sciences Annual Meeting, National Academy of Sciences April 27, 2009, For Immediate Release'. Washington, DC: The White House Office of the Press Secretary, located at http://www.osa.org/News/publicpolicy/WashingtonUpdates/NASspeechtranscript.pdf (accessed 26 October 2009).

Office for National Statistics (2007) *Labour Market Statistics, First Release*. 19 January 2008.

Oldenburg, R. (1999) *The Great Good Place: Cafes, Coffee Shops, Bookstores, Bars, Hair Salons, and Other Hangouts at the Heart of the Community*, 3rd edn. New York: Marlowe and Company.

Parker, D. and Song, M. (2006) 'New ethnicities online: reflexive racialisation and the internet', *The Sociological Review*, 54(3): 575–594.

Parton, N. (2008) 'Changes in the form of knowledge in social work: from the "social" to the "informational"?', *British Journal of Social Work* 38(2): 253–269.

Paul, C. (2007) 'The database as system and cultural form: anatomies of cultural narratives', in V. Vesna (ed.) *Database Aesthetics*. Minneapolis: University of Minnesota Press, pp. 95–110.

Perri 6 (1998) *The Future of Privacy*. London: Demos.

Pink, D. (2005) 'The book stops here'. *Wired* 13(3), located at http://www.wired.com/wired/archive/13.03/wili.html (accessed 25 March 2009).

Plant, S. (1997) *Zeroes and Ones: Digital Women and the New Technoculture.* London: Fourth Estate.

Porat, M. (1977) *The Information Economy: Definition and Measurement.* Washington, DC: US Government Printing Office.

Poster, M. (1990) *The Mode of Information: Poststructuralism and Social Context.* Cambridge: Polity.

Poster, M. (1995) *The Second Media Age.* Cambridge: Polity.

Poster, M. (2001) *What's the Matter with the Internet?* Minneapolis: University of Minnesota Press.

Poster, M. (2006) *Information Please: Culture and Politics in the Age of Digital Machines.* Durham: Duke University Press.

Prensky, M. (2001) *Digital Games Base Learning.* New York: McGraw-Hill.

Putnam, R. (2000) *Bowling Alone: The Collapse and Revival of American Community.* New York and London: Simon & Schuster.

Quah, D. (1999) 'The weightless economy in growth', *The Business Economist*, 30(1): 40–53.

Rabon, L. (2001) 'Technology outlook 2001: US suppliers weather winds of change', *Bobbin*, 42(Jan): 54–60.

Raisinghani, M., Benoit, A., Ding, J., Gomez, M., Gupta, K., Gusila, V. and Power, D. (2004) 'Ambient intelligence: changing forms of human–computer interaction and their social implications', *Journal of Digital Information*, 5(4): 1–8.

Rak, J. (2005) 'The digital queer: weblogs and internet identity', *Biography*, 28(1): 166–182.

Reinert, E. and Reinert, H. (2006) 'Creative destruction in economics: Nietzsche, Sombart, Schumpeter', in Backhaus, J. Drechsler and W. Drechsler (eds) *Friedrich Nietzsche 1844–2000: Economy and Society.* New York, Springer, pp. 55–85.

Resnik, S. and Wolff, R. (1982) 'Marxist epistemology: the critique of economic determinism', *Social Text*, 6(3): 31–72.

Reuters (2008) 'Global cellphone penetration reaches 50 pct.', located at http://investing. reuters.co.uk/news/articleinvesting.aspx?type=media&storyID=nL29172095 (accessed 30 July 2008).

Rheingold, H. (1993) *The Virtual Community: Homesteading on the Electronic Frontier.* Reading, MA: Addison-Wesley Pub.

Rheingold, H. (2000) *The Virtual Community: Homesteading on the Electronic Frontier*, 2nd edn. Cambridge MA: MIT Press. (Originally published in 1993 by Addison Weseley.)

Rheingold, H. (2002) *Smart Mobs: The Next Social Revolution.* Cambridge, Mass: Basic Books.

Richardson, I. (2007) 'Pocket technospaces: the bodily incorporation of mobile media', *Continuum*, 21(2): 205–215.

Rideout, V., Roberts, D. and Foehr, D. (2005) *Generation M: Media in the Lives of 8–18 Year Olds.* The Henry J. Kaiser Family Foundation, located at http://www.kff.org/ entmedia/upload/Executive-Summary-Generation-M-Media-in-the-lives-f8-18-year-olds. pdf (accessed 25 January 2009).

Rimer, S. (2009) 'A lesson in modern manners: no texting at the dinner table', *The New York Times*, 7 June 2008. p. 7.

Ritzer, G. (1998) *The McDonaldization Thesis: Expansions and Extensions.* London: Sage.

Riva, G. (2003) 'Ambient intelligence in health care', *CyberPsychology & Behavior*, 6(3): 295–300.

Rivett, M. (2000) 'Approaches to analysing the web text: a consideration of the web site as an emergent cultural form', *Convergence* 6(3): 34–56.

Robinett, W. (2003) 'Foreword', in M. Wolf and B. Perron (eds) *The Video Game Theory Reader*. New York and London: Routledge, pp. vii–xxi.

Robins, K. and Webster, F. (1986) *Information Technology: A Luddite Analysis*. Norwood, NJ: Ablex.

Robinson, N. (2002) 'The politics of the fuel protests: towards a multi-dimensional explanation', *The Political Quarterly*, 73(1): 58– 67.

Robinson, W. and Harris, T. (2000) 'Towards a global ruling class? Globalization and the transnational capitalist class', *Science and Society*, 64(1): 11–54.

Roman, A. (2009) 'Texting God: SMS and religion in the Phillipines', *Journal of the Asian Research Center for Religion and Social Communication*, 3(1), located at http://www. stjohn.ac.th/arc/texting%20god.pdf (accessed 12 November 2009).

Ross, M. (2005) 'Typing, doing, and being: sexuality and the Internet', *Journal of Sex Research*, 42(4): 342–352.

Rubin, M. and Huber, M. (1986) *The Knowledge Industry in the United States 1960–1980*. Princeton: Princeton University Press.

Savage, M., Bagnall, G. and Longhurst, B. (2005) *Globalization and Belonging*. London: Sage.

Schau, H. and Gilly, M. (2003) 'We are what we post? Self-presentation in personal web space', *Journal of Consumer Research*, 30(3): 385–404.

Scheeres, J. (2003) 'Suicide 101: lessons before dying', *Wired* 02/03/03, located at http:// www.wired.com/culture/lifestyle/news/2003/02/57444 (accessed 4 December 2009).

Schiller, H. (1986) *Information and the Crisis Economy*. New York: Oxford University Press.

Schiller, H. (1999) *Digital Capitalism: Networking the Global Market System*. Cambridge, MA: MIT Press.

Schmidt, J. (2007) 'Blogging practices: an analytical framework', *Journal of Computer-mediated Communication*, 12(4): 1409–1420.

Schneider, J. (2000) 'Effect of cybersex addiction on the family', *Sexual Addiction and Compulsivity*, 7(1): 31–58.

Schneider, J. and Weiss, R. (2001) *Cybersex Exposed: Simple Fantasy or Obsession?* Center City, MN: Hazelden.

Schulman, A. (2001) 'The extent of systematic monitoring of employee e-mail and internet use', *Privacy Foundation Report*, located at http://www.sonic.net/~undoc/extent.htm (accessed 15 September 2009).

Schumpeter, J. (1939) *Business Cycles: A Theoretical, Historical and Statistical Analysis of the Capitalist Process*. New York: McGraw-Hill.

Scott, N., Batchelor, S., Ridley, J. and Jorgensen, B. (2004) *The Impact of Mobile Phones in Africa*. Report prepared for the Commission of Africa, ref: CNTR 026, located at http:// www.commissionforafrica.org/english/report/background/scott_et_al_background.pdf (accessed 2 August 2008).

Selinger, E. and Engström, T. (2007) 'On naturally embodied cyborgs: identities, metaphors, and models', *Janus Head*, 9(2): 553–584.

Selwyn, N. (2004) 'Reconsidering political and popular understandings of the digital divide.' *New Media & Society*, 6(3): 341–362.

Sennet, R. (1998) *The Corrosion of Character: The Personal Consequences of Work in the New Capitalism*. New York and London: Norton & Co.

Shaw, W. (1979) '"The handmill gives you the feudal lord": Marx's technological determinism', *History and Theory*, 18(2): 155–176.

Shields, R. (2003) *The Virtual*. London: Routledge.

Shilling, C. (1993) *The Body and Social Theory*. London: Sage.

Shilling, C. (2005) *The Body in Culture, Technology and Society*. London: Sage.

Shiva, V. (1997) *Biopiracy: The Plunder of Nature and Knowledge*. Boston: South End Press.

Shiva, V. (2001) *Protect or Plunder? Understanding Intellectual Property Rights*. London: Zed Books.

Simmel, G. (1950) 'The metropolis and mental life', in K. Wolff (trans and ed.) *The Sociology of Georg Simmel*. Glencoe, ILL: The Free Press.

Simmel, G. (1971) 'Social forms and inner needs', in D. Levine (ed.) *Georg Simmel on Individuality and Social Forms*. Chicago: University of Chicago Press, pp. 11–99.

Slater, D. (2002) 'Social relationships and identity online and offline', in L. Lievrouw and S. Livingstone (eds) *Handbook of New Media*. London: Sage, pp. 533–546.

Snyder, C. (2008) 'Google ordered to unmask mystery blogger in India', *Wired*, August 14, located at http://www.wired.com/epicenter/2008/08/google-ordered/ (accessed 18 September 2009).

Snyder, I. (2007) 'New media and cultural form: narrative versus database', in A. Adams and S. Brindley (eds) *Teaching Secondary English with ICT*. London: Open University Press, pp. 67–79.

Solomon, S. (1987) *Phases of Economic Growth, 1850–1973: Kondratieff Waves and Kuznets Swings*. Cambridge: Cambridge University Press.

Somers, M. (1994) 'The narrative constitution of identity: a relational and network approach', *Theory and Society*, 23(5): 605–649.

Souter, D., Scott, N., Garforth, C., Jain, R., Mascrarenhas, O. and McKemey, K. (2007) *The Economic Impact of Telecommunications on Rural Livelihoods and Poverty Reduction: A Study of Rural Communities in India (Gujarat), Mazambique, and Tanzania*. Commonwealth Telecommunications Organisation for UK Department for International Development 2005, located at http://www.telafrica.org/R8437/files/pdfs/FinalReport.pdf (accessed on 5 August 2008).

Spinello, R. (2003) *CyberEthics: Morality and Law in Cyberspace*, 2nd edn. London: Jones and Bartlett Pubs.

Stanley, S. (2001) 'Disembodiment is a cyberspace myth: discourse and the self in real space', *CyberPsychology & Behavior*, 4(1): 77–93.

Stark, E. (2006) 'Free culture and the internet: a new semiotic democracy', *openDemocracy*, located at http://www.opendemocracy.net/arts-commons/semiotic_3662.jsp (accessed 6 January 2010).

Statistics Canada (2008) *Statistics Canada Labour Force Survey*, located at Statscan.ca/English/subjects/labour/LFS/lfs-en.htm (accessed 5 March 2008).

Steuer, J. (1992) 'Defining virtual reality: dimensions determining telepresence', *Journal of Communication*, 4(2): 73–93.

Stewert, S. (2001) 'The A.I. Web Game', located at http://www.seanstewart.org/beast/intro/ (accessed 14 April 2009).

Stivale, C. (1998) *The Two-fold Thought of Deleuze and Guattari*. London: Guildford.

Stock, G. (2003) *Redesigning Humans: Choosing our Genes, Changing our Future*. New York: Mariner Books.

Stone, A.R. (1995) *The War of Desire and Technology at the Close of the Mechanical Age*. Cambridge, MA: MIT Press.

Strano, M. (2008) 'User descriptions and interpretations of self-presentation through *Facebook* profile images', *Cyberpsychology: Journal of Psychological Research on Cyberspace*,

2(2), article 1, located at http://cyberpsychology.eu/view.php?cisloclanku=2008110402& article=1 (accessed 15 March 2009).

Stroud, N. (2008) 'Media use and political predispositions: revisiting the concept of selective exposure', *Political Behavior*, 30(3): 341–366.

Suler, J. (2004) 'The online disinhibition effect', located at http://www-usr.rider.edu/~suler/psycyber/disinhibit.html (accessed 15 December 2009).

Sunstein, C. (2001) *Republic.com*. Oxford: Princeton University Press.

Swain, S. (2008) 'UK's financial services share rises to 9.4% of GDP in '06', *The Financial Express*, 2 January, located at http://www.financialexpress.com/news/uks-financial-services-share-rises-to-9.4-of-gdp-in-06/256893/ (accessed 21 October 2009).

Taylor, R., Caeti, T., Loper, D., Fritsch, E. and Liederbach, J. (2006) *Digital Crime and Digital Terrorism*. Upper Saddle River, NJ: Pearson.

Taylor, T. (2002) 'Living digitally: embodiment in virtual worlds', in R. Schroeder (ed.) *The Social Life of Avatars: Presence and Interaction in Shared Virtual Environments*. London: Springer-Verlag, pp 40–62.

Tepper, S. and Hargittai, E. (2009) 'Pathways to music exploration in the digital age', *Poetics*, 37(3): 227–249.

Thacker, E. (2003) 'Data made flesh: biotechnology and the discourse of the posthuman', *Cultural Critique,* 53(3): 72–97.

The Economist (2009) 'Beyond voice: special report on telecommunications in emerging markets', 24 September, located at http://www.economist.com/specialreports/display story.cfm?story_id=14483848# (accessed 24 October 2009).

Thompson, H. and Garbacz, C. (2007) 'Mobile, fixed line and internet services effects on global productive efficiency', *Information Economics and Policy* 19(2): 189–214.

Tierney, J. (2007) 'Are scientists playing God? It depends on your religion', *The New York Times*, 20 November, located at http://www.nytimes.com/2007/11/20/science/20tier. html (accessed 23 June 2009).

Toffler, A. (1970) *Future Shock*. New York: Random House.

Toffler, A. (1980) *The Third Wave*. New York: Bantam Books.

Tonkiss, F. (2006) *Contemporary Economic Sociology: Globalisation, Production and Inequality*. London: Routledge.

Tönnies, F. (1955) *Community and Association* (trans C. Loomis). London: Routledge & Keegan Paul.

Touraine, A. (1971) *The Post-industrial Society: Tomorrow's Social History; Classes, Conflicts and Culture in the Programmed Society*. New York: Random House.

Trippi, J. (2004) *The Revolution Will Not Be Televised: Democracy, the Internet, and the Overthrow of Everything*. New York: Reagan Books.

Turkel, S. (1996) *Life on the Screen: Identity in the Age of the Internet*. London: Weidenfeld & Nicolson.

Turkel, S. (1999) 'Cyberspace and identity', *Contemporary Sociology*, 28(6): 643–648.

Turner, B. (1984) *The Body and Society: Explorations in Social Theory*. Oxford: Blackwell.

Tutt, D. (2005) 'Mobile performances of a teenager: a study of situated mobile phone activity in the living room', *Convergence: The International Journal of Research into New Media Technologies*, 11(2): 58–75.

UNCTAD (2007) *World Investment Report: Transnational Corporations, Extractive Industries and World Development*. New York and Geneva: United Nations.

Urry, J. (2000) *Sociology Beyond Societies: Mobilities for the Twenty-first Century*. London: Routledge.

Valeknberg, P., Schouten, A. and Peter, J. (2005) 'Adolescents' identity experiments on the internet', *New Media & Society*, 7(3): 383–402.

Van de Donk, W., Loader, B., Nixon, P. and Rucht, D. (eds) (2003) *Cyberprotest: New Media, Citizens and Social Movements*. London: Routledge.

Van den Berg, B. (2009) 'The situated self: identity in a world of ambient intelligence'. PhD Dissertation, Erasmus Universiteit: Rotterdam, located at http://publishing.eur. nl/ir/repub/asset/15586/Van%20den%20Berg%20-%20Dissertation%20-%20final%20-%20 march%202009.pdf (accessed 12 July 2009).

Van Dijk, J. (2000) 'Models of democracy and concepts of communication', in K. Hacker and J. van Dijk (eds) *Digital Democracy, Issues of Theory and Practice*. London: Sage, pp. 30–53.

Van Dijk, J. (2005) *The Deepening Divide: Inequality and the Information Society*. London: Sage.

Van Dijk, J. (2006) *The Network Society*, 2nd edn. London: Sage.

Vasalou, A., Joinson, A., Bänziger, T., Goldie, P. and Pitt, J. (2008) 'Avatars in social media: balancing accuracy, playfulness and embodied messages', *International Journal of Human–Computer Studies*, 66(11): 801–811.

Verton, D. (2003) *Black Ice: The Invisible Threat of Cyber-Terrorism*. New York: McGraw-Hill.

Vetere, F., Howard, S. and Gibbs, M. (2005) 'Phatic technologies: sustaining sociability through ubiquitous computing'. *Proceedings of CHI*, 2005, located at http://www.vs.inf. ethz.ch/events/ubisoc2005/UbiSoc%202005%20submissions/12-Vetere-Frank.pdf (accessed 15 October 2007).

Vichot, R. (2009) '"Doing it for the lulz?": online communities of practice and offline tactical media', MA thesis, Georgia Institute of Technology: Atlanta, located at http:// smartech.gatech.edu/bitstream/1853/28098/1/vichot_ray_200905_mast.pdf (accessed 1 September 2009).

Virilio, P. (1992) 'Big Optics' (trans. Jorg von Stein), in Peter Weibel (ed.) *Zur Rechtfertigung der hypothetischen Natur de Kunst und der Nicht-Identitdt in der Objektwelt/ On Justifying the Hypothetical Nature of Art and the Non-Identicality within the Object World*. Koln: Galerie Tanja Grunert, pp. 82–93.

Vodafone (2005) *Africa: The Impact of Mobile Phones: Moving the Debate Forward*. Vodaphone Policy Paper Series #3, located at http://www.vodaphone.com/ect/medialib/ attachments/cr_downloads (accessed 15 July 2008).

Voida, A., Grinter, R. and Ducheneault, N. (2006) 'Social practices around *iTunes*', in K. O'Hara and B. Brown (eds) *Consuming Music Together: Social and Collaborative Aspects of Music Consumption Technologies*. London: Springer, pp. 57–83.

Wagner, M. (2007) 'Sex in *Second Life*', *InformationWeek*, 26 May, located at http://www. informationweek.com/news/software/hosted/showArticle.jhtml?articleID=199701944 (accessed 27 December 2009).

Wajcman, J. (1991). *Feminism Confronts Technology*. University Park: Pennsylvania State University Press.

Wajcman, J. (2004) *TechnoFeminism*. Cambridge: Polity.

Waldby, C. (2007) *The Visible Human Project: Informatic Bodies and Posthuman Medicine*. New York: Routledge.

Walker, K. (2000) '"It's difficult to hide it": the presentation of self on internet home pages', *Qualitative Sociology*, 23(1): 99–120.

Warf, B. (2003) 'Mergers and acquisitions in the telecommunications industry', *Growth and Change*, 34(3): 321–344.

Warschaur, M. (2004) *Technology and Social Inclusion: Rethinking the Digital Divide*. London: MIT Press.

Watts, E. (2001) '"Voice" and "voicelessness"', *Rhetorical Studies QJS*, 87: 79–196.

Waverman, L., Meschi, M. and Fuss, M. (2005) 'The impact of telecoms on economic growth in developing countries', in Vodafone (2005) *Africa: The Impact of Mobile Phones: Moving the Debate Forward*. Vodaphone Policy Paper Series #3. pp 10–23, located at http://www.vodaphone.com/ect/medialib/attachments/cr_downloads (accessed 15 July 2008).

Weber, M. (1978) 'The city (non-legitimate domination)', in G. Roth and C. Wittich (eds) *Economy and Society*, Vol. 2. Berkeley: University of California Press, pp. 1212–1372.

Webster, F. (1995) *Theories of the Information Society*. London: Routledge.

Wellman, B. (1979) 'The community question: the intimate networks of East Yorkers', *The American Journal of Sociology*, 84(5): 1201–1231.

Wellman, B. (1997) 'The road to utopia and dystopia on the information highway', *Contemporary Sociology*, 26(4): 455–459.

Wellman, B. (2001) 'The persistence and transformation of community: from neighbourhood groups to social networks'. A Report to the Law Commission of Canada. 30 October, located at http://www.chass.utoronto.ca/~wellman/publications/lawcomm/lawcomm7.PDF (accessed 1 August 2009).

Wellman, B. (2002) 'Little boxes, glocalization, and networked individualism', in M. Tanabe, P. van den Besselaar and T. Ishida (eds) *Digital Cities II: Computational and Sociological Approaches*. Berlin: Springer, pp. 10–25.

Wellman, B. and Gulia, M. (1996) 'Net surfers don't ride alone: virtual communities as communities', in P. Kollock and M. Smith (eds) *Communities in Cyberspace*, Berkeley: University of California Press, pp. 167–194.

Wellman, B., Boase, J. and Chen, W. (2002) 'The networked nature of community: offline and online', *IT & Society*, 1(1): 151–165.

Wellman, B., Haase, A., Witte, J. and Hampton, K. (2001) 'Does the Internet increase, decrease, or supplement social capital? Social networks, participation and community commitment', *American Behavioral Scientist*, 45(3): 436–455.

Whitty, M. (2007) 'Revealing the "real" me, searching for the "actual" you: presentations of self on an internet dating site', *Computers in Human Behavior*, 24(4): 1707–1723.

Wilcox, C. (2008) 'Internet fundraising in 2008: a new model?', *The Forum*, 6(1): 1–13.

Williams, D., Yee, N. and Caplan, S. (2008) 'Who plays, how much, and why? Debunking the stereotypical gamer profile', *Journal of Computer-mediated Communication*. 13(4): 993–1018.

Williams, M. (2005) 'Mobile networks and foreign direct investment in developing countries', in Vodafone. (2005) *Africa: The Impact of Mobile Phones: Moving the Debate Forward*. Vodaphone Policy Paper Series #3. pp. 24–40, located at http://www.vodafone.com/ect/medialib/attachments/cr_downloads (accessed 15 July 2008).

William, R. (1990 [1975]) *Television: Technology and Cultural Form*. London: Routledge.

Williams, S. and Bendelow, G. (1998) *The Lived Body: Sociological Themes, Embodied Issues*. London: Routledge.

Willson, M. (1997) 'Community in the abstract: a practical and ethical dilemma?', in D. Holmes (ed.) *Virtual Politics: Identity and Community in Cyberspace*, London: Sage, pp. 145–165.

Winseck, D. (1998) 'Pursuing the holy grail: information highways and media reconvergence in Britain and Canada', *European Journal of Communication*, 13(3): 337–374.

WIPO (2009) *World Intellectual Property Indicators: 2009 Edition*, located at http://www.wipo.int/export/sites/www/ipstats/en/statistics/patents/pdf/wipo_pub_941.pdf (accessed 26 October 2009).

Wirth, L. (1938) 'Urbanism as a way of life', *The American Journal of Sociology*, 44(1): 1–24.

Wirtz, B. (2001) 'Reconfiguration of value chains in converging media and communications markets', *Long Range Planning*, 34: 489–506.

Wise, J. (1997) *Exploring Technology and Social Space*. London: Sage.

Wittel, A. (2001) 'Toward a network sociality' *Theory, Culture & Society*, 18(6): 51–76.

Wolf, G. (2004) 'How the Internet invented Howard Dean', *Wired*, 12(1), located at http://www.wired.com/wired/archive/12.01/dean.html (accessed on 2 September 2009).

Wolf, M. and Perron, B. (eds) (2003) *The Video Game Theory Reader*. New York and London: Routledge.

Wolfendale, J. (2007) 'My avatar, my self: virtual harm and attachment', *Ethics & Information Technology*, 9(2): 111–119.

Wray, S. (1999) 'On electronic civil disobedience', *Peace Review*, 11(1): 107–111.

Wright, S. (2009) 'Political blogs, representation and the public sphere', *Aslib Proceedings: New Information Perspectives*, 61(2): 155–169.

Wynn, E. and Katz, J. (1997) 'Hyperbole over cyberspace: self-presentation and social boundaries in internet home pages and discourse', *The Information Society*, 13(4): 297–327.

Yar, M. (2006) *Cybercrime and Society*. London: Sage.

Zazlow, J. (2002) 'If TiVo thinks you are gay, here's how to set it straight', *The Wall Street Journal*, 26 November 2002.

Zhao, S., Grasmuck, S. and Martin, J. (2008) 'Identity construction on Facebook: digital empowerment in anchored relationships', *Computers in Human Behavior*, 24(5): 1816–1836.

Zwick, D. and Dholakia, N. (2004) 'Whose identity is it anyway? Consumer representation in an age of database marketing', *Journal of Macromarketing*, 24(1): 31–43.

Zwick, D. and Knott, J. (2009) 'Manufacturing customers: the database as a new means of production', *Journal of Consumer Culture*, 9(2): 221–247.

INDEX